Robert Louis Stevenson

AN INLAND VOYAGE

AND

TRAVELS WITH A DONKEY

BY

ROBERT LOUIS STEVENSON

EDITED BY

JAMES CLOYD BOWMAN, M.A.

ASSOCIATE PROFESSOR OF ENGLISH
IN THE IOWA STATE COLLEGE

ALLYN AND BACON

Boston   New York   Chicago

COPYRIGHT, 1918, BY

JAMES CLOYD BOWMAN

Norwood Press
J. S. Cushing Co. — Berwick & Smith Co.
Norwood, Mass., U.S.A.

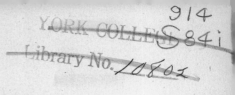

PREFACE

An Inland Voyage and *Travels with a Donkey* are to be enjoyed rather than studied pedantically. They are to be read for the interest of the style and for the charm of the author's personality. Incidentally, they fascinate through the veiled beauty with which they clothe commonplace things, and the manner in which they make the most trivial experience interesting and human. The editor has worked with this in mind.

After the student has enjoyed the excursions, he may then find it valuable to study carefully certain definite portions which have especially appealed to him. When he has mastered these somewhat, he will find it profitable to take some experience of his own, and try to write it out as Stevenson would have done. This can do no more harm than to show him what a wonderfully clever writer Stevenson really is; and besides, it can hardly fail to make him more conscious of a number of possible ways of adding neatness to his own expression.

Full as has been the charm of these journeys in the past, they now have an added interest in that the one was taken through a part of the same country that is being fought over on the Western Front.

J. C. B.

May 20, 1918.

CONTENTS

MAPS AND ILLUSTRATIONS

INTRODUCTION

ROBERT LOUIS STEVENSON

I

BIOGRAPHICAL SKETCH

ROBERT LOUIS STEVENSON was born in Edinburgh, Scotland, on November 13, 1850. On his father's side he was descended from a family of distinguished lighthouse engineers; his father, his grandfather, and his great-grandfather, were not alone builders of the best lighthouses of the North; their inventions and improvements were equally noteworthy. From these men Stevenson inherited a great love of adventure, a vagabond joy for the sea and for the open road.

His maternal grandfather, Louis Balfour, was a Professor of Moral Philosophy and a Minister. It was in his house that Stevenson spent the greater part of his boyhood. "Now I often wonder," says Stevenson, "what I inherited from this old minister. I must suppose, indeed, that he was fond of preaching sermons, and so am I, though I never heard it maintained that either of us loved to hear them." From his forbears, then, Stevenson received a rare blend of personality.

From his mother, Stevenson inherited a diseased throat and weak lungs. These kept him almost constantly in the "land of counterpane" during the winter. His nurse, the while, beguiled many tedious hours by reading from the Bible and the lives of the old Covenanters. During the summer he was encouraged to run out-of-doors, and despite his frailty, he proved himself wilder and more care-free than any of his companions.

At the age of eleven his health mended sufficiently so that his parents began to prepare him for the University of Edinburgh. They planned for him to follow the profession of his father. During this period he also read widely, and enjoyed especially, Shakespeare, Scott, Bunyan, and *The Arabian Nights*.

He entered the University at the age of seventeen, but soon discovered that he had neither the scientific mind nor the physical endurance to succeed as an engineer. When his father took him for a voyage, he found — instead of being interested in lighthouse construction — that his mind was teeming with wonderful romances about the coast and islands which they visited.

Although his father was firm, he finally allowed Stevenson to decide upon literature as a career, — but first he thought it wise that the son should finish a course in law, so that he might, in necessity, have a profession to fall back upon. Stevenson submitted to the decision, and finally at the age of twenty-five succeeded in passing the examinations for admission to the bar, though not until he had nearly ruined his health through work and worry. It was the father's lack of understanding that led the son to the following protest:

> Say not of me that weakly I declined
> The labours of my sires, and fled the sea,
> The towers we founded and the lamps we lit,
> To play at home with paper like a child.

The four years that followed were spent largely in travel, and in search for a hospitable climate. He made long and frequent visits at Fontainebleau, Barbizon, Grez, and Nemours, in intimate association with the colonies of artists. Here it was that he first met Mrs. Osborne, his future wife. Often he visited the galleries and theatres of Paris. During this period, too, he made many of his most intimate and lasting friends.

Among these were Sidney Colvin, his biographer and literary executor; W. E. Henley, his collaborator in dramatic composition; Mrs. Sitwell, who helped him past his religious crisis; Andrew Lang, Edmund Gosse, and Leslie Stephen, writers and critics all. He also made the journeys which are described in *An Inland Voyage* and *Travels with a Donkey*. In addition he wrote twenty or more articles and essays which appeared in various magazines. Although it seemed to his parents that he was wasting much valuable time in idleness at Siron's Inn, he was in reality constantly studying to perfect his style of writing and broaden his knowledge of life; gradually he was emerging as a man of letters.

When Stevenson and Mrs. Osborne met in France in 1789, they loved at first sight. A few months later when she returned to her home in California, Stevenson determined to follow. Those of his friends in whom he confided advised strongly against the proposed journey. Knowing his father's temper, he sailed without even notifying his parent. He took steerage passage on the *Devonian*, partly to lessen the expense and partly for the novelty of the voyage.

From New York he travelled to California by emigrant train. These experiences he later gave the world in *An*

Amateur Emigrant and *Across the Plains*. However valuable the literary material thus secured, the hardships of such travel were too great for Stevenson's frail constitution; he was all but a dead man when he reached Monterey. In the mountains above this town he was nursed back to life by two generous ranchers.

It was December, 1879, when he found himself sufficiently recovered to go to San Francisco. Here for several months he struggled "all alone on forty-five cents a day, and sometimes less, with quantities of hard work and many heavy thoughts," in an effort to support himself through his writing; but before the end of the winter his health broke completely, and he found himself at death's door, with a galloping consumption.

It was then that Mrs. Osborne — now free from her husband — heroically came to Stevenson's bedside, and nursed him through the crisis. "After a while," he wrote, "my spirit got up again in divine frenzy, and has since kicked and spurred my vile body forward with great emphasis and success." When his father was made aware of the son's condition, he cabled him the financial support which he had romantically abandoned when he started for America.

In May, 1880, he was married, when, as he says, he was "a mere complication of cough and bones, much fitter for an emblem of mortality than a bridegroom." With his wife and her son, Lloyd, he went up into the hills a little way from San Francisco, and lived for a time at a deserted mining camp; this experience he published in *The Silverado Squatters*. In August of the same year he sailed from New York with his family, and found his parents and his friend, Sidney Colvin, on the wharf at

Stevenson, however, a number of the individual traits which contribute to the effect are easily discerned.

Stevenson is one of the most companionable of authors. His chief motive is autobiographical. With the seeming genial egotism of a child, he admits the reader to the intimacies of his soul, and relates his motives, his tastes, his opinions, his faults. He chats so pleasantly about the people he meets, the books he reads, even the methods he employs in accomplishing his effects in writing, that the reader soon feels on the inmost terms of friendship with him. And yet all without the trace of vanity. The reader is so captivated that soon he finds himself turning the pages of the travels and the essays again and again, with the feeling that these personal secrets are intended alone for him. This quality is so marked in Stevenson that many have felt as does Henley: "The man himself is so much greater than even the best of his works."

Stevenson was a wanderer from his birth. "I travel not to go anywhere," he says, "but to go." Remaining long in any one place "tells on my old gypsy nature; like a violin hung up, I begin to lose what music there is in me; and with the music, I do not know what besides, or do not know what to call it, but something radically part of life, a rhythm, perhaps, in one's old and brutally overridden nerves, or perhaps a kind of variety of blood that the heart has come to look for." This trait kept alive in Stevenson a boyish craving for adventure: "He ran to embrace life like a lover." This it is in him which gives voice to the finest melody he uttered:

Under the wide and starry sky,
Dig the grave and let me lie;
Glad did I live and gladly die,
And I laid me down with a will.

> This be the verse you grave for me:
> *Here he lies where he longed to be;*
> *Home is the sailor, home from the sea,*
> *And the hunter home from the hill.*

It is this ceaseless struggle for adventure, this very masculine vigor, this restless romance, which keeps his soul constantly alert and young, and which many consider in him the greatest quality of all.

In his wanderings, it is the out-of-doors — the mountains, the valleys, the rivers, the ocean — not the city — for which Stevenson hankers. "To wash in one of God's rivers in the open air" is a tonic for soul and body. He is never so healthy as when tramping the hills or sailing the seas. Not alone is it nature that takes him afield; it is the untrammelled, wild, natural, masculine life of the valleys and the mountains, and especially of the ocean that appeals to him. For me, he says "not the shoddy sham of cities, clubs, and colleges, but the world where men still live a man's life." And again: "God knows I don't care who I chum with; perhaps I like sailors best; but to go round and sue and sneak to keep a crowd together — never." The wish expressed in his *Envoy* is not alone for others; it is his desire for himself:

> A living river by the door,
> A nightingale in the sycamore.

Stevenson never grew up; his wonder and imagination, his buoyant simplicity and curiosity, are those of a child. He retains, in such extraordinary freshness, the memory of himself as a child that he has but to wink one eye in order to transform himself into the lad of his dreams. When he is too sick or too exhausted to work, he drags his ailing body into the unused attic, and there with Lloyd Osborne plays unfagged, for hours at a time, a boyish game of war.

To him life is ever fresh. He is never bored with the monotony of existence. Every day he jumps out of his trundle bed afresh to gaze upon the wonderful world. He has an interest in everything and in everybody. Bohemian and open-minded, with no animosity against those who oppose him, he is constantly a learner. Boy and man, he often plays the truant, and often seems wasting himself in idleness, because he is intently studying things about him. "Do you think I have an empty life?" he writes from Vailima, "or that a man jogging to his club has so much to interest and amuse him?"

There is, too, a sort of uncanny, haunting presence that surrounds him; it is as if he has, under the magic of his wand, an invisible, winged-footed Ariel to do his bidding. This is the quality which makes many of his stories, such as *Thrawn Janet* and *Dr. Jekyll and Mr. Hyde*, haunting, unforgettable memories. Truly he is, as Barrie has said, "a spirit of boyhood tugging at the skirts of this old world of ours and compelling it to come back and play."

In spite of constitutional weakness and chronic pain, Stevenson displayed the courage and indomitable will that has endeared him to the whole world. In this respect he is not unlike Scott. In spite of the complicated miseries that surround him, "up a high hill he heaves a huge round stone." Although often "groggy afoot and vague in the head," although incapacitated by scrivener's cramp, he despairs not. When others would have slighted their work, he toils rigorously, and ceases not until he has produced the exact effect he desires.

Whatever the cost, he maintains his ideal: "Every piece of work which is not as good as you can make it, which you have palmed off, imperfect, meagrely thought, niggardly in execution, upon mankind who is your pay-master on parole and in a sense your pupil, every hasty or slovenly or untrue performance, should rise up against you in the court of your own heart and condemn you for a thief." And not only did Stevenson work, but he smiled. Instead of airing his troubles, he converses charmingly of his pleasures. He has the rare capacity of making others feel as he feels:

> The world is so full of a number of things,
> I'm sure we should all be as happy as kings.

Stevenson is fundamentally religious: this does not mean that he holds to any narrow creed, for he does not. "I believe in the ultimate decency of things," he says, "ay, and if I woke in hell, I should still believe it." In spirit, he never gets very far away from the Puritan influence of his childhood and youth. The voice of "Cummie," his faithful nurse, rings in his ears to the end: "We are all nobly born; fortunate those who know it; blessed those who remember."

This influence keeps his mind wholesome, sweet, and clean. Witness one of his household prayers for use at Vailima: "At morning. The day returns and brings us the petty round of irritating concerns and duties. Help us to play the man, help us to perform them with laughter and kind faces, let cheerfulness abound with industry. Give us to go blithely on our business all this day, bring us to our resting beds weary and content and undishonored, and grant us in the end the gift of sleep." About him there is "no flurry, no high words, no long faces; only hard work and honest thought." He makes his practice a reflection of his philosophy; in his creed as in his life he is always the soldier and the gentleman. He purges the mind and sets the feet upon the honest, manly journey.

The charm of Stevenson's personality carries over into his style. There is an unusual harmony between the man and his books. In grace, appeal, and melody, his style is practically perfect. "I have one feather in my cap," he says, "and that is I am not a sloven." During his formative years he associated intimately with the genre painters of France, and formed the habit of studying his words as the artist studies his colors. He loves the striking epithet and the harmonious sentence. He is the born artist and knows how to mingle the rhythm with the sound in an infinitely varied and irresistible pattern.

"Too many of us," he counsels, "read by the eye, but the man who means to write, must, whether he articulates or not, read everything by the ear. In short, as a musician reads score and can hear harmony, so the literary man, even while skimming with the eye, must be able to hear all the uttered words." His love of style for its own sake, together with his artistic sensitiveness and ceaseless labor, produces a beauty of rhythm and sound, an avoidance of artifice, and a perfect concord between sound and sense. Yes, and there runs like a golden thread through all that he writes a freshness and a masculine vigor which is unmistakable. Withal, as in his personality, there is an exquisite blending of pathos and humor, melody and wisdom.

But one must end somewhere in this enumeration, although not half through dissecting the motley person-

ality.   There remains still the man of the world, the ob-
solete soldier of fortune, the whimsical child, the critic.
But at whatever length one continues, one must feel that
one has failed to give any definite conception of the charm
which must be felt through reading the author, if it is to
be appreciated.   It is all too much like tearing a bit of
protoplasm into its elements, and then expecting the
nitrogen and the oxygen and the hydrogen to have life.
After all, is it not in the infinitely complex blending of all
these qualities that the charm of Stevenson really exists?
Perhaps his friend Henley has come nearest expressing this:

> Thin-legged, thin-chested, slight unspeakably,
> Neat-footed and weak-fingered : in his face —
> Lean, large-boned, curved of beak, and touched with race,
> Bold-lipped, rich-tinted, mutable as the sea,
> The brown eyes radiant with vivacity —
> There shone a brilliant and romantic grace,
> A spirit intense and rare, with trace on trace
> Of passion, impudence, and energy.
> Valiant in velvet, light in ragged luck,
> Most vain, most generous, sternly critical,
> Buffoon and poet, lover and sensualist;
> A deal of Ariel, just a streak of Puck,
> Much Antony, of Hamlet most of all,
> And something of the Shorter Catechist.

III

An Inland Voyage and Travels with a Donkey

It is the companionable Stevenson that one accompanies
in *An Inland Voyage* and *Travels with a Donkey*.   His
mind is as open and as fresh as that of a child.   He is un-
afraid and confiding.   He does not attempt to force theories

upon one nor to slap one constantly with cocksure convictions: he simply allows his mind to take color from each passing sight and sound along the way; and he is so surcharged with wit and pathos, insight and wisdom, and is so cheerful and natural about it all, that one cannot help being captivated. The grace and harmony of the expression is but a small part of the potent charm; the larger part lies in the strangeness and picturesqueness with which every commonplace thing is enveloped, and in the revelation that — if one has but the eye to see it — everything in the world is flooded with artistry and beauty.

In *An Inland Voyage* Stevenson gives the log of a canoeing journey which he took during September, 1876, from Antwerp, through Belgium and northern France, to Pontoise, a town on the Oise near Paris. On this voyage he was accompanied by his old friend, Walter Simpson, with whom he had previously taken many and varied excursions. The voyage lasted for seventeen days. "I have been wet through nearly every day of travel since the second (inclusive); besides this, I have had to fight against pretty mouldy health; so that, on the whole, the essayist and reviewer has shown, I think, some pluck."

Yet in the report he gives us, we have but a veiled suggestion here and there of the disagreeable weather and the poor health. One feels instead that "he who is of the brotherhood does not voyage in quest of the picturesque but of certain jolly humors — of the hope and spirit with which the march begins at morning, and the peace and spiritual reflections of the evening's rest." From almost every page there radiates the white sunlight of a joyous spirit.

Travels with a Donkey is Stevenson's log of his walking

journey over the Cévennes in southeastern France. He left Le Monastier the last week of September, 1878, and after spending twelve days in the company of Modestine, reached Alais, on the Gardon. His journey lay in the present departments of Ardeche and Lozere, though Stevenson preferred to use the names of the corresponding old districts, Viveras and Gevaudan. The general direction of his foot-steps lay toward the south, though his winding, irregular way often took him toward almost every other point of the compass. He pays more attention than in the *Voyage* to the people he meets, and his eyes turn oftener to the stars.

In each of the stories he reverts again and again to his joy in personal freedom. He is sure he would "rather be a bargee than occupy any position under heaven that requires attendance at an office." In each there is much of the feeling and philosophy of the gypsy and the vagabond.

IV

BIBLIOGRAPHY

LIST OF STEVENSON'S BOOKS:

1878. An Inland Voyage
1879. Travels with a Donkey in the Cévennes
1881. Virginibus Puerisque, and Other Papers
1882. Familiar Studies of Men and Books
1882. New Arabian Nights
1883. Treasure Island
1885. Prince Otto
1885. A Child's Garden of Verses
1885. The Dynamiter: More New Arabian Nights

EDITIONS OF STEVENSON'S WORKS:

The Thistle Edition. This edition in twenty-six volumes contains the author's *Life* by Balfour, and his *Letters* by Colvin.

The Biographical Edition. This edition in twenty-seven volumes contains instructive and entertaining prefaces by Mrs. Stevenson.

BIOGRAPHIES OF STEVENSON:

Graham Balfour.

> *Life of Robert Louis Stevenson.* London, 1901. This is the authoritative life of Stevenson.

John Alexander Hammerton.

> *Stevensonia; an Anecdotal Life and Appreciation.* Edinburgh (Second Edition), 1907. A collection of interesting and valuable materials from various sources.

Richard Ashley Rice.

> *Robert Louis Stevenson; How to Know Him.* Indianapolis, 1916. A recent popular biography in an interesting series.

BIBLIOGRAPHIES OF STEVENSON:

W. F. Prideaux.

> *Bibliography of the Works of Robert Louis Stevenson.* Revised edition, edited and supplemented by Mrs. Luther S. Livingston. London, 1918.

John Herbert Slater.

> *Robert Louis Stevenson; a Bibliography of His Complete Works.* 1914.

CRITICAL ESSAYS:

Walter Raleigh.

> *Robert Louis Stevenson.* 1895.

Arthur Quiller-Couch.

> *Robert Louis Stevenson* in *Adventures in Criticism.* 1896.

William Lyon Phelps.

> *Robert Louis Stevenson* in *Essays on Modern Novelists.* 1910.

J. A. Hammerton.

> *In the Track of R. L. Stevenson.*   1907.   The author
> follows the course over which Stevenson jour-
> neyed in *An Inland Voyage* and *Travels with a
> Donkey.* He discourses pleasantly about the
> country and the people, and presents numerous
> photographs.   These illustrations are valuable
> in that they show many of the exact scenes
> described by Stevenson.

AN INLAND VOYAGE

BY

ROBERT LOUIS STEVENSON

EDITED FOR SCHOOL USE, WITH INTRODUCTION AND NOTES

JAMES CLOYD BOWMAN, M.A.
ASSOCIATE PROFESSOR OF ENGLISH IN
THE IOWA STATE COLLEGE

———o‹o›‹o›o———

ALLYN AND BACON

Boston   New York   Chicago

SIR WALTER GRINDLAY SIMPSON, BART.

My dear *Cigarette*,

It was enough that you should have shared so liberally in the rams and portages of our voyage; that you should have had so hard a battle to recover the derelict *Arethusa* on the flooded Oise; and that you should thenceforth have piloted a mere wreck of mankind to Origny Sainte-Benoîte and a supper so eagerly desired. It was perhaps more than enough, as you once somewhat piteously complained, that I should have set down all the strong language to you, and kept the appropriate reflexions for myself. I could not in decency expose you to share the disgrace of another and more public shipwreck. But now that this voyage of ours is going into a cheap edition, that peril, we shall hope, is at an end, and I may put your name on the burgee.

But I cannot pause till I have lamented the fate of our two ships. That, sir, was not a fortunate day when we projected the possession of a canal barge; it was not a fortunate day when we shared our day-dream with the most hopeful of day-dreamers. For a while, indeed, the world looked smilingly. The barge was procured and christened, and as the *Eleven Thousand Virgins of Cologne*, lay for some months, the admired of all admirers, in a pleasant river and under the walls of an ancient town. M. Mattras, the accomplished carpenter of Moret, had made her a centre of emulous labour; and you will not have forgotten the amount of sweet champagne consumed in the inn at the bridge end, to give zeal to the workmen and speed to the work. On the financial aspect, I would not willingly dwell. The *Eleven Thousand Virgins of Cologne* rotted in the stream where she was beautified. She felt not the impulse of the breeze; she was never harnessed to the patient track-horse. And when at length she was sold, by the indignant carpenter of Moret, there were sold along with her the *Arethusa* and the *Cigarette*, she of cedar, she, as we knew so keenly on a portage, of solid-hearted English oak. Now these historic vessels fly the tricolor and are known by new and alien names.

R. L. S.

PREFACE

To equip so small a book with a preface is, I am half afraid, to sin against proportion. But a preface is more than an author can resist, for it is the reward of his labours. When the foundation stone is laid, the architect appears with his plans, and struts for an hour before the public eye. So with the writer in his preface : he may have never a word to say, but he must show himself for a moment in the portico, hat in hand, and with an urbane demeanour.

It is best, in such circumstance, to represent a delicate shade of manner between humility and superiority : as if the book had been written by some one else, and you had merely run over it and inserted what was good. But for my part I have not yet learned the trick to that perfection ; I am not yet able to dissemble the warmth of my sentiments towards a reader ; and if I meet him on the threshold, it is to invite him in with country cordiality.

To say truth, I had no sooner finished reading this little book in proof than I was seized upon by a distressing apprehension.

It occurred to me that I might not only be the first to read these pages, but the last as well ; that I might have pioneered this very smiling tract of country all in vain, and find not a soul to follow in my steps. The more I thought, the more I disliked the notion ; until the distaste grew into a sort of panic terror, and I rushed into this Preface, which is no more than an advertisement for readers.

What am I to say for my book? Caleb and Joshua brought back from Palestine a formidable bunch of grapes; alas! my book produces naught so nourishing; and for the matter of that, we live in an age when people prefer a definition to any quantity of fruit.

I wonder, would a negative be found enticing? for, from the negative point of view, I flatter myself this volume has a certain stamp. Although it runs to considerably upwards of two hundred pages, it contains not a single reference to the imbecility of God's universe, nor so much as a single hint that I could have made a better one myself, — I really do not know where my head can have been. I seemed to have forgotten all that makes it glorious to be man. 'T is an omission that renders the book philosophically unimportant; but I am in hopes the eccentricity may please in frivolous circles.

To the friend who accompanied me I owe many thanks already, indeed I wish I owed him nothing else; but at this moment I feel towards him an almost exaggerated tenderness. He, at least, will become my reader — if it were only to follow his own travels alongside of mine.

R. L. S.

CONTENTS

MAP OF *An Inland Voyage*

AN INLAND VOYAGE

ANTWERP TO BOOM

WE made a great stir in Antwerp Docks. A stevedore and a lot of dock porters took up the two canoes, and ran with them for the slip. A crowd of children followed cheering. The *Cigarette* went off in a splash and a bubble of small breaking water. Next moment the *Arethusa* was after her. A steamer was coming down, men on the paddle-box shouted hoarse warnings, the stevedore and his porters were bawling from the quay. But in a stroke or two the canoes were away out in the middle of the Scheldt, and all steamers, and stevedores, and other 'longshore vanities were left behind.

The sun shone brightly; the tide was making — four jolly miles an hour; the wind blew steadily, with occasional squalls. For my part, I had never been in a canoe under sail in my life; and my first experiment out in the middle of this big river was not made without some trepidation. What would happen when the wind first caught my little canvas? I suppose it was almost as trying a venture into the regions of the unknown as to publish a first book, or to marry. But my doubts were not of long duration; and in five minutes you will not be surprised to learn that I had tied my sheet.

I own I was a little struck by this circumstance myself; of course, in company with the rest of my fellow-men, I had always tied the sheet in a sailing-boat; but in so little and crank a concern as a canoe, and with these charging squalls, I was not prepared to find myself follow the same principle; and it inspired me with some contemptuous views of our regard for life. It is certainly easier to smoke with the sheet fastened; but I had never before weighed a comfortable pipe of tobacco against an obvious risk, and gravely elected for the comfortable pipe. It is a commonplace, that we cannot answer for ourselves before we have been tried. But it is not so common a reflection, and surely more consoling that we usually find ourselves a great deal braver and better than we thought. I believe this is every one's experience: but an apprehension that they may belie themselves in the future prevents mankind from trumpeting this cheerful sentiment abroad. I wish sincerely, for it would have saved me much trouble, there had been some one to put me in a good heart about life when I was younger; to tell me how dangers are most portentous on a distant sight; and how the good in a man's spirit will not suffer itself to be overlaid, and rarely or never deserts him in the hour of need. But we are all for tootling on the sentimental flute in literature; and not a man among us will go to the head of the march to sound the heady drums.

It was agreeable upon the river. A barge or two went past laden with hay. Reeds and willows bordered the stream; and cattle and grey, venerable horses came and hung their mild heads over the embankment. Here and there was a pleasant village among trees, with a noisy shipping-yard; here and there a villa in a lawn. The wind served us well up the Scheldt and thereafter up the

THE CATHEDRAL AT ANTWERP

Rupel; and we were running pretty free when we began to sight the brickyards of Boom, lying for a long way on the right bank of the river. The left bank was still green and pastoral, with alleys of trees along the embankment, and here and there a flight of steps to serve a ferry, where perhaps there sat a woman with her elbows on her knees, or an old gentleman with a staff and silver spectacles. But Boom and its brickyards grew smokier and shabbier with every minute; until a great church with a clock, and a wooden bridge over the river, indicated the central quarters of the town.

Boom is not a nice place, and is only remarkable for one thing: that the majority of the inhabitants have a private opinion that they can speak English, which is not justified by fact. This gave a kind of haziness to our intercourse. As for the Hôtel de la Navigation, I think it is the worst feature of the place. It boasts of a sanded parlour, with a bar at one end, looking on the street; and another sanded parlour, darker and colder, with an empty bird-cage and a tricolor subscription box by way of sole adornment, where we made shift to dine in the company of three uncommunicative engineer apprentices and a silent bagman. The food, as usual in Belgium, was of a nondescript occasional character; indeed I have never been able to detect anything in the nature of a meal among this pleasing people; they seem to peck and trifle with viands all day long in an amateur spirit: tentatively French, truly German, and somehow falling between the two.

The empty bird-cage, swept and garnished, and with no trace of the old piping favourite, save where two wires had been pushed apart to hold its lump of sugar, carried

with it a sort of graveyard cheer. The engineer apprentices would have nothing to say to us, nor indeed to the
bagman; but talked low and sparingly to one another,
or raked us in the gaslight with a gleam of spectacles.
For though handsome lads, they were all (in the Scotch
phrase) barnacled.

There was an English maid in the hotel, who had been
long enough out of England to pick up all sorts of funny
foreign idioms, and all sorts of curious foreign ways, which
need not here be specified. She spoke to us very flu-
ently in her jargon, asked us information as to the manners
of the present day in England, and obligingly corrected
us when we attempted to answer. But as we were deal-
ing with a woman, perhaps our information was not so
much thrown away as it appeared. The sex likes to
pick up knowledge and yet preserve its superiority. It
is good policy, and almost necessary in the circumstances.
If a man finds a woman admires him, were it only for his
acquaintance with geography, he will begin at once to
build upon the admiration. It is only by unintermittent
snubbing that the pretty ones can keep us in our place.
Men, as Miss Howe or Miss Harlowe would have said,
"are such *encroachers*." For my part, I am body and
soul with the women; and after a well-married couple,
there is nothing so beautiful in the world as the myth of
the divine huntress. It is no use for a man to take to
the woods; we know him; Anthony tried the same thing
long ago, and had a pitiful time of it by all accounts. But
there is this about some women, which overtops the best
gymnosophist among men, that they suffice to themselves,
and can walk in a high and cold zone without the countenance of any trousered being. I declare, although the

reverse of a professed ascetic, I am more obliged to women for this ideal than I should be to the majority of them, or indeed to any but one, for a spontaneous kiss. There is nothing so encouraging as the spectacle of self-sufficiency. And when I think of the slim and lovely maidens, running the woods all night to the note of Diana's horn; moving among the old oaks, as fancy-free as they; things of the forest and the starlight, not touched by the commotion of man's hot and turbid life — although there are plenty other ideals that I should prefer — I find my heart beat at the thought of this one. 'Tis to fail in life, but to fail with what a grace! That is not lost which is not regretted. And where — here slips out the male — where would be much of the glory of inspiring love, if there were no contempt to overcome?

ON THE WILLEBROEK CANAL

NEXT morning, when we set forth on the Willebroek Canal, the rain began heavy and chill. The water of the canal stood at about the drinking temperature of tea; and under this cold aspersion, the surface was covered with steam. The exhilaration of departure, and the easy motion of the boats under each stroke of the paddles, supported us through this misfortune while it lasted; and when the cloud passed and the sun came out again, our spirits went up above the range of stay-at-home humours. A good breeze rustled and shivered in the rows of trees that bordered the canal. The leaves flickered in and out of the light in tumultuous masses. It seemed sailing weather to eye and ear; but down between the banks, the wind reached us only in faint and desultory puffs. There was hardly enough to steer by. Progress was intermittent and unsatisfactory. A jocular person, of marine antecedents, hailed us from the tow-path with a *"C'est vite, mais c'est long."*

The canal was busy enough. Every now and then we met or overtook a long string of boats, with great green tillers; high sterns with a window on either side of the rudder, and perhaps a jug or a flower-pot in one of the windows; a dingy following behind; a woman busied about the day's dinner, and a handful of children. These barges were all tied one behind the other with tow-ropes, to the number of twenty-five or thirty; and the

6

line was headed and kept in motion by a steamer of
strange construction. It had neither paddlewheel nor
screw; but by some gear not rightly comprehensible to
the unmechanical mind, it fetched up over its bow a small
bright chain which lay along the bottom of the canal,
and paying it out again over the stern, dragged itself
forward, link by link, with its whole retinue of loaded
scows. Until one had found out the key to the enigma,
there was something solemn and uncomfortable in the
progress of one of these trains, as it moved gently along
the water with nothing to mark its advance but an eddy
alongside dying away into the wake.

Of all the creatures of commercial enterprise, a canal
barge is by far the most delightful to consider. It may
spread its sails, and then you see it sailing high above the
tree-tops and the wind-mill, sailing on the aqueduct,
sailing through the green corn-lands : the most picturesque
of things amphibious. Or the horse plods along at a foot-
pace as if there were no such thing as business in the
world; and the man dreaming at the tiller sees the same
spire on the horizon all day long. It is a mystery how
things ever get to their destination at this rate; and to
see the barges waiting their turn at a lock, affords a fine
lesson of how easily the world may be taken. There
should be many contented spirits on board, for such a life
is both to travel and to stay at home.

The chimney smokes for dinner as you go along; the
banks of the canal slowly unroll their scenery to con-
templative eyes; the barge floats by great forests and
through great cities with their public buildings and their
lamps at night; and for the bargee, in his floating home,
"travelling abed," it is merely as if he were listening to

another man's story or turning the leaves of a picture book in which he had no concern. He may take his afternoon walk in some foreign country on the banks of the canal, and then come home to dinner at his own fireside.

There is not enough exercise in such a life for any high measure of health; but a high measure of health is only necessary for unhealthy people. The slug of a fellow, who is never ill nor well, has a quiet time of it in life, and dies all the easier.

I am sure I would rather be a bargee than occupy any position under Heaven that required attendance at an office. There are few callings, I should say, where a man gives up less of his liberty in return for regular meals. The bargee is on shipboard; he is master in his own ship; he can land whenever he will; he can never be kept beating off a lee-shore a whole frosty night when the sheets are as hard as iron; and so far as I can make out, time stands as nearly still with him as is compatible with the return of bedtime or the dinner-hour. It is not easy to see why a bargee should ever die.

Half-way between Willebroek and Villevorde, in a beautiful reach of canal like a squire's avenue, we went ashore to lunch. There were two eggs, a junk of bread, and a bottle of wine on board the *Arethusa;* and two eggs and an Etna cooking apparatus on board the *Cigarette*. The master of the latter boat smashed one of the eggs in the course of disembarkation; but observing pleasantly that it might still be cooked *à la papier*, he dropped it into the Etna, in its covering of Flemish newspaper. We landed in a blink of fine weather; but we had not been two minutes ashore before the wind fresh-

ened into half a gale, and the rain began to patter on our
shoulders. We sat as close about the Etna as we could.
The spirits burned with great ostentation; the grass
caught flame every minute or two, and had to be trodden
out; and before long there were several burnt fingers of
the party. But the solid quantity of cookery accomplished was out of proportion with so much display;
and when we desisted, after two applications of the fire,
the sound egg was a little more than loo-warm; and
as for *à la papier*, it was a cold and sordid *fricassée* of
printer's ink and broken eggshell. We made shift to
roast the other two by putting them close to the burning
spirits, and that with better success. And then we uncorked the bottle of wine, and sat down in a ditch with our
canoe aprons over our knees. It rained smartly. Dis-
comfort, when it is honestly uncomfortable and makes
no nauseous pretensions to the contrary, is a vastly
humorous business; and people well steeped and stupefied
in the open air are in a good vein for laughter. From this
point of view, even egg *à la papier* offered by way of
food may pass muster as a sort of accessory to the fun.
But this manner of jest, although it may be taken in good
part, does not invite repetition; and from that time forward the Etna voyaged like a gentleman in the locker of
the *Cigarette*.

It is almost unnecessary to mention that when lunch
was over and we got aboard again and made sail, the
wind promptly died away. The rest of the journey to
Villevorde we still spread our canvas to the unfavouring
air, and with now and then a puff, and now and then a
spell of paddling, drifted along from lock to lock between
the orderly trees.

It was a fine, green, fat landscape, or rather a mere green water-lane going on from village to village. Things had a settled look, as in places long lived in. Crop-headed children spat upon us from the bridges as we went below, with a true conservative feeling. But even more conservative were the fishermen, intent upon their floats, who let us go by without one glance. They perched upon sterlings and buttresses and along the slope of the embankment, gently occupied. They were indifferent like pieces of dead nature. They did not move any more than if they had been fishing in an old Dutch print. The leaves fluttered, the water lapped, but they continued in one stay, like so many churches established by law. You might have trepanned every one of their innocent heads and found no more than so much coiled fishing-line below their skulls. I do not care for your stalwart fellows in india-rubber stockings breasting up mountain torrents with a salmon rod; but I do dearly love the class of man who plies his unfruitful art for ever and a day by still and depopulated waters.

At the lock just beyond Villevorde there was a lock mistress who spoke French comprehensibly, and told us we were still a couple of leagues from Brussels. At the same place the rain began again. It fell in straight, parallel lines, and the surface of the canal was thrown up into an infinity of little crystal fountains. There were no beds to be had in the neighbourhood. Nothing for it but to lay the sails aside and address ourselves to steady paddling in the rain.

Beautiful country houses, with clocks and long lines of shuttered windows, and fine old trees standing in groves and avenues, gave a rich and sombre aspect in

the rain and the deepening dusk to the shores of the
canal. I seem to have seen something of the same effect
in engravings: opulent landscapes, deserted and overhung with the passage of storm. And throughout we
had the escort of a hooded cart, which trotted shabbily
along the tow-path, and kept at an almost uniform distance in our wake.

THE ROYAL SPORT NAUTIQUE

THE rain took off near Laeken. But the sun was already down; the air was chill; and we had scarcely a dry stitch between the pair of us. Nay, now we found ourselves near the end of the Allée Verte, and on the very threshold of Brussels we were confronted by a serious difficulty. The shores were closely lined by canal boats waiting their turn at the lock. Nowhere was there any convenient landing-place; nowhere so much as a stable-yard to leave the canoes in for the night. We scrambled ashore and entered an *estaminet* where some sorry fellows were drinking with the landlord. The landlord was pretty round with us; he knew of no coach-house or stable-yard, nothing of the sort; and seeing we had come with no mind to drink, he did not conceal his impatience to be rid of us. One of the sorry fellows came to the rescue. Somewhere in the corner of the basin there was a slip, he informed us, and something else besides, not very clearly defined by him, but hopefully construed by his hearers.

Sure enough there was the slip in the corner of the basin; and at the top of it two nice-looking lads in boating clothes. The *Arethusa* addressed himself to these. One of them said there would be no difficulty about a night's lodging for our boats; and the other, taking a cigarette from his lips, inquired if they were made by Searle & Son. The name was quite an introduction.

Half-a-dozen other young men came out of a boat-house bearing the superscription ROYAL SPORT NAUTIQUE, and joined in the talk. They were all very polite, voluble, and enthusiastic; and their discourse was interlarded with English boating-terms, and the names of English boat-builders and English clubs. I do not know, to my shame, any spot in my native land, where I should have been so warmly received by the same number of people. We were English boating-men, and the Belgian boating-men fell upon our necks. I wonder if French Huguenots were as cordially greeted by English Protestants when they came across the Channel out of great tribulation. But, after all, what religion knits people so closely as common sport?

The canoes were carried into the boat-house; they were washed down for us by the club servants, the sails were hung out to dry, and everything made as snug and tidy as a picture. And in the meanwhile we were led upstairs by our new-found brethren, for so more than one of them stated the relationship, and made free of their lavatory. This one lent us soap, that one a towel, a third and fourth helped us to undo our bags. And all the time such questions, such assurances of respect and sympathy! I declare I never knew what glory was before.

"Yes, yes, the *Royal Sport Nautique* is the oldest club in Belgium."

"We number two hundred."

"We" — this is not a substantive speech, but an abstract of many speeches, the impression left upon my mind after a great deal of talk; and very youthful, pleasant, natural, and patriotic it seems to me to be —

"We have gained all races, except those where we were cheated by the French."

"You must leave all your wet things to be dried."

"O! *entre frères!* In any boat-house in England we should find the same." (I cordially hope they might.)

"*En Angleterre, vous employez des sliding-seats, n'est-ce pas?*"

"We are all employed in commerce during the day; but in the evening, *voyez-vous, nous sommes sérieux.*"

These were the words. They were all employed over the frivolous mercantile concerns of Belgium during the day; but in the evening they found some hours for the serious concerns of life. I may have a wrong idea of wisdom, but I think that was a very wise remark. People connected with literature and philosophy are busy all their days in getting rid of second-hand notions and false standards. It is their profession, in the sweat of their brows, by dogged thinking, to recover their old fresh view of life, and distinguish what they really and originally like from what they have only learned to tolerate perforce. And these Royal Nautical Sportsmen had the distinction still quite legible in their hearts. They had still those clean perceptions of what is nice and nasty, what is interesting and what is dull, which envious old gentlemen refer to as illusions. The nightmare illusion of middle age, the bear's hug of custom gradually squeezing the life out of a man's soul, had not yet begun for these happy-star'd young Belgians. They still knew that the interest they took in their business was a trifling affair compared to their spontaneous, long-suffering affection for nautical sports. To know what you prefer, instead of humbly saying Amen to what the world tells

you you ought to prefer, is to have kept your soul alive.
Such a man may be generous; he may be honest in
something more than the commercial sense; he may love
his friends with an elective, personal sympathy, and not
accept them as an adjunct of the station to which he has
been called. He may be a man, in short, acting on his
own instincts, keeping in his own shape that God made
him in; and not a mere crank in the social enginehouse,
welded on principles that he does not understand, and
for purposes that he does not care for.

For will any one dare to tell me that business is more
entertaining than fooling among boats? He must have
never seen a boat, or never seen an office, who says so.
And for certain the one is a great deal better for the
health. There should be nothing so much a man's
business as his amusements. Nothing but money-
grubbing can be put forward to the contrary; no one but

> Mammon, the least erected spirit that fell
> From Heaven,

durst risk a word in answer. It is but a lying cant that
would represent the merchant and the banker as people
disinterestedly toiling for mankind, and then most useful
when they are most absorbed in their transactions; for
the man is more important than his services. And when
my Royal Nautical Sportsman shall have so far fallen
from his hopeful youth that he cannot pluck up an enthusiasm over anything but his ledger, I venture to doubt
whether he will be near so nice a fellow, and whether he
would welcome, with so good a grace, a couple of drenched
Englishmen paddling into Brussels in the dusk.

When we had changed our wet clothes and drunk a

glass of pale ale to the club's prosperity, one of their number escorted us to a hotel. He would not join us at our dinner, but he had no objection to a glass of wine. Enthusiasm is very wearing; and I begin to understand why prophets were unpopular in Judæa, where they were best known. For three stricken hours did this excellent young man sit beside us to dilate on boats and boat-races; and before he left, he was kind enough to order our bed-room candles.

We endeavoured now and again to change the subject; but the diversion did not last a moment: the Royal Nautical Sportsman bridled, shied, answered the question, and then breasted once more into the swelling tide of his subject. I call it his subject; but I think it was he who was subjected. The *Arethusa*, who holds all racing as a creature of the devil, found himself in a pitiful dilemma. He durst not own his ignorance for the honour of old England, and spoke away about English clubs and English oarsmen whose fame had never before come to his ears. Several times, and once, above all, on the question of sliding-seats, he was within an ace of exposure. As for the *Cigarette*, who has rowed races in the heat of his blood, but now disowns these slips of his wanton youth, his case was still more desperate; for the Royal Nautical proposed that he should take an oar in one of their eights on the morrow, to compare the English with the Belgian stroke. I could see my friend perspiring in his chair whenever that particular topic came up. And there was yet another proposal which had the same effect on both of us. It appeared that the champion canoeist of Europe (as well as most other champions) was a Royal Nautical Sportsman. And if we would only wait until

the Sunday, this infernal paddler would be so condescend-
ing as to accompany us on our next stage. Neither of
us had the least desire to drive the coursers of the sun
against Apollo.

When the young man was gone, we countermanded our
candles, and ordered some brandy and water. The great
billows had gone over our head. The Royal Nautical
Sportsmen were as nice young fellows as a man would
wish to see, but they were a trifle too young and a thought
too nautical for us. We began to see that we were old
and cynical; we liked ease and the agreeable rambling
of the human mind about this and the other subject;
we did not want to disgrace our native land by messing
at eight, or toiling pitifully in the wake of the champion
canoeist. In short, we had recourse to flight. It seemed
ungrateful, but we tried to make that good on a card
loaded with sincere compliments. And indeed it was no
time for scruples; we seemed to feel the hot breath of
the champion on our necks.

AT MAUBEUGE

PARTLY from the terror we had of our good friends the Royal Nauticals, partly from the fact that there were no fewer than fifty-five locks between Brussels and Charleroi, we concluded that we should travel by train across the frontier, boats and all. Fifty-five locks in a day's journey was pretty well tantamount to trudging the whole distance on foot, with the canoes upon our shoulders, an object of astonishment to the trees on the canal-side, and of honest derision to all right-thinking children.

To pass the frontier, even in a train, is a difficult matter for the *Arethusa*. He is, somehow or other, a marked man for the official eye. Wherever he journeys, there are the officers gathered together. Treaties are solemnly signed, foreign ministers, ambassadors, and consuls sit throned in state from China to Peru, and the union jack flutters on all the winds of heaven. Under these safe-guards, portly clergymen, school-mistresses, gentlemen in grey tweed suits, and all the ruck and rabble of British touristry pour unhindered, *Murray* in hand, over the railways of the Continent, and yet the slim person of the *Arethusa* is taken in the meshes, while these great fish go on their way rejoicing. If he travels without a passport, he is cast, without any figure about the matter, into noisome dungeons: if his papers are in order, he is suffered to go his way indeed, but not until he has been humiliated by a general incredulity. He is a born British

subject, yet he has never succeeded in persuading a single
official of his nationality. He flatters himself he is indifferent honest; yet he is rarely known for anything
better than a spy, and there is no absurd and disreputable
means of livelihood but has been attributed to him in
some heat of official or popular distrust. . . .

For the life of me I cannot understand it. I, too,
have been knolled to church and sat at good men's feasts,
but I bear no mark of it. I am as strange as a Jack
Indian to their official spectacles. I might come from
any part of the globe, it seems, except from where I do.
My ancestors have laboured in vain, and the glorious
Constitution cannot protect me in my walks abroad. It is
a great thing, believe me, to present a good normal type
of the nation you belong to.

Nobody else was asked for his papers on the way to
Maubeuge, but I was; and although I clung to my rights,
I had to choose at last between accepting the humiliation
and being left behind by the train. I was sorry to give
way, but I wanted to get to Maubeuge.

Maubeuge is a fortified town with a very good inn,
the *Grand Cerf*. It seemed to be inhabited principally
by soldiers and bagmen; at least, these were all that we
saw except the hotel servants. We had to stay there
some time, for the canoes were in no hurry to follow us,
and at last stuck hopelessly in the custom-house until
we went back to liberate them. There was nothing to
do, nothing to see. We had good meals, which was a
great matter, but that was all.

The *Cigarette* was nearly taken up upon a charge of
drawing the fortifications: a feat of which he was hopelessly incapable. And besides, as I suppose each bellig-

erent nation has a plan of the other's fortified places already, these precautions are of the nature of shutting the stable door after the steed is away. But I have no doubt they help to keep up a good spirit at home. It is a great thing if you can persuade people that they are somehow or other partakers in a mystery. It makes them feel bigger. Even the Freemasons, who have been shown up to satiety, preserve a kind of pride; and not a grocer among them, however honest, harmless, and empty-headed he may feel himself to be at bottom, but comes home from one of their *cænacula* with a portentous significance for himself.

It is an odd thing how happily two people, if there are two, can live in a place where they have no acquaintance. I think the spectacle of a whole life in which you have no part paralyses personal desire. You are content to become a mere spectator. The baker stands in his door; the colonel with his three medals goes by to the *café* at night; the troops drum and trumpet and man the ramparts as bold as so many lions. It would task language to say how placidly you behold all this. In a place where you have taken some root you are provoked out of your indifference; you have a hand in the game, — your friends are fighting with the army. But in a strange town, not small enough to grow too soon familiar, nor so large as to have laid itself out for travellers, you stand so far apart from the business that you positively forget it would be possible to go nearer; you have so little human interest around you that you do not remember yourself to be a man. Perhaps in a very short time you would be one no longer. Gymnosophists go into a wood with all nature seething around them, with romance on every side; it

would be much more to the purpose if they took up their
abode in a dull country town where they should see just
so much of humanity as to keep them from desiring more,
and only the stale externals of man's life.   These externals
are as dead to us as so many formalities, and speak a dead
language in our eyes and ears.   They have no more meaning than an oath or a salutation.   We are so much accustomed to see married couples going to church of a
Sunday that we have clean forgotten what they represent;
and novelists are driven to rehabilitate adultery, no less,
when they wish to show us what a beautiful thing it is
for a man and a woman to live for each other.

One person in Maubeuge, however, showed me something more than his outside.   That was the driver of
the hotel omnibus: a mean enough looking little man, as
well as I can remember, but with a spark of something
human in his soul.   He had heard of our little journey,
and came to me at once in envious sympathy.   How he
longed to travel! he told me.   How he longed to be
somewhere else, and see the round world before he
went into the grave!   "Here I am," said he.   "I
drive to the station.   Well.   And then I drive back
again to the hotel.   And so on every day and all the
week round.   My God, is that life?"   I could not say
I thought it was — for him.   He pressed me to tell him
where I had been, and where I hoped to go; and as he
listened, I declare the fellow sighed.   Might not this
have been a brave African traveller, or gone to the Indies
after Drake?   But it is an evil age for the gipsily inclined
among men.   He who can sit squarest on a three-legged
stool, he it is who has the wealth and glory.

I wonder if my friend is still driving the omnibus for

the *Grand Cerf!* Not very likely, I believe; for I think
he was on the eve of mutiny when we passed through,
and perhaps our passage determined him for good. Better
a thousand times that he should be a tramp, and mend
pots and pans by the wayside, and sleep under trees,
and see the dawn and the sunset every day above a new
horizon. I think I hear you say that it is a respectable
position to drive an omnibus? Very well. What right
has he who likes it not to keep those who would like it
dearly out of this respectable position? Suppose a dish
were not to my taste, and you told me that it was a
favourite among the rest of the company, what should
I conclude from that? Not to finish the dish against my
stomach, I suppose.

Respectability is a very good thing in its way, but it
does not rise superior to all considerations. I would not
for a moment venture to hint that it was a matter of
taste; but I think I will go as far as this: that if a position
is admittedly unkind, uncomfortable, unnecessary, and
superfluously useless, although it were as respectable
as the Church of England, the sooner a man is out of it,
the better for himself, and all concerned.

ON THE SAMBRE CANALISED

To Quartes

ABOUT three in the afternoon the whole establishment of the *Grand Cerf* accompanied us to the water's edge. The man of the omnibus was there with haggard eyes. Poor cage-bird! Do I not remember the time when I myself haunted the station, to watch train after train carry its complement of freemen into the night, and read the names of distant places on the time-bills with indescribable longings?

We were not clear of the fortifications before the rain began. The wind was contrary, and blew in furious gusts; nor were the aspects of nature any more clement than the doings of the sky. For we passed through a blighted country, sparsely covered with brush, but handsomely enough diversified with factory chimneys. We landed in a soiled meadow among some pollards, and there smoked a pipe in a flaw of fair weather. But the wind blew so hard we could get little else to smoke. There were no natural objects in the neighbourhood, but some sordid workshops. A group of children, headed by a tall girl, stood and watched us from a little distance all the time we stayed. I heartily wonder what they thought of us.

At Hautmont, the lock was almost impassable; the landing-place being steep and high, and the launch at a long distance. Near a dozen grimy workmen lent us a hand. They refused any reward; and, what is much

better, refused it handsomely, without conveying any
sense of insult. "It is a way we have in our country-side,"
said they. And a very becoming way it is. In Scotland, where also you will get services for nothing, the good
people reject your money as if you had been trying to
corrupt a voter. When people take the trouble to do dignified acts, it is worth while to take a little more, and
allow the dignity to be common to all concerned. But
in our brave Saxon countries, where we plod threescore
years and ten in the mud, and the wind keeps singing in
our ears from birth to burial, we do our good and bad with
a high hand and almost offensively; and make even our
alms a witness-bearing and an act of war against the wrong.

After Hautmont, the sun came forth again and the wind
went down; and a little paddling took us beyond the
iron works and through a delectable land. The river
wound among low hills, so that sometimes the sun was at
our backs and sometimes it stood right ahead, and the
river before us was one sheet of intolerable glory. On
either hand meadows and orchards bordered, with a margin of sedge and water flowers, upon the river. The hedges
were of great height, woven about the trunks of hedgerow
elms; and the fields, as they were often very small, looked
like a series of bowers along the stream. There was never
any prospect; sometimes a hill-top with its trees would
look over the nearest hedgerow, just to make a middle
distance for the sky; but that was all. The heaven
was bare of clouds. The atmosphere, after the rain, was
of enchanting purity. The river doubled among the
hillocks, a shining strip of mirror glass; and the dip of
the paddles set the flowers shaking along the brink.

In the meadows wandered black and white cattle

fantastically marked. One beast, with a white head and the rest of the body glossy black, came to the edge to drink, and stood gravely twitching his ears at me as I went by, like some sort of preposterous clergyman in a play. A moment after I heard a loud plunge, and, turning my head, saw the clergyman struggling to shore. The bank had given way under his feet.

Besides the cattle, we saw no living things except a few birds and a great many fishermen. These sat along the edges of the meadows, sometimes with one rod, sometimes with as many as half a score. They seemed stupefied with contentment; and, when we induced them to exchange a few words with us about the weather, their voices sounded quiet and far away. There was a strange diversity of opinion among them as to the kind of fish for which they set their lures; although they were all agreed in this, that the river was abundantly supplied. Where it was plain that no two of them had ever caught the same kind of fish, we could not help suspecting that perhaps not any one of them had ever caught a fish at all. I hope, since the afternoon was so lovely, that they were one and all rewarded; and that a silver booty went home in every basket for the pot. Some of my friends would cry shame on me for this; but I prefer a man were he only an angler, to the bravest pair of gills in all God's waters. I do not affect fishes unless when cooked in sauce; whereas an angler is an important piece of river scenery, and hence deserves some recognition among canoeists. He can always tell you where you are, after a mild fashion; and his quiet presence serves to accentuate the solitude and stillness, and remind you of the glittering citizens below your boat.

The Sambre turned so industriously to and fro among his little hills that it was past six before we drew near the lock at Quartes. There were some children on the tow-path, with whom the *Cigarette* fell into a chaffing talk as they ran along beside us. It was in vain that I warned him. In vain I told him in English that boys were the most dangerous creatures; and if once you began with them, it was safe to end in a shower of stones. For my own part, whenever anything was addressed to me, I smiled gently and shook my head, as though I were an inoffensive person inadequately acquainted with French. For indeed, I have had such an experience at home that I would sooner meet many wild animals than a troop of healthy urchins.

But I was doing injustice to these peaceable young Hainaulters. When the *Cigarette* went off to make inquiries, I got out upon the bank to smoke a pipe and superintend the boats, and became at once the centre of much amiable curiosity. The children had been joined by this time by a young woman and a mild lad who had lost an arm; and this gave me more security. When I let slip my first word or so in French, a little girl nodded her head with a comical grown-up air. "Ah, you see," she said, "he understands well enough now; he was just making believe." And the little group laughed together very good-naturedly.

They were much impressed when they heard we came from England; and the little girl proffered the information that England was an island "and a far way from here — *bien loin d'ici.*"

"Ay, you may say that, a far way from here," said the lad with one arm.

I was nearly as homesick as ever I was in my life; they seemed to make it such an incalculable distance to the place where I first saw the day.

They admired the canoes very much. And I observed one piece of delicacy in these children which is worthy of record. They had been deafening us for the last hundred yards with petitions for a sail; ay, and they deafened us to the same tune next morning when we came to start; but then, when the canoes were lying empty, there was no word of any such petition. Delicacy? or perhaps a bit of fear for the water in so crank a vessel? I hate cynicism a great deal worse than I do the devil; unless perhaps, the two were the same thing? And yet 'tis a good tonic; the cold tub and bath-towel of the sentiments; and positively necessary to life in cases of advanced sensibility.

From the boats they turned to my costume. They could not make enough of my red sash; and my knife filled them with awe.

"They make them like that in England," said the boy with one arm. I was glad he did not know how badly we make them in England nowadays. "They are for people who go away to sea," he added, "and to defend one's life against great fish."

I felt I was becoming a more and more romantic figure to the little group at every word. And so I suppose I was. Even my pipe, although it was an ordinary French clay, pretty well "trousered," as they call it, would have a rarity in their eyes, as a thing coming from so far away. And if my feathers were not very fine in themselves, they were all from over seas. One thing in my outfit, however, tickled them out of all politeness; and that was the bemired condition of my canvas shoes. I

suppose they were sure the mud at any rate was a home
product. The little girl (who was the genius of the
party) displayed her own sabots in competition; and I
wish you could have seen how gracefully and merrily she
did it.

The young woman's milk-can, a great amphora of
hammered brass, stood some way off upon the sward. I
was glad of an opportunity to divert public attention from
myself and return some of the compliments I had received.
So I admired it cordially both for form and colour, telling
them, and very truly, that it was as beautiful as gold. They
were not surprised. The things were plainly the boast
of the country-side. And the children expatiated on the
costliness of these amphoræ, which sell sometimes as high
as thirty francs apiece; told me how they were carried
on donkeys, one on either side of the saddle, a brave
caparison in themselves; and how they were to be seen
all over the district, and at the larger farms in great number and of great size.

PONT-SUR-SAMBRE

We are Pedlars

THE *Cigarette* returned with good news. There were beds to be had some ten minutes' walk from where we were, at a place called Pont. We stowed the canoes in a granary, and asked among the children for a guide. The circle at once widened round us, and our offers of reward were received in dispiriting silence. We were plainly a pair of Bluebeards to the children; they might speak to us in public places, and where they had the advantage of numbers; but it was another thing to venture off alone with two uncouth and legendary characters, who had dropped from the clouds upon their hamlet this quiet afternoon, sashed and beknived, and with a flavour of great voyages. The owner of the granary came to our assistance, singled out one little fellow, and threatened him with corporalities; or I suspect we should have had to find the way for ourselves. As it was, he was more frightened at the granary man than the strangers, having perhaps had some experience of the former. But I fancy his little heart must have been going at a fine rate, for he kept trotting at a respectful distance in front, and looking back at us with scared eyes. Not otherwise may the children of the young world have guided Jove or one of his Olympian compeers on an adventure.

A miry lane led us up from Quartes, with its church

and bickering wind-mill. The hinds were trudging home-
wards from the fields. A brisk little old woman passed
us by. She was seated across a donkey between a pair
of glittering milk-cans, and, as she went, she kicked jauntily
with her heels upon the donkey's side, and scattered
shrill remarks among the wayfarers. It was notable that
none of the tired men took the trouble to reply. Our
conductor soon led us out of the lane and across country.
The sun had gone down, but the west in front of us was
one lake of level gold. The path wandered awhile in the
open, and then passed under a trellis like a bower in-
definitely prolonged. On either hand were shadowy
orchards; cottages lay low among the leaves and sent
their smoke to heaven; every here and there, in an opening, appeared the great gold face of the west.

I never saw the *Cigarette* in such an idyllic frame of
mind. He waxed positively lyrical in praise of country
scenes. I was little less exhilarated myself; the mild
air of the evening, the shadows, the rich lights, and the
silence made a symphonious accompaniment about our
walk; and we both determined to avoid towns for the
future and sleep in hamlets.

At last the path went between two houses, and turned
the party out into a wide, muddy highroad, bordered,
as far as the eye could reach on either hand, by an unsightly village. The houses stood well back, leaving a
ribbon of waste land on either side of the road, where
there were stacks of firewood, carts, barrows, rubbish
heaps, and a little doubtful grass. Away on the left, a
gaunt tower stood in the middle of the street. What
it had been in past ages I know not: probably a hold in
time of war; but nowadays it bore an illegible dial-plate

in its upper parts, and near the bottom an iron letter-box.

The inn to which we had been recommended at Quartes was full, or else the landlady did not like our looks. I ought to say, that with our long, damp india-rubber bags, we presented rather a doubtful type of civilisation : like rag-and-bone men, the *Cigarette* imagined. "These gentlemen are pedlars? — *Ces messieurs sont des marchands?*" — asked the landlady. And then, without waiting for an answer, which I suppose she thought superfluous in so plain a case, recommended us to a butcher who lived hard by the tower and took in travellers to lodge.

Thither went we. But the butcher was flitting, and all his beds were taken down. Or else he didn't like our looks. As a parting shot, we had, "These gentlemen are pedlars?"

It began to grow dark in earnest. We could no longer distinguish the faces of the people who passed us by with an inarticulate good-evening. And the householders of Pont seemed very economical with their oil, for we saw not a single window lighted in all that long village. I believe it is the longest village in the world; but I dare say in our predicament every pace counted three times over. We were much cast down when we came to the last auberge, and, looking in at the dark door, asked timidly if we could sleep there for the night. A female voice assented, in no very friendly tones. We clapped the bags down and found our way to chairs.

The place was in total darkness, save a red glow in the chinks and ventilators of the stove. But now the landlady lit a lamp to see her new guests; I suppose the darkness was what saved us another expulsion, for I

cannot say she looked gratified at our appearance. We
were in a large, bare apartment, adorned with two alle-
gorical prints of Music and Painting, and a copy of the
Law against ·Public Drunkenness. On one side there was
a bit of a bar, with some half-a-dozen bottles. Two
labourers sat waiting supper, in attitudes of extreme
weariness; a plain-looking lass bustled about with a
sleepy child of two, and the landlady began to derange
the pots upon the stove and set some beefsteak to grill.

"These gentlemen are pedlars?" she asked sharply;
and that was all the conversation forthcoming. We
began to think we might be pedlars, after all. I never
knew a population with so narrow a range of conjecture
as the innkeepers of Pont-sur-Sambre. But manners
and bearing have not a wider currency than bank-notes.
You have only to get far enough out of your beat, and
all your accomplished airs will go for nothing. These
Hainaulters could see no difference between us and the
average pedlar. Indeed, we had some grounds for reflection while the steak was getting ready, to see how perfectly they accepted us at their own valuation, and how
our best politeness and best efforts at entertainment
seemed to fit quite suitably with the character of pack-
men. At least it seemed a good account of the profession
in France, that even before such judges we could not
beat them at our own weapons.

At last we were called to table. The two hinds (and
one of them looked sadly worn and white in the face, as
though sick with over-work and under-feeding) supped
off a single plate of some sort of bread-berry, some potatoes in their jackets, a small cup of coffee sweetened
with sugar candy, and one tumbler of swipes. The land-

lady, her son, and the lass aforesaid took the same. Our meal was quite a banquet by comparison. We had some beefsteak, not so tender as it might have been, some of the potatoes, some cheese, an extra glass of the swipes, and white sugar in our coffee.

You see what it is to be a gentleman, — I beg your pardon, what it is to be a pedlar. It had not before

THE TOWN HALL AT NOYON (See page 92)

occurred to me that a pedlar was a great man in a labourer's alehouse; but now that I had to enact the part for the evening, I found that so it was. He has in his hedge quarters somewhat the same pre-eminence as the man who takes a private parlour in a hotel. The more you look into it the more infinite are the class distinctions among men; and possibly, by a happy dispensation there is no one at all at the bottom of the scale; no one but can find some superiority over somebody else, to keep up his pride withal.

We were displeased enough with our fare. Particularly the *Cigarette;* for I tried to make believe that I was amused with the adventure, tough beefsteak and all. According to the Lucretian maxim, our steak should have been flavoured by the look of the other people's bread-berry; but we did not find it so in practice. You may have a head knowledge that other people live more poorly than yourself, but it is not agreeable — I was going to say, it is against the etiquette of the universe — to sit at the same table and pick your own superior diet from among their crusts. I had not seen such a thing done since the greedy boy at school with his birthday cake. It was odious enough to witness, I could remember; and I had never thought to play the part myself. But there, again, you see what it is to be a pedlar.

There is no doubt that the poorer classes in our country are much more charitably disposed than their superiors in wealth. And I fancy it must arise a great deal from the comparative indistinction of the easy and the not so easy in these ranks. A workman or a pedlar cannot shutter himself off from his less comfortable neighbours. If he treats himself to a luxury, he must do it in the face of a dozen who cannot. And what should more directly lead to charitable thoughts? . . . Thus the poor man, camping out in life, sees it as it is, and knows that every mouthful he puts in his belly has been wrenched out of the fingers of the hungry.

But at a certain stage of prosperity, as in a balloon ascent, the fortunate person passes through a zone of clouds, and sublunary matters are thenceforward hidden from his view. He sees nothing but the heavenly bodies, all in admirable order and positively as good as new. He finds himself surrounded in the most touching manner by the attentions of Providence, and compares himself involuntarily with the lilies and the skylarks. He does not precisely sing, of course; but then he looks so unassuming in his open Landau! If all the world dined at one table, this philosophy would meet with some rude knocks.

PONT–SUR–SAMBRE

The Travelling Merchant

LIKE the lackeys in Molière's farce, when the true nobleman broke in on their high life below stairs, we were destined to be confronted with a real pedlar. To make the lesson still more poignant for fallen gentlemen like us, he was a pedlar of infinitely more consideration than the sort of scurvy fellows we were taken for; like a lion among mice, or a ship of war bearing down upon two cockboats. Indeed, he did not deserve the name of pedlar at all; he was a travelling merchant.

I suppose it was about half-past eight when this worthy, Monsieur Hector Gilliard, of Maubeuge, turned up at the alehouse door in a tilt cart drawn by a donkey, and cried cheerily on the inhabitants. He was a lean, nervous flibber-tigibbet of a man, with something the look of an actor and something the look of a horse jockey. He had evidently prospered without any of the favours of education, for he adhered with stern simplicity to the masculine gender, and in the course of the evening passed off some fancy futures in a very florid style of architecture. With him came his wife, a comely young woman, with her hair tied in a yellow kerchief, and their son, a little fellow of four, in a blouse and military *képi*. It was notable that the child was many degrees better dressed than either of the parents. We were informed he was already at a boarding-school; but the holidays having just commenced, he was off to spend them with his parents on a cruise. An enchanting holiday occupation, was it not? to travel all day with father and mother in the tilt cart full of countless treasures; the green country rattling by on either side, and the children in all the villages contemplating him with envy and wonder. It is better fun, during the holidays, to be the son of a travelling merchant, than son and heir to the greatest cotton spinner in creation. And as for being a reigning prince, — indeed, I never saw one if it was not Master Gilliard !

While M. Hector and the son of the house were putting up the donkey and getting all the valuables under lock and key, the landlady warmed up the remains of our beefsteak and fried the cold potatoes in slices, and Madame Gilliard set herself to waken the boy, who had come far that day, and was peevish and dazzled by the light. He was no sooner awake than he began to prepare himself for supper by eating galette, unripe pears, and cold potatoes, with, so far as I could judge, positive benefit to his appetite.

The landlady, fired with motherly emulation, awoke her own little girl, and the two children were confronted. Master Gilliard looked at her for a moment, very much as a dog looks at his own reflection in a mirror before he turns away. He was at that time absorbed in the galette. His mother seemed crestfallen that he should display so little inclination towards the other sex, and expressed her disappointment with some candour and a very proper reference to the influence of years.

Sure enough a time will come when he will pay more attention to the girls, and think a great deal less of his mother; let us hope she will like it as well as she seemed to fancy. But it is odd enough; the very women who profess most contempt for mankind as a sex seem to find even its ugliest particulars rather lively and high-minded in their own sons.

The little girl looked longer and with more interest, probably because she was in her own house, while he was a traveller and accustomed to strange sights. And, besides, there was no galette in the case with her.

All the time of supper there was nothing spoken of but my young lord. The two parents were both absurdly fond of their child. Monsieur kept insisting on his sagacity; how he knew all the children at school by name, and when this utterly failed on trial, how he was cautious and exact to a strange degree, and if asked anything, he would sit and think — and think, and if he did not know it, "my faith, he wouldn't tell you at all — *ma foi, il ne vous le dira pas.*" Which is certainly a very high degree of caution. At intervals, M. Hector would appeal to his wife, with his mouth full of beefsteak, as to the little fellow's age at such or such a time when he had said or done something memorable; and I noticed that Madame usually poohpooed these inquiries. She herself was not boastful in her vein; but she never had her fill of caressing the child; and she seemed to take a gentle pleasure in recalling all that was fortunate in his little existence. No school-boy could have talked more of the holidays which were just beginning and less of the black school-time which must inevitably follow after. She showed, with a pride perhaps partly mercantile in origin, his pockets preposterously swollen with tops, and whistles, and string. When she called at a house in the way of business, it appeared he kept her company; and, whenever a sale was made, received a sou out of the profit. Indeed, they spoiled him vastly, these two good people. But they had an eye to his manners, for all that, and reproved him for some little faults in breeding which occurred from time to time during supper.

On the whole, I was not much hurt at being taken for a pedlar. I might think that I ate with greater delicacy, or that my mistakes in French belonged to a different order; but it was plain that these distinctions would be thrown away upon the landlady and the two labourers. In all essential things we and the Gilliards cut very much the same figure in the alehouse kitchen. M. Hector was more at home, indeed, and took a higher tone with the world; but that was explicable on the ground of his driving a donkey-cart, while we poor bodies tramped afoot. I dare say the rest of the company thought us dying with envy, though in no ill sense, to be as far up in the profession as the new arrival.

And of one thing I am sure; that every one thawed and became more humanised and conversible as soon as these innocent people appeared upon the scene. I would not very readily trust the travelling merchant with any extravagant sum of money, but I am sure his heart was in the right place. In this mixed world, if you can find one or two sensible places in a man; above all, if you should find a whole family living together on such pleasant terms, you may surely be satisfied, and take the rest for granted; or, what is a great deal better, boldly make up your mind that you can do perfectly well without the rest, and that ten thousand bad traits cannot make a single good one any the less good.

It was getting late. M. Hector lit a stable lantern and went off to his cart for some arrangement, and my young gentleman proceeded to divest himself of the better part of his raiment and play gymnastics on his mother's lap, and thence on to the floor, with accompaniment of laughter.

"Are you going to sleep alone?" asked the servant lass.

"There's little fear of that," says Master Gilliard.

"You sleep alone at school," objected his mother. "Come, come, you must be a man."

But he protested that school was a different matter from the holidays; that there were dormitories at school, and silenced the discussion with kisses, his mother smiling, no one better pleased than she.

There certainly was, as he phrased it, very little fear that he should sleep alone, for there was but one bed for the trio. We, on our part, had firmly protested against one man's accommodation for two; and we had a double bedded pen in the loft of the house, furnished, beside the beds, with exactly three hat pegs and one table. There was not so much as a glass of water. But the window would open, by good fortune.

Some time before I fell asleep the loft was full of the sound of mighty snoring; the Gilliards, and the labourers, and the people of the inn, all at it, I suppose, with one consent. The young moon outside shone very clearly over *Pont-sur-Sambre*, and down upon the alehouse where all we pedlars were abed.

ON THE SAMBRE CANALISED

To Landrecies

In the morning, when we came down-stairs the land-lady pointed out to us two pails of water behind the street door. "*Voilà de l'eau pour vous débarbouiller*," says she. And so there we made a shift to wash ourselves, while Madame Gilliard brushed the family boots on the outer doorstep, and M. Hector, whistling cheerily, arranged some small goods for the day's campaign in a portable chest of drawers, which formed a part of his baggage. Meanwhile the child was letting off Waterloo crackers all over the floor.

I wonder, by the way, what they call Waterloo crackers in France; perhaps Austerlitz crackers. There is a great deal in the point of view. Do you remember the French-man who, travelling by way of Southampton, was put down in Waterloo Station, and had to drive across Water-loo Bridge? He had a mind to go home again, it seems.

Pont itself is on the river, but whereas it is ten minutes' walk from Quartes by dry land, it is six weary kilometres by water. We left our bags at the inn and walked to our canoes through the wet orchards unencumbered. Some of the children were there to see us off, but we were no longer the mysterious beings of the night before. A de-parture is much less romantic than an unexplained arrival in the golden evening. Although we might be greatly taken at a ghost's first appearance, we should behold him vanish with comparative equanimity.

The good folks of the inn at Pont, when we called there for the bags, were overcome with marvelling. At the sight of these two dainty little boats, with a fluttering union jack on each, and all the varnish shining from the sponge, they began to perceive that they had entertained angels unawares. The landlady stood upon the bridge, probably lamenting she had charged so little; the son ran to and fro, and called out the neighbours to enjoy the sight; and we paddled away from quite a crowd of rapt observers. These gentlemen pedlars, indeed! Now you see their quality too late.

The whole day was showery, with occasional drenching plumps. We were soaked to the skin, then partially dried in the sun, then soaked once more. But there were some calm intervals, and one notably, when we were skirting the forest of Mormal, a sinister name to the ear, but a place most gratifying to sight and smell. It looked solemn along the river-side, drooping its boughs into the water, and piling them up aloft into a wall of leaves. What is a forest but a city of nature's own, full of hardy and innocuous living things, where there is nothing dead and nothing made with the hands, but the citizens themselves are the houses and public monuments? There is nothing so much alive and yet so quiet as a woodland; and a pair of people, swinging past in canoes, feel very small and bustling by comparison.

And, surely, of all smells in the world the smell of many trees is the sweetest and most fortifying. The sea has a rude pistolling sort of odour, that takes you in the nostrils like snuff, and carries with it a fine sentiment of open water and tall ships; but the smell of a forest, which comes nearest to this in tonic quality, surpasses it by many de-

grees in the quality of softness. Again, the smell of the
sea has little variety, but the smell of a forest is infinitely
changeful; it varies with the hour of the day, not in
strength merely, but in character; and the different
sorts of trees, as you go from one zone of the wood to another, seem to live among different kinds of atmosphere.
Usually the rosin of the fir predominates. But some
woods are more coquettish in their habits; and the breath
of the forest Mormal, as it came aboard upon us that
showery afternoon, was perfumed with nothing less delicate than sweetbrier.

I wish our way had always lain among woods. Trees
are the most civil society. An old oak that has been
growing where he stands since before the Reformation,
taller than many spires, more stately than the greater part
of mountains, and yet a living thing, liable to sicknesses
and death, like you and me: is not that in itself a speaking lesson in history? But acres on acres full of such
patriarchs contiguously rooted, their green tops billow-
ing in the wind, their stalwart younglings pushing up
about their knees; a whole forest, healthy and beautiful,
giving colour to the light, giving perfume to the air;
what is this but the most imposing piece in nature's
repertory? Heine wished to lie like Merlin under the
oaks of Broceliande. I should not be satisfied with one
tree; but if the wood grew together like a banyan grove,
I would be buried under the taproot of the whole; my
parts should circulate from oak to oak; and my consciousness should be diffused abroad in all the forest, and give
a common heart to that assembly of green spires, so that
it, also, might rejoice in its own loveliness and dignity.
I think I feel a thousand squirrels leaping from bough to

bough in my vast mausoleum; and the birds and the winds merrily coursing over its uneven, leafy surface.

Alas! the forest of Mormal is only a little bit of a wood, and it was but for a little way that we skirted by its boundaries. And the rest of the time the rain kept coming in squirts and the wind in squalls, until one's heart grew weary of such fitful, scolding weather. It was odd how the showers began when we had to carry the boats over a lock and must expose our legs. They always did. This is a sort of thing that readily begets a personal feeling against nature. There seems no reason why the shower should not come five minutes before or five minutes after, unless you suppose an intention to affront you. The *Cigarette* had a mackintosh which put him more or less above these contrarieties. But I had to bear the brunt uncovered. I began to remember that nature was a woman. My companion, in a rosier temper, listened with great satisfaction to my jeremiads, and ironically concurred. He instanced, as a cognate matter, the action of the tides, "which," said he, "was altogether designed for the confusion of canoeists, except in so far as it was calculated to minister to a barren vanity on the part of the moon."

At the last lock, some little way out of Landrecies, I refused to go any farther; and sat in a drift of rain by the side of the bank, to have a reviving pipe. A vivacious old man, whom I took to have been the devil, drew near, and questioned me about our journey. In the fulness of my heart I laid bare our plans before him. He said it was the silliest enterprise that ever he heard of. Why, did I not know, he asked me, that it was nothing but locks, locks, locks, the whole way? not to mention that, at this season of the year, we would find the Oise quite dry? "Get into a train, my little young man," said he, "and go you away home to your parents." I was so astounded at the man's malice that I could only stare at him in silence. A tree would never have spoken to me like this. At last I got out with some words. We had come from Antwerp already, I told him, which was a good long way; and we should do the rest in spite of him. Yes, I said, if there were no other reason, I would do it now, just because he had dared to say we could not. The pleasant old gentleman looked at me sneeringly, made an allusion to my canoe, and marched off, wagging his head.

I was still inwardly fuming when up came a pair of young fellows, who imagined I was the *Cigarette's* servant, on a comparison, I suppose, of my bare jersey with the other's mackintosh, and asked me many questions about my place and my master's character. I said he was a good enough fellow, but had this absurd voyage on the head. "Oh, no, no," said one, "you must not say that; it is not absurd; it is very courageous of him." I believe these were a couple of angels sent to give me heart again. It was truly fortifying to reproduce all the old man's insinuations, as if they were original to me in my character of a malcontent footman, and have them brushed away like so many flies by these admirable young men.

When I recounted this affair to the *Cigarette*, "They must have a curious idea of how English servants behave," says he, drily, "for you treated me like a brute beast at the lock."

I was a good deal mortified; but my temper had suffered, it is a fact.

AT LANDRECIES

At Landrecies the rain still fell and the wind still blew; but we found a double-bedded room with plenty of furniture, real water-jugs with real water in them, and dinner, a real dinner, not innocent of real wine. After having been a pedlar for one night, and a butt for the elements during the whole of the next day, these comfortable circumstances fell on my heart like sunshine. There was an English fruiterer at dinner, travelling with a Belgian fruiterer; in the evening at the *café* we watched our compatriot drop a good deal of money at corks, and I don't know why, but this pleased us.

It turned out that we were to see more of Landrecies than we expected; for the weather next day was simply bedlamite. It is not the place one would have chosen for a day's rest, for it consists almost entirely of fortifications. Within the ramparts, a few blocks of houses, a long row of barracks, and a church figure, with what countenance they may, as the town. There seems to be no trade, and a shop-keeper from whom I bought a sixpenny flint and steel was so much affected that he filled my pockets with spare flints into the bargain. The only public buildings that had any interest for us were the hotel and the *café*. But we visited the church. There lies Marshal Clarke. But as neither of us had ever heard of that military hero, we bore the associations of the spot with fortitude.

In all garrison towns, guard-calls, and *réveilles*, and

such like, make a fine, romantic interlude in civic business. Bugles, and drums, and fifes are of themselves most excellent things in nature, and when they carry the mind to marching armies and the picturesque vicissitudes of war they stir up something proud in the heart. But in a shadow of a town like Landrecies, with little else moving, these points of war made a proportionate commotion. Indeed, they were the only things to remember. It was just the place to hear the round going by at night in the darkness, with the solid tramp of men marching, and the startling reverberations of the drum. It reminded you that even this place was a point in the great warfaring system of Europe, and might on some future day be ringed about with cannon smoke and thunder, and make itself a name among strong towns.

The drum, at any rate, from its martial voice and notable physiological effect, nay, even from its cumbrous and comical shape, stands alone among the instruments of noise. And if it be true, as I have heard it said, that drums are covered with asses' skin, what a picturesque irony is there in that! As if this long-suffering animal's hide had not been sufficiently belaboured during life, now by Lyonnese costermongers, now by presumptuous Hebrew prophets, it must be stripped from his poor hinder quarters after death, stretched on a drum, and beaten night after night round the streets of every garrison town in Europe. And up the heights of Alma and Spicheren, and wherever death has his red flag a-flying, and sounds his own potent tuck upon the cannons, there also must the drummer boy, hurrying with white face over fallen comrades, batter and bemaul this slip of skin from the loins of peaceable donkeys.

Generally a man is never more uselessly employed than when he is at this trick of bastinadoing asses' hide. We know what effect it has in life, and how your dull ass will not mend his pace with beating. But in this state of mummy and melancholy survival of itself, when the hollow skin reverberates to the drummer's wrist, and each dub-a-dub goes direct to a man's heart, and puts madness there, and that disposition of the pulses which we, in our big way of talking, nickname Heroism, — is there not something in the nature of a revenge upon the donkey's persecutors? Of old, he might say, you drubbed me up hill and down dale and I must endure; but now that I am dead those dull thwacks that were scarcely audible in country lanes have become stirring music in front of the brigade, and for every blow that you lay on my old great-coat, you will see a comrade stumble and fall.

Not long after the drums had passed the *café*, the *Cigarette* and the *Arethusa* began to grow sleepy, and set out for the hotel, which was only a door or two away. But although we had been somewhat indifferent to Landrecies, Landrecies had not been indifferent to us. All day, we learned, people had been running out between the squalls to visit our two boats. Hundreds of persons, so said report, although it fitted ill with our idea of the town, — hundreds of persons had inspected them where they lay in a coal-shed. We were becoming lions in Landrecies, who had been only pedlars the night before in Pont.

And now, when we left the *café*, we were pursued and overtaken at the hotel door by no less a person than the Juge de Paix; a functionary, as far as I can make out, of the character of a Scotch Sheriff Substitute. He gave

us his card and invited us to sup with him on the spot,
very neatly, very gracefully, as Frenchmen can do these
things. It was for the credit of Landrecies, said he; and
although we knew very well how little credit we could do
the place, we must have been churlish fellows to refuse
an invitation so politely introduced.

The house of the judge was close by; it was a well-
appointed bachelor's establishment, with a curious collection of old brass warming-pans upon the walls. Some
of these were most elaborately carved. It seemed a picturesque idea for a collector. You could not help thinking how many nightcaps had wagged over these warming-
pans in past generations; what jests may have been made
and kisses taken while they were in service; and how
often they had been uselessly paraded in the bed of death.
If they could only speak at what absurd, indecorous, and
tragical scenes had they not been present?

The wine was excellent. When we made the judge our
compliments upon a bottle, "I do not give it you as my
worst," said he. I wonder when Englishmen will learn
these hospitable graces. They are worth learning; they
set off life and make ordinary moments ornamental.

There were two other Landrecienses present. One
was the collector of something or other, I forget what;
the other, we were told, was the principal notary of the
place. So it happened that we all five more or less followed the law. At this rate, the talk was pretty certain
to become technical. The *Cigarette* expounded the poor
laws very magisterially. And a little later I found myself laying down the Scotch law of illegitimacy, of which
I am glad to say I know nothing. The collector and
the notary, who were both married men, accused the

judge, who was a bachelor, of having started the subject. He deprecated the charge, with a conscious, pleased air, just like all the men I have ever seen, be they French or English. How strange that we should all, in our unguarded moments, rather like to be thought a bit of a rogue with the women!

As the evening went on the wine grew more to my taste; the spirits proved better than the wine; the company was genial. This was the highest water mark of popular favour on the whole cruise. After all, being in a judge's house, was there not something semi-official in the tribute? And so, remembering what a great country France is, we did full justice to our entertainment. Landrecies had been a long while asleep before we returned to the hotel; and the sentries on the ramparts were already looking for daybreak.

SAMBRE AND OISE CANAL

Canal Boats

NEXT day we made a late start in the rain. The judge politely escorted us to the end of the lock under an umbrella. We had now brought ourselves to a pitch of humility, in the matter of weather, not often attained except in the Scotch Highlands. A rag of blue sky or a glimpse of sunshine set our hearts singing; and when the rain was not heavy we counted the day almost fair.

Long lines of barges lay one after another along the canal, many of them looking mighty spruce and shipshape in their jerkin of Archangel tar picked out with white and green. Some carried gay iron railings and quite a parterre of flowerpots. Children played on the decks, as heedless of the rain as if they had been brought up on Loch Caron side; men fished over the gunwale, some of them under umbrellas; women did their washing; and every barge boasted its mongrel cur by way of watchdog. Each one barked furiously at the canoes, running alongside until he had got to the end of his own ship, and so passing on the word to the dog aboard the next. We must have seen something like a hundred of these embarkations in the course of that day's paddle, ranged one after another like the houses in a street; and from not one of them were we disappointed of this accompaniment. It was like visiting a menagerie, the *Cigarette* remarked.

These little cities by the canal-side had a very odd effect upon the mind. They seemed, with their flower-pots and smoking chimneys, their washings and dinners, a rooted piece of nature in the scene; and yet if only the canal below were to open, one junk after another would hoist sail or harness horses and swim away into all parts of France; and the impromptu hamlet would separate, house by house, to the four winds. The children who played together to-day by the Sambre and Oise Canal, each at his own father's threshold, when and where might they next meet?

For some time past the subject of barges had occupied a great deal of our talk, and we had projected an old age on the canals of Europe. It was to be the most leisurely of progresses, now on a swift river at the tail of a steam-boat, now waiting horses for days together on some inconsiderable junction. We should be seen pottering on deck in all the dignity of years, our white beards falling into our laps. We were ever to be busied among paint-pots, so that there should be no white fresher and no green more emerald than ours, in all the navy of the canals. There should be books in the cabin, and tobacco jars, and some old Burgundy as red as a November sunset and as odorous as a violet in April. There should be a flageolet whence the *Cigarette*, with cunning touch, should draw melting music under the stars; or perhaps, laying that aside, upraise his voice — somewhat thinner than of yore, and with here and there a quaver, or call it a natural grace note — in rich and solemn psalmody.

All this simmering in my mind set me wishing to go aboard one of these ideal houses of lounging. I had plenty to choose from, as I coasted one after another and the dogs bayed at me for a vagrant. At last I saw a nice old man and his wife looking at me with some interest, so I gave them good-day and pulled up alongside. I began with a remark upon their dog, which had somewhat the look of a pointer; thence I slid into a compliment on Madame's flowers, and thence into a word in praise of their way of life.

If you ventured on such an experiment in England you would get a slap in the face at once. The life would be shown to be a vile one, not without a side shot at your better fortune. Now, what I like so much in France is the clear, unflinching recognition by everybody of his own luck. They all know on which side their bread is buttered, and take a pleasure in showing it to others, which is surely the better part of religion. And they scorn to make a poor mouth over their poverty, which I take to be the better part of manliness. I have heard a woman in quite a better position at home, with a good bit of money in hand, refer to her own child with a horrid whine as "a poor man's child." I would not say such a thing to the Duke of Westminster. And the French are full of this spirit of independence. Perhaps it is the result of republican institutions, as they call them. Much more likely it is because there are so few people really poor that the whiners are not enough to keep each other in countenance.

The people on the barge were delighted to hear that I admired their state. They understood perfectly well, they told me, how Monsieur envied them. Without doubt Monsieur was rich, and in that case he might make a canal boat as pretty as a villa — *joli comme un château.* And with that they invited me on board their own water villa. They apologised for their cabin; they had not been rich enough to make it as it ought to be.

"The fire should have been here, at this side," explained the husband. "Then one might have a writing-table in the middle — books — and" (comprehensively) "all. It would be quite coquettish — *ça serait tout-à-fait coquet.*" And he looked about him as though the improvements were already made. It was plainly not the first time that he had thus beautified his cabin in imagination; and when next he makes a hit, I should expect to see the writing-table in the middle.

Madame had three birds in a cage. They were no great thing, she explained. Fine birds were so dear. They had sought to get a *Hollandais* last winter in Rouen (Rouen, thought I; and is this whole mansion, with its dogs, and birds, and smoking chimneys, so far a traveller as that, and as homely an object among the cliffs and orchards of the Seine as on the green plains of Sambre?) — they had sought to get a *Hollandais* last winter in Rouen; but these cost fifteen francs apiece — picture it — fifteen francs!

"*Pour un tout petit oiseau* —For quite a little bird," added the husband.

As I continued to admire, the apologetics died away, and the good people began to brag of their barge and their happy condition in life, as if they had been Emperor and Empress of the Indies. It was, in the Scotch phrase, a good hearing, and put me in good-humour with the world. If people knew what an inspiriting thing it is to hear a man boasting, so long as he boasts of what he really has, I believe they would do it more freely and with a better grace.

They began to ask about our voyage. You should have seen how they sympathised. They seemed half ready to give up their barge and follow us. But these *canaletti* are only gipsies semi-domesticated. The semi-domestication came out in rather a pretty form. Suddenly Madame's brow darkened. *"Cependant,"* she began, and then stopped; and then began again by asking me if I were single.

"Yes," said I.

"And your friend who went by just now?"

He also was unmarried.

Oh, then, all was well. She could not have wives left alone at home; but since there were no wives in the question, we were doing the best we could.

"To see about one in the world," said the husband, *"il n'y a que ça —* there is nothing else worth while. A man, look you, who sticks in his own village like a bear," he went on, "very well, he sees nothing. And then death is the end of all. And he has seen nothing."

Madame reminded her husband of an Englishman who had come up this canal in a steamer.

"Perhaps Mr. Moens in the *Ytene,*" I suggested.

"That's it," assented the husband. "He had his wife and family with him, and servants. He came ashore at all the locks and asked the name of the villages, whether from boatmen or lockkeepers; and then he wrote, wrote them down. Oh, he wrote enormously! I suppose it was a wager."

A wager was a common enough explanation for our own exploits, but it seemed an original reason for taking notes.

THE OISE IN FLOOD

Before nine next morning the two canoes were in-
stalled on a light country cart at Etreux; and we were
soon following them along the side of a pleasant valley
full of hop-gardens and poplars. Agreeable villages lay
here and there on the slope of the hill : notably, Tupigny,
with the hop-poles hanging their garlands in the very
street, and the houses clustered with grapes. There was
a faint enthusiasm on our passage; weavers put their
heads to the windows; children cried out in ecstasy at
sight of the two "boaties" — *barquettes;* and bloused
pedestrians, who were acquainted with our charioteer,
jested with him on the nature of his freight.

We had a shower or two, but light and flying. The air
was clean and sweet among all these green fields and
green things growing. There was not a touch of autumn
in the weather. And when, at Vadencourt, we launched
from a little lawn opposite a mill, the sun broke forth and
set all the leaves shining in the valley of the Oise.

The river was swollen with the long rains. From Vadencourt all the way to Origny it ran with ever-quickening
speed, taking fresh heart at each mile, and racing as
though it already smelt the sea. The water was yellow
and turbulent, swung with an angry eddy among half-sub-
merged willows, and made an angry clatter along stony
shores. The course kept turning and turning in a narrow and well-timbered valley. Now the river would ap-

proach the side, and run gliding along the chalky base of
the hill, and show us a few open colza fields among the
trees. Now it would skirt the garden-walls of houses,
where we might catch a glimpse through a doorway, and
see a priest pacing in the checkered sunlight. Again, the
foliage closed so thickly in front that there seemed to be
no issue; only a thicket of willows overtopped by elms
and poplars, under which the river ran flush and fleet,
and where a kingfisher flew past like a piece of the blue
sky. On these different manifestations the sun poured its
clear and catholic looks. The shadows lay as solid on
the swift surface of the stream as on the stable meadows.
The light sparkled golden in the dancing poplar leaves,
and brought the hills into communion with our eyes.
And all the while the river never stopped running or took
breath; and the reeds along the whole valley stood shivering from top to toe.

There should be some myth (but if there is, I know it
not) founded on the shivering of the reeds. There are
not many things in nature more striking to man's eye.
It is such an eloquent pantomime of terror; and to see
such a number of terrified creatures taking sanctuary in
every nook along the shore is enough to infect a silly
human with alarm. Perhaps they are only acold, and
no wonder, standing waist deep in the stream. Or, perhaps, they have never got accustomed to the speed and
fury of the river's flux, or the miracle of its continuous
body. Pan once played upon their forefathers; and so,
by the hands of his river, he still plays upon these later
generations down all the valley of the Oise; and plays the
same air, both sweet and shrill, to tell us of the beauty
and the terror of the world.

The canoe was like a leaf in the current. It took it up and shook it, and carried it masterfully away, like a Centaur carrying off a nymph. To keep some command on our direction required hard and diligent plying of the paddle. The river was in such a hurry for the sea! Every drop of water ran in a panic, like so many people in a frightened crowd. But what crowd was ever so numerous or so single-minded? All the objects of sight went by at a dance measure; the eyesight raced with the racing river; the exigencies of every moment kept the pegs screwed so tight that our being quivered like a well-tuned instrument, and the blood shook off its lethargy, and trotted through all the highways and byways of the veins and arteries, and in and out of the heart, as if circulation were but a holiday journey and not the daily moil of threescore years and ten. The reeds might nod their heads in warning, and with tremulous gestures tell how the river was as cruel as it was strong and cold, and how death lurked in the eddy underneath the willows. But the reeds had to stand where they were; and those who stand still are always timid advisers. As for us, we could have shouted aloud. If this lively and beautiful river were, indeed, a thing of death's contrivance, the old ashen rogue had famously outwitted himself with us. I was living three to the minute. I was scoring points against him every stroke of my paddle, every turn of the stream. I have rarely had better profit of my life.

For I think we may look upon our little private war with death somewhat in this light. If a man knows he will sooner or later be robbed upon a journey, he will have a bottle of the best in every inn, and look upon all his extravagances as so much gained upon the thieves. And above all, where, instead of simply spending, he makes a profitable investment for some of his money, when it will be out of risk of loss. So every bit of brisk living, and above all when it is healthful, is just so much gained upon the wholesale filcher, death. We shall have the less in our pockets, the more in our stomachs, when he cries, Stand and deliver. A swift stream is a favourite artifice of his, and one that brings him in a comfortable thing per annum; but when he and I come to settle our accounts I shall whistle in his face for these hours upon the upper Oise.

Towards afternoon we got fairly drunken with the sunshine and the exhilaration of the pace. We could no longer contain ourselves and our content. The canoes were too small for us; we must be out and stretch ourselves on shore. And so in a green meadow we bestowed our limbs on the grass, and smoked deifying tobacco, and proclaimed the world excellent. It was the last good hour of the day, and I dwell upon it with extreme complacency.

On one side of the valley, high upon the chalky summit of the hill, a ploughman with his team appeared and disappeared at regular intervals. At each revelation he stood still for a few seconds against the sky, for all the world (as the *Cigarette* declared) like a toy Burns who had just ploughed up the Mountain Daisy. He was the only living thing within view, unless we are to count the river.

On the other side of the valley a group of red roofs and a belfry showed among the foliage. Thence some inspired bell-ringer made the afternoon musical on a chime of bells. There was something very sweet and taking in the air he played, and we thought we had never heard bells

speak so intelligibly or sing so melodiously as these.   It
must have been to some such measure that the spinners
and the young maids sang, "Come away, Death," in the
Shakespearian Illyria.   There is so often a threatening
note, something blatant and metallic, in the voice of
bells, that I believe we have fully more pain than pleasure
from hearing them; but these, as they sounded abroad,
now high, now low, now with a plaintive cadence that
caught the ear like the burden of a popular song, were
always moderate and tunable, and seemed to fall in with
the spirit· of still, rustic places, like the noise of a waterfall or the babble of a rookery in spring.   I could have
asked the bell-ringer for his blessing, good, sedate old
man, who swung the rope so gently to the time of his
meditations.   I could have blessed the priest or the heritors, or whoever may be concerned with such affairs in
France, who had left these sweet old bells to gladden the
afternoon, and not held meetings, and made collections,
and had their names repeatedly printed in the local paper,
to rig up a peal of brand-new, brazen, Birmingham-hearted
substitutes, who should bombard their sides to the provocation of a brand-new bell-ringer, and fill the echoes of
the valley with terror and riot.

At last the bells ceased, and with their note the sun
withdrew.   The piece was at an end; shadow and silence
possessed the valley of the Oise.   We took to the paddle
with glad hearts, like people who have sat out a noble
performance and return to work.   The river was more
dangerous here; it ran swifter, the eddies were more
sudden and violent.   All the way down we had had our
fill of difficulties.   Sometimes it was a weir which could
be shot, sometimes one so shallow and full of stakes that

we must withdraw the boats from the water and carry
them round. But the chief sort of obstacle was a consequence of the late high winds. Every two or three hundred yards a tree had fallen across the river, and usually
involved more than another in its fall. Often there was
free water at the end, and we could steer round the leafy
promontory and hear the water sucking and bubbling

THE REFECTORY AT THE REAR OF NOYON CATHEDRAL (See page 92)

among the twigs. Often, again, when the tree reached
from bank to bank, there was room, by lying close, to
shoot through underneath, canoe and all. Sometimes it
was necessary to get out upon the trunk itself and pull
the boats across; and sometimes, where the stream was
too impetuous for this, there was nothing for it but to
land and "carry over." This made a fine series of

accidents in the day's career, and kept us aware of ourselves.

Shortly after our re-embarkation, while I was leading by a long way, and still full of a noble, exulting spirit in honour of the sun, the swift pace, and the church bells, the river made one of its leonine pounces round a corner, and I was aware of another fallen tree within a stone-cast. I had my back-board down in a trice, and aimed for a place where the trunk seemed high enough above the water, and the branches not too thick to let me slip below. When a man has just vowed eternal brotherhood with the universe he is not in a temper to take great determinations coolly, and this, which might have been a very important determination for me, had not been taken under a happy star. The tree caught me about the chest, and while I was yet struggling to make less of myself and get through, the river took the matter out of my hands and bereaved me of my boat. The *Arethusa* swung round broadside on, leaned over, ejected so much of me as still remained on board, and, thus disencumbered, whipped under the tree, righted, and went merrily away down stream.

I do not know how long it was before I scrambled on to the tree to which I was left clinging, but it was longer than I cared about. My thoughts were of a grave and almost sombre character, but I still clung to my paddle. The stream ran away with my heels as fast as I could pull up my shoulders, and I seemed, by the weight, to have all the water of the Oise in my trousers' pockets. You can never know, till you try it, what a dead pull a river makes against a man. Death himself had me by the heels, for this was his last ambuscade, and he must now join personally in the fray. And still I held to my paddle. At last I dragged myself on to my stomach on the trunk, and lay there a breathless sop, with a mingled sense of humour and injustice. A poor figure I must have presented to Burns upon the hill-top with his team. But there was the paddle in my hand. On my tomb, if ever I have one, I mean to get these words inscribed: "He clung to his paddle."

The *Cigarette* had gone past awhile before; for, as I might have observed, if I had been a little less pleased with the universe at the moment, there was a clear way round the tree-top at the farther side. He had offered his services to haul me out, but, as I was then already on my elbows, I had declined and sent him down stream after the truant *Arethusa*. The stream was too rapid for a man to mount with one canoe, let alone two, upon his hands. So I crawled along the trunk to shore, and proceeded down the meadows by the riverside. I was so cold that my heart was sore. I had now an idea of my own why the reeds so bitterly shivered. I could have given any of them a lesson. The *Cigarette* remarked, facetiously, that he thought I was "taking exercise" as I drew near, until he made out for certain that I was only twittering with cold. I had a rub-down with a towel, and donned a dry suit from the india-rubber bag. But I was not my own man again for the rest of the voyage. I had a queasy sense that I wore my last dry clothes upon my body. The struggle had tired me; and, perhaps, whether I knew it or not, I was a little dashed in spirit. The devouring element in the universe had leaped out against me, in this green valley quickened by a running stream. The bells were all very pretty in their way, but

I had heard some of the hollow notes of Pan's music. Would the wicked river drag me down by the heels, indeed? and look so beautiful all the time? Nature's good-humour was only skin deep, after all.

There was still a long way to go by the winding course of the stream, and darkness had fallen, and a late bell was ringing in Origny Sainte-Benoîte when we arrived.

ORIGNY SAINTE-BENOÎTE

A By-Day

THE next day was Sunday, and the church bells had little rest; indeed, I do not think I remember anywhere else so great a choice of services as were here offered to the devout. And while the bells made merry in the sunshine, all the world with his dog was out shooting among the beets and colza.

In the morning a hawker and his wife went down the street at a foot-pace, singing to a very slow, lamentable music, "*O France, mes amours.*" It brought everybody to the door; and when our landlady called in the man to buy the words, he had not a copy of them left. She was not the first nor the second who had been taken with the song. There is something very pathetic in the love of the French people, since the war, for dismal patriotic music-making. I have watched a forester from Alsace while some one was singing "*Les malheurs de la France,*" at a baptismal party in the neighbourhood of Fontainebleau. He arose from the table and took his son aside, close by where I was standing. "Listen, listen," he said, bearing on the boy's shoulder, "and remember this, my son." A little after he went out into the garden suddenly, and I could hear him sobbing in the darkness.

The humiliation of their arms and the loss of Alsace and Lorraine made a sore pull on the endurance of this sensitive people; and their hearts are still hot, not so much against Germany as against the Empire. In what other country will you find a patriotic ditty bring all the world into the street? But affliction heightens love; and we shall never know we are Englishmen until we have lost India. Independent America is still the cross of my existence; I cannot think of Farmer George without abhorrence; and I never feel more warmly to my own land than when I see the stars and stripes, and remember what our empire might have been.

The hawker's little book, which I purchased, was a curious mixture. Side by side with the flippant, rowdy nonsense of the Paris music-halls there were many pastoral pieces, not without a touch of poetry, I thought, and instinct with the brave independence of the poorer class in France. There you might read how the woodcutter gloried in his axe, and the gardener scorned to be ashamed of his spade. It was not very well written, this poetry of labour, but the pluck of the sentiment redeemed what was weak or wordy in the expression. The martial and the patriotic pieces, on the other hand, were tearful, womanish productions one and all. The poet had passed under the Caudine Forks; he sang for an army visiting the tomb of its old renown, with arms reversed; and sang not of victory, but of death. There was a number in the hawker's collection called *Conscrits Français*, which may rank among the most dissuasive war-lyrics on record. It would not be possible to fight at all in such a spirit. The bravest conscript would turn pale if such a ditty were struck up beside him on the morning of battle; and whole regiments would pile their arms to its tune.

If Fletcher of Saltoun is in the right about the influence of national songs, you would say France was come to a poor pass. But the thing will work its own cure, and a sound-hearted and courageous people weary at length of snivelling over their disasters. Already Paul Déroulède has written some manly military verses. There is not much of the trumpet note in them, perhaps, to stir a man's heart in his bosom; they lack the lyrical elation, and move slowly; but they are written in a grave, honourable, stoical spirit, which should carry soldiers far in a good cause. One feels as if one would like to trust Déroulède with something. It will be happy if he can so far inoculate his fellow-countrymen that they may be trusted with their own future. And, in the meantime, here is an antidote to "French Conscripts" and much other doleful versification.

We had left the boats over night in the custody of one whom we shall call Carnival. I did not properly catch his name, and perhaps that was not unfortunate for him, as I am not in a position to hand him down with honour to posterity. To this person's premises we strolled in the course of the day, and found quite a little deputation inspecting the canoes. There was a stout gentleman with a knowledge of the river, which he seemed eager to impart. There was a very elegant young gentleman in a black coat, with a smattering of English, who led the talk at once to the Oxford and Cambridge boat race. And then there were three handsome girls from fifteen to twenty; and an old gentleman in a blouse, with no teeth to speak of, and a strong country accent. Quite the pick of Origny, I should suppose.

The *Cigarette* had some mysteries to perform with his rigging in the coach-house; so I was left to do the parade single-handed. I found myself very much of a hero

whether I would or not.   The girls were full of little shud-
derings over the dangers of our journey.   And I thought
it would be ungallant not to take my cue from the ladies.
My mishap of yesterday, told in an offhand way, produced a deep sensation.   It was Othello over again, with
no less than three Desdemonas and a sprinkling of sym-
pathetic senators in the background.   Never were the
canoes more flattered, or flattered more adroitly.

"It is like a violin," cried one of the girls in an ecstasy.

"I thank you for the word, mademoiselle," said I.
"All the more since there are people who call out to me
that it is like a coffin."

"Oh! but it is really like a violin.   It is finished like
a violin," she went on.

"And polished like a violin," added a senator.

"One has only to stretch the cords," concluded another,
"and then tum-tumty-tum"; he imitated the result
with spirit.

Was not this a graceful little ovation?   Where this
people finds the secret of its pretty speeches I cannot
imagine, unless the secret should be no other than a sincere desire to please.   But then no disgrace is attached
in France to saying a thing neatly; whereas in England,
to talk like a book is to give in one's resignation to society.

The old gentleman in the blouse stole into the coach-
house, and somewhat irrelevantly informed the *Cigarette*
that he was the father of the three girls and four more;
quite an exploit for a Frenchman.

"You are very fortunate," answered the *Cigarette*
politely.

And the old gentleman, having apparently gained his
point, stole away again.

We all got very friendly together. The girls proposed
to start with us on the morrow, if you please. And, jest-
ing apart, every one was anxious to know the hour of our
departure. Now, when you are going to crawl into your
canoe from a bad launch, a crowd, however friendly, is
undesirable, and so we told them not before twelve, and
mentally determined to be off by ten at latest.

Towards evening we went abroad again to post some
letters. It was cool and pleasant; the long village was
quite empty, except for one or two urchins who followed
us as they might have followed a menagerie; the hills
and the tree-tops looked in from all sides through the
clear air, and the bells were chiming for yet another
service.

Suddenly we sighted the three girls, standing, with a
fourth sister, in front of a shop on the wide selvage of
the roadway. We had been very merry with them a
little while ago, to be sure. But what was the etiquette
of Origny? Had it been a country road, of course we
should have spoken to them; but here, under the eyes of
all the gossips, ought we to do even as much as bow?
I consulted the *Cigarette*.

"Look," said he.

I looked. There were the four girls on the same spot;
but now four backs were turned to us, very upright and
conscious. Corporal Modesty had given the word of
command, and the well-disciplined picket had gone right-
about-face like a single person. They maintained this
formation all the while we were in sight; but we heard
them tittering among themselves, and the girl whom
we had not met laughed with open mouth, and even
looked over her shoulder at the enemy. I wonder was

it altogether modesty after all, or in part a sort of country provocation?

As we were returning to the inn we beheld something floating in the ample field of golden evening sky, above the chalk cliffs and the trees that grow along their summit. It was too high up, too large, and too steady for a kite; and, as it was dark, it could not be a star. For, although a star were as black as ink and as rugged as a walnut, so amply does the sun bathe heaven with radiance that it would sparkle like a point of light for us. The village was dotted with people with their heads in air; and the children were in a bustle all along the street and far up the straight road that climbs the hill, where we could still see them running in loose knots. It was a balloon, we learned, which had left St. Quentin at half-past five that evening. Mighty composedly the majority of the grown people took it. But we were English, and were soon running up the hill with the best. Being travellers ourselves in a small way, we would fain have seen these other travellers alight.

The spectacle was over by the time we gained the top of the hill. All the gold had withered out of the sky, and the balloon had disappeared. Whither? I ask myself; caught up into the seventh heaven? or come safely to land somewhere in that blue, uneven distance, into which the roadway dipped and melted before our eyes? Probably the aëronauts were already warming themselves at a farm chimney, for they say it is cold in these unhomely regions of the air. The night fell swiftly. Roadside trees and disappointed sightseers, returning through the meadows, stood out in black against a margin of low, red sunset. It was cheerfuller to face the other way, and so down the hill we went, with a full moon, the colour of a melon, swinging high above the wooded valley, and the white cliffs behind us faintly reddened by the fire of the chalk-kilns.

The lamps were lighted, and the salads were being made in Origny Sainte-Benoîte by the river.

ORIGNY SAINTE–BENOÎTE

The Company at Table

ALTHOUGH we came late for dinner, the company at table treated us to sparkling wine. "That is how we are in France," said one. "Those who sit down with us are our friends." And the rest applauded.

They were three altogether, and an odd trio to pass the Sunday with.

Two of them were guests like ourselves, both men of the north. One ruddy, and of a full habit of body, with copious black hair and beard, the intrepid hunter of France, who thought nothing so small, not even a lark or minnow, but he might vindicate his prowess by its capture. For such a great, healthy man, his hair flourishing like Samson's, his arteries running buckets of red blood, to boast of these infinitesimal exploits, produced a feeling of disproportion in the world, as when a steam-hammer is set to cracking nuts. The other was a quiet, subdued person, blond, and lymphatic, and sad, with something the look of a Dane: *"Tristes têtes de Danois!"* as Gaston Lafenestre used to say.

I must not let that name go by without a word for the best of all good fellows, now gone down into the dust. We shall never again see Gaston in his forest costume, — he was Gaston with all the world, in affection, not in disrespect, — nor hear him wake the echoes of Fontainebleau with the woodland horn.   Never again shall his kind smile put peace among all races of artistic men, and make the Englishman at home in France.   Never more shall the sheep, who were not more innocent at heart than he, sit all unconsciously for his industrious pencil.   He died too early, at the very moment when he was beginning to put forth fresh sprouts and blossom into something worthy of himself; and yet none who knew him will think he lived in vain.   I never knew a man so little, for whom yet I had so much affection; and I find it a good test of others, how much they had learned to understand and value him. His was, indeed, a good influence in life while he was still among us; he had a fresh laugh; it did you good to see him; and, however sad he may have been at heart, he always bore a bold and cheerful countenance and took fortune's worst as it were the showers of spring.   But now his mother sits alone by the side of Fontainebleau woods, where he gathered mushrooms in his hardy and penurious youth.

Many of his pictures found their way across the Channel; besides those which were stolen, when a dastardly Yankee left him alone in London with two English pence, and, perhaps, twice as many words of English.   If any one who reads these lines should have a scene of sheep, in the manner of Jacques, with this fine creature's signature, let him tell himself that one of the kindest and bravest of men has lent a hand to decorate his lodging.   There may be better pictures in the National Gallery; but not a painter among the generations had a better heart. Precious in the sight of the Lord of humanity, the Psalms tell us, is the death of his saints.   It had need to be precious; for it is very costly, when, by a stroke, a mother is left desolate, and the peace-maker and *peace looker* of a whole society is laid in the ground with Cæsar and the Twelve Apostles.

There is something lacking among the oaks of Fontainebleau; and when the dessert comes in at Barbizon, people look to the door for a figure that is gone.

The third of our companions at Origny was no less a person than the landlady's husband; not properly the landlord, since he worked himself in a factory during the day, and came to his own house at evening as a guest; a man worn to skin and bone by perpetual excitement, with baldish head, sharp features, and swift, shining eyes. On Saturday, describing some paltry adventure at a duck hunt, he broke a plate into a score of fragments. Whenever he made a remark he would look all round the table with his chin raised and a spark of green light in either eye, seeking approval. His wife appeared now and again in the doorway of the room, where she was superintending dinner, with a "Henri, you forget yourself," or a "Henri, you can surely talk without making such a noise." Indeed, that was what the honest fellow could not do. On the most trifling matter his eyes kindled, his fist visited the table, and his voice rolled abroad in changeful thunder. I never saw such a petard of a man; I think the devil was in him. He had two favourite expressions, "It is logical," or illogical, as the case might be; and this other thrown out with a certain bravado as a man might unfurl a banner, at the beginning of many a long and sonorous story: "I am a proletarian, you see." Indeed, we saw it very well. God forbid that ever I should find him handling a gun in Paris streets. That will not be a good moment for the general public.

I thought his two phrases very much represented the good and evil of his class, and, to some extent, of his country. It is a strong thing to say what one is, and not be ashamed of it; even although it be in doubtful taste to repeat the statement too often in one evening. I should not admire it in a duke, of course; but as times go the trait is honourable in a workman. On the other hand, it is not at all a strong thing to put one's reliance upon logic; and our own logic particularly, for it is generally wrong. We never know where we are to end if once we begin following words or doctors. There is an upright stock in a man's own heart that is trustier than any syllogism; and the eyes, and the sympathies, and appetites know a thing or two that have never yet been stated in controversy. Reasons are as plentiful as blackberries; and, like fisticuffs, they serve impartially with all sides. Doctrines do not stand or fall by their proofs and are only logical in so far as they are cleverly put. An able controversialist no more than an able general demonstrates the justice of his cause. But France is all gone wandering after one or two big words; it will take some time before they can be satisfied that they are no more than words, however big; and, when once that is done, they will perhaps find logic less diverting.

The conversation opened with details of the day's shooting. When all the sportsmen of a village shoot over the village territory *pro indiviso*, it is plain that many questions of etiquette and priority must arise.

"Here now," cried the landlord, brandishing a plate, "here is a field of beet-root. Well. Here am I, then. I advance, do I not? *Eh bien!* sacristi"; and the statement, waxing louder, rolls off into a reverberation of oaths, the speaker glaring about for sympathy, and everybody nodding his head to him in the name of peace.

The ruddy Northman told some tales of his own prowess in keeping order: notably one of a Marquis.

"Marquis," I said, "if you take another step I fire upon you. You have committed a dirtiness, Marquis."

Whereupon, it appeared, the Marquis touched his cap and withdrew.

The landlord applauded noisily. "It was well done," he said. "He did all that he could. He admitted he was wrong." And then oath upon oath. He was no marquis-lover, either, but he had a sense of justice in him, this proletarian host of ours.

From the matter of hunting, the talk veered into a general comparison of Paris and the country. The proletarian beat the table like a drum in praise of Paris. "What is Paris? Paris is the cream of France. There are no Parisians; it is you, and I, and everybody who are Parisians. A man has eighty chances per cent to get on in the world in Paris." And he drew a vivid sketch of the workman in a den no bigger than a dog-hutch, making articles that were to go all over the world. *"Eh bien, quoi, c'est magnifique, ça!"* cried he.

The sad Northman interfered in praise of a peasant's life; he thought Paris bad for men and women. "Centralisation," said he —

But the landlord was at his throat in a moment. It was all logical, he showed him, and all magnificent. "What a spectacle! What a glance for an eye!" And the dishes reeled upon the table under a cannonade of blows.

Seeking to make peace, I threw in a word in praise of

the liberty of opinion in France. I could hardly have shot more amiss. There was an instant silence and a great wagging of significant heads. They did not fancy the subject, it was plain, but they gave me to understand that the sad Northman was a martyr on account of his views. "Ask him a bit," said they. "Just ask him."

"Yes, sir," said he in his quiet way, answering me, although I had not spoken, "I am afraid there is less liberty of opinion in France than you may imagine." And with that he dropped his eyes and seemed to consider the subject at an end.

Our curiosity was mightily excited at this. How, or why, or when was this lymphatic bagman martyred? We concluded at once it was on some religious question, and brushed up our memories of the Inquisition, which were principally drawn from Poe's horrid story, and the sermon in *Tristram Shandy*, I believe.

On the morrow we had an opportunity of going further into the question; for when we rose very early to avoid a sympathising deputation at our departure, we found the hero up before us. He was breaking his fast on white wine and raw onions, in order to keep up the character of martyr, I conclude. We had a long conversation, and made out what we wanted in spite of his reserve. But here was a truly curious circumstance. It seems possible for two Scotchmen and a Frenchman to discuss during a long half-hour, and each nationality have a different idea in view throughout. It was not till the very end that we discovered his heresy had been political, or that he suspected our mistake. The terms and spirit in which he spoke of his political beliefs were, in our eyes, suited to religious beliefs. And *vice versa*.

Nothing could be more characteristic of the two countries. Politics are the religion of France; as Nanty
Ewart would have said, "A d——d bad religion," while
we, at home, keep most of our bitterness for all differences
about a hymn-book or a Hebrew word which, perhaps,
neither of the parties can translate. And perhaps the
misconception is typical of many others that may never
be cleared up; not only between people of different race,
but between those of different sex.

As for our friend's martyrdom, he was a Communist,
or perhaps only a Communard, which is a very different
thing, and had lost one or more situations in consequence.
I think he had also been rejected in marriage; but perhaps he had a sentimental way of considering business
which deceived me. He was a mild, gentle creature,
anyway, and I hope he has got a better situation and
married a more suitable wife since then.

DOWN THE OISE

To Moy

CARNIVAL notoriously cheated us at first. Finding us easy in our ways, he regretted having let us off so cheaply, and, taking me aside, told me a cock-and-bull story, with the moral of another five francs for the narrator. The thing was palpably absurd; but I paid up, and at once dropped all friendliness of manner and kept him in his place as an inferior, with freezing British dignity. He saw in a moment that he had gone too far and killed a willing horse; his face fell; I am sure he would have refunded if he could only have thought of a decent pretext. He wished me to drink with him, but I would none of his drinks. He grew pathetically tender in his professions, but I walked beside him in silence or answered him in stately courtesies, and, when we got to the landing-place, passed the word in English slang to the *Cigarette*.

In spite of the false scent we had thrown out the day before, there must have been fifty people about the bridge. We were as pleasant as we could be with all but Carnival. We said good-bye, shaking hands with the old gentleman who knew the river and the young gentleman who had a smattering of English, but never a word for Carnival. Poor Carnival, here was a humiliation. He who had been so much identified with the canoes, who had given orders in our name, who had shown off the boats and even the boatmen like a private exhibition of his own, to be now so publicly shamed by the lions of his caravan! I never saw anybody look more crestfallen than he. He hung in the background, coming timidly forward ever and again as he thought he saw some symptom of a relenting humour and falling hurriedly back when he encountered a cold stare. Let us hope it will be a lesson to him.

I would not have mentioned Carnival's peccadillo had not the thing been so uncommon in France. This, for instance, was the only case of dishonesty or even sharp practice in our whole voyage. We talk very much about our honesty in England. It is a good rule to be on your guard wherever you hear great professions about a very little piece of virtue. If the English could only hear how they are spoken of abroad, they might confine themselves for awhile to remedying the fact, and perhaps even when that was done, give us fewer of their airs.

The young ladies, the graces of Origny, were not present at our start; but when we got round to the second bridge, behold, it was black with sight-seers! We were loudly cheered, and for a good way below young lads and lasses ran along the bank, still cheering. What with current and paddling, we were flashing along like swallows. It was no joke to keep up with us upon the woody shore. But the girls picked up their skirts, as if they were sure they had good ankles, and followed until their breath was out. The last to weary were the three graces and a couple of companions; and just as they, too, had had enough, the foremost of the three leaped upon a tree-stump and kissed her hand to the canoeists. Not Diana herself, although this was more of a Venus, after all, could have done a graceful thing more gracefully. "Come back again!" she cried; and all the others echoed her; and the hills about Origny repeated the words, "Come back." But the river had us round an angle in a twinkling, and we were alone with the green trees and running water.

Come back? There is no coming back, young ladies, on the impetuous stream of life.

> The merchant bows unto the seaman's star,
> The ploughman from the sun his season takes.

And we must all set our pocket watches by the clock of fate. There is a headlong, forthright tide, that bears away man with his fancies like straw, and runs fast in time and space. It is full of curves like this, your winding river of the Oise; and lingers and returns in pleasant pastorals; and yet, rightly thought upon, never returns at all. For though it should revisit the same acre of meadow in the same hour, it will have made an ample sweep between whiles; many little streams will have fallen in; many exhalations risen towards the sun; and even although it were the same acre, it will not be the same river Oise. And thus, O graces of Origny, although the wandering fortune of my life should carry me back again to where you await death's whistle by the river, that will not be the old I who walks the streeet; and those wives and mothers, say, will those be you?

There was never any mistake about the Oise, as a matter of fact. In these upper reaches it was still in a prodigious hurry for the sea. It ran so fast and merrily, through all the windings of its channel, that I strained my thumb fighting with the rapids, and had to paddle all the rest of the way with one hand turned up. Sometimes it had to serve mills; and being still a little river, ran very dry and shallow in the meanwhile. We had to put our legs out of the boat, and shove ourselves off the sand of the bottom with our feet. And still it went on its way singing among the poplars, and making a green valley in the world. After a good woman, and a good book, and tobacco, there is nothing so agreeable on earth as a river. I forgave it its attempt on my life; which was, after all, one part owing to the unruly winds of heaven that had blown down the tree, one part to my own mismanagement, and only a third part to the river itself, and that not out of malice, but from its great preoccupation over its own business of getting to the sea. A difficult business, too; for the detours it had to make are not to be counted. The geographers seem to have given up the attempt; for I found no map represent the infinite contortion of its course. A fact will say more than any of them. After we had been some hours, three, if I mistake not, flitting by the trees at this smooth, breakneck gallop, when we came upon a hamlet and asked where we were, we had got no further than four kilometres (say two miles and a half) from Origny. If it were not for the honour of the thing (in the Scotch saying), we might almost as well have been standing still.

We lunched on a meadow inside a parallelogram of poplars. The leaves danced and prattled in the wind all around about us. The river hurried on meanwhile, and seemed to chide at our delay. Little we cared. The river knew where it was going; not so we; the less our hurry, where we found good quarters, and a pleasant theatre for a pipe. At that hour stock-brokers were shouting in Paris Bourse for two or three per cent; but we minded them as little as the sliding stream, and sacrificed a hecatomb of minutes to the gods of tobacco and digestion. Hurry is the resource of the faithless. Where a man can trust his own heart, and those of his friends, to-morrow is as good as to-day. And if he die in the meanwhile, why, then, there he dies, and the question is solved.

We had to take to the canal in the course of the afternoon; because where it crossed the river there was, not a bridge, but a siphon. If it had not been for an excited fellow on the bank we should have paddled right into the siphon, and thenceforward not paddled any more. We met a man, a gentleman, on the tow-path, who was much interested in our cruise. And I was witness to a strange seizure of lying suffered by the *Cigarette;* who, because his knife came from Norway, narrated all sorts of adventures in that country, where he has never been. He was quite feverish at the end, and pleaded demoniacal possession.

Moy (pronounce Moÿ) was a pleasant little village, gathered round a chateau in a moat. The air was perfumed with hemp from neighbouring fields. At the Golden Sheep we found excellent entertainment. German shells from the siege of La Fère, Nürnberg figures, gold-fish in a bowl, and all manner of knick-knacks, embellished the public room. The landlady was a stout, plain, short-sighted, motherly body, with something not far short of a genius for cookery. She had a guess of her excellence herself. After every dish was sent in, she would come and look on at the dinner for awhile, with puckered, blinking eyes. *"C'est bon, n'est-ce pas?"* she would say; and, when she had received a proper answer, she disappeared into the kitchen. That common French dish, partridge and cabbages, became a new thing in my eyes at the Golden Sheep; and many subsequent dinners have bitterly disappointed me in consequence. Sweet was our rest in the Golden Sheep at Moy.

LA FÈRE OF CURSED MEMORY

WE lingered in Moy a good part of the day, for we were fond of being philosophical, and scorned long journeys and early starts on principle. The place, moreover, invited to repose. People in elaborate shooting-costumes sallied from the chateau with guns and game-bags; and this was a pleasure in itself, to remain behind while these elegant pleasure-seekers took the first of the morning. In this way all the world may be an aristocrat, and play the duke among marquises, and the reigning monarch among dukes, if he will only outvie them in tranquillity. An imperturbable demeanour comes from perfect patience. Quiet minds cannot be perplexed or frightened, but go on in fortune or misfortune at their own private pace, like a clock during a thunder-storm.

We made a very short day of it to La Fère; but the dusk was falling and a small rain had begun before we stowed the boats. La Fère is a fortified town in a plain, and has two belts of rampart. Between the first and the second extends a region of waste land and cultivated patches. Here and there along the wayside were posters forbidding trespass in the name of military engineering. At last a second gateway admitted us to the town itself. Lighted windows looked gladsome, whiffs of comfortable cookery came abroad upon the air. The town was full of the military reserve, out for the French Autumn manœuvres, and the reservists walked speedily and wore their formidable great-coats. It was a fine night to be within doors over dinner, and hear the rain upon the windows.

The *Cigarette* and I could not sufficiently congratulate each other on the prospect, for we had been told there was a capital inn at La Fère. Such a dinner as we were going to eat! such beds as we were to sleep in! and all the while the rain raining on houseless folk over all the pop-lared country-side. It made our mouths water. The inn bore the name of some woodland animal, stag, or hart, or hind, I forget which. But I shall never forget how spacious and how eminently habitable it looked as we drew near. The carriage entry was lighted up not by intention, but from the mere superfluity of fire and candle in the house. A rattle of many dishes came to our ears; we sighted a great field of tablecloth; the kitchen glowed like a forge and smelt like a garden of things to eat.

Into this, the inmost shrine and physiological heart of a hostelry, with all its furnaces in action and all its dressers charged with viands, you are now to suppose us making our triumphal entry, a pair of damp rag-and-bone men, each with a limp india-rubber bag upon his arm. I do not believe I have a sound view of that kitchen; I saw it through a sort of glory, but it seemed to me crowded with the snowy caps of cookmen, who all turned round from their saucepans and looked at us with surprise. There was no doubt about the landlady, however; there she was, heading her army, a flushed, angry woman, full of affairs. Her I asked politely — too politely, thinks the *Cigarette* — if we could have beds, she surveying us coldly from head to foot.

"You will find beds in the suburb," she remarked. "We are too busy for the like of you."

If we could make an entrance, change our clothes, and order a bottle of wine, I felt sure we could put things right; so said I, "If we cannot sleep, we may at least dine," — and was for depositing my bag.

What a terrible convulsion of nature was that which followed in the landlady's face! She made a run at us and stamped her foot.

"Out with you, — out of the door!" she screeched. "*Sortez! sortez! sortez par la porte!*"

I do not know how it happened, but next moment we were out in the rain and darkness, and I was cursing before the carriage entry like a disappointed mendicant. Where were the boating-men of Belgium? where the judge and his good wines? and where the graces of Origny? Black, black was the night after the firelit kitchen, but what was that to the blackness in our heart? This was not the first time that I have been refused a lodging. Often and often have I planned what I should do if such a misadventure happened to me again. And nothing is easier to plan. But to put in execution, with the heart boiling at the indignity? Try it; try it only once, and tell me what you did.

It is all very fine to talk about tramps and morality. Six hours of police surveillance (such as I have had) or one brutal rejection from an inn door change your views upon the subject like a course of lectures. As long as you keep in the upper regions, with all the world bowing to you as you go, social arrangements have a very handsome air; but once get under the wheels and you wish society were at the devil. I will give most respectable men a fortnight of such a life, and then I will offer them twopence for what remains of their morality.

For my part, when I was turned out of the Stag, or the Hind, or whatever it was, I would have set the temple of Diana on fire if it had been handy. There was no crime complete enough to express my disapproval of human institutions. As for the *Cigarette*, I never knew a man so altered. "We have been taken for pedlars again," said he. "Good God, what it must be to be a pedlar in reality!" He particularised a complaint for every joint in the landlady's body. Timon was a philanthropist alongside of him. And then, when he was at the top of his maledictory bent, he would suddenly break away and begin whimperingly to commiserate the poor. "I hope to God," he said, — and I trust the prayer was answered, — "that I shall never be uncivil to a pedlar." Was this the imperturbable *Cigarette*? This, this was he. Oh, change beyond report, thought, or belief!

Meantime the heaven wept upon our heads; and the windows grew brighter as the night increased in darkness. We trudged in and out of La Fère streets; we saw shops, and private houses where people were copiously dining; we saw stables where carters' nags had plenty of fodder and clean straw; we saw no end of reservists, who were very sorry for themselves this wet night, I doubt not, and yearned for their country homes; but had they not each man his place in La Fère barracks? And we, what had we?

There seemed to be no other inn in the whole town. People gave us directions, which we followed as best we could, generally with the effect of bringing us out again upon the scene of our disgrace. We were very sad people indeed, by the time we had gone all over La Fère; and the *Cigarette* had already made up his mind to lie under a poplar and sup off a loaf of bread. But right at the other end, the house next the town gate was full of light and bustle. "*Bazin, aubergiste, loge à pied*," was the sign. "*À la Croix de Malte.*" There were we received.

The room was full of noisy reservists drinking and smoking; and we were very glad indeed when the drums and bugles began to go about the streets, and one and all had to snatch shakoes and be off for the barracks.

Bazin was a tall man, running to fat; soft-spoken, with a delicate, gentle face. We asked him to share our wine; but he excused himself, having pledged reservists all day long. This was a very different type of the workman-innkeeper from the bawling, disputatious fellow at Origny. He also loved Paris, where he had worked as a decorative painter in his youth. There were such opportunities for self-instruction there, he said. And if any one has read Zola's description of the workman's marriage party visiting the Louvre they would do well to have heard Bazin by way of antidote. He had delighted in the museums in his youth. "One sees there little miracles of work," he said; "that is what makes a good workman; it kindles a spark." We asked him how he managed in La Fère. "I am married," he said, "and I have my pretty children. But frankly, it is no life at all. From morning to night I pledge a pack of good-enough fellows who know nothing.".

It faired as the night went on, and the moon came out of the clouds. We sat in front of the door, talking softly with Bazin. At the guardhouse opposite the guard was being for ever turned out, as trains of field artillery kept clanking in out of the night or patrols of horsemen trotted by in their cloaks. Madame Bazin came out after awhile; she was tired with her day's work, I suppose; and she nestled up to her husband and laid her head upon his breast. He had his arm about her and kept gently patting her on the shoulder. I think Bazin was right, and he was really married. Of how few people can the same be said!

Little did the Bazins know how much they served us. We were charged for candles, for food and drink, and for the beds we slept in. But there was nothing in the bill for the husband's pleasant talk; nor for the pretty spectacle of their married life. And there was yet another item uncharged. For these people's politeness really set us up again in our own esteem. We had a thirst for consideration; the sense of insult was still hot in our spirits; and civil usage seemed to restore us to our position in the world.

How little we pay our way in life! Although we have our purses continually in our hand, the better part of service goes still unrewarded. But I like to fancy that a grateful spirit gives as good as it gets. Perhaps the Bazins knew how much I liked them? perhaps they, also, were healed of some slights by the thanks that I gave them in my manner?

DOWN THE OISE

Through the Golden Valley

BELOW La Fère the river runs through a piece of open pastoral country; green, opulent, loved by breeders; called the Golden Valley. In wide sweeps, and with a swift and equable gallop, the ceaseless stream of water visits and makes green the fields. Kine, and horses, and little humorous donkeys browse together in the meadows, and come down in troops to the riverside to drink. They make a strange feature in the landscape; above all when startled, and you see them galloping to and fro, with their incongruous forms and faces. It gives a feeling as of great, unfenced pampas, and the herds of wandering nations. There were hills in the distance upon either hand; and on one side, the river sometimes bordered on the wooded spurs of Coucy and St. Gobain.

The artillery were practising at La Fère; and soon the cannon of heaven joined in that loud play. Two continents of cloud met and exchanged salvos overhead; while all round the horizon we could see sunshine and clear air upon the hills. What with the guns and the thunder, the herds were all frightened in the Golden Valley. We could see them tossing their heads, and running to and fro in timorous indecision; and when they had made up their minds, and the donkey followed the horse, and the cow was after the donkey, we could hear their hoofs thundering abroad over the meadows. It had a martial sound, like cavalry charges. And altogether, as far as the ears are concerned, we had a very rousing battle piece performed for our amusement.

At last, the guns and the thunder dropped off; the sun shone on the wet meadows; the air was scented with the breath of rejoicing trees and grass; and the river kept unweariedly carrying us on at its best pace. There was a manufacturing district about Chauny; and after that the banks grew so high that they hid the adjacent country, and we could see nothing but clay sides, and one willow after another. Only here and there we passed by a village or a ferry, and some wondering child upon the bank would stare after us until we turned the corner. I dare say we continued to paddle in that child's dreams for many a night after.

Sun and shower alternated like day and night, making the hours longer by their variety. When the showers were heavy I could feel each drop striking through my jersey to my warm skin; and the accumulation of small shocks put me nearly beside myself. I decided I should buy a mackintosh at Noyon. It is nothing to get wet; but the misery of these individual pricks of cold all over my body at the same instant of time made me flail the water with my paddle like a madman. The *Cigarette* was greatly amused by these ebullitions. It gave him something else to look at besides clay banks and willows.

All the time the river stole away like a thief in straight places, or swung round corners with an eddy; the willows nodded and were undermined all day long; the clay banks tumbled in; the Oise, which had been so many centuries making the Golden Valley, seemed to have changed its fancy and be bent upon undoing its performance. What a number of things a river does by simply following Gravity in the innocence of its heart!

NOYON CATHEDRAL

NOYON stands about a mile from the river, in a little plain surrounded by wooded hills, and entirely covers an eminence with its tile roofs, surmounted by a long, straight-backed cathedral with two stiff towers. As we got into the town, the tile roofs seemed to tumble up-hill one upon another, in the oddest disorder; but for all their scrambling they did not attain above the knees of the cathedral, which stood, upright and solemn, over all. As the streets drew near to this presiding genius, through the market-place under the Hôtel de Ville, they grew emptier and more composed. Blank walls and shuttered windows were turned to the great edifice, and grass grew on the white causeway. "Put off thy shoes from off thy feet, for the place whereon thou standest is holy ground." The Hôtel du Nord, nevertheless, lights its secular tapers within a stone-cast of the church; and we had the superb east end before our eyes all morning from the window of our bedroom. I have seldom looked on the east end of a church with more complete sympathy. As it flanges out in three wide terraces, and settles down broadly on the earth, it looks like the poop of some great old battle-ship. Hollow-backed buttresses carry vases, which figure for the stern lanterns. There is a roll in the ground, and the towers just appear above the pitch of the roof, as though the good ship were bowing lazily over an Atlantic swell. At any moment it might be a hundred feet away from you, climbing the next billow. At any moment a window might open, and some old admiral thrust forth a cocked hat and proceed to take an observation. The old admirals sail the sea no longer; the old ships of battle are all broken up, and live only in pictures; but this, that was a church before ever they were thought upon, is still a church, and makes as brave an appearance by the Oise. The cathedral and the river

THE CATHEDRAL AT NOYON

are probably the two oldest things for miles around; and certainly they have both a grand old age.

The Sacristan took us to the top of one of the towers, and showed us the five bells hanging in their loft. From above the town was a tessellated pavement of roofs and gardens; the old line of rampart was plainly traceable; and the Sacristan pointed out to us, far across the plain, in a bit of gleaming sky between two clouds, the towers of Château Coucy.

I find I never weary of great churches. It is my favourite kind of mountain scenery. Mankind was never so happily inspired as when it made a cathedral : a thing as single and specious as a statue to the first glance, and yet, on examination, as lively and interesting as a forest in detail. The height of spires cannot be taken by trigonometry; they measure absurdly short, but how tall they are to the admiring eye! And where we have so many elegant proportions, growing one out of the other, and all together into one, it seems as if proportion transcended itself and became something different and more imposing. I could never fathom how a man dares to lift up his voice to preach in a cathedral. What is he to say that will not be an anti-climax? For though I have heard a considerable variety of sermons, I never yet heard one that was so expressive as a cathedral. 'Tis the best preacher itself, and preaches day and night; not only telling you of man's art and aspirations in the past, but convicting your own soul of ardent sympathies; or rather, like all good preachers, it sets you preaching to yourself, — and every man is his own doctor of divinity in the last resort.

As I sat outside of the hotel in the course of the afternoon, the sweet, groaning thunder of the organ floated out of the church like a summons. I was not averse, liking the theatre so well, to sit out an act or two of the play, but I could never rightly make out the nature of the service I beheld. Four or five priests and as many choristers were singing *Miserere* before the high altar when I went in. There was no congregation but a few old women on chairs and old men kneeling on the pavement. After awhile a long train of young girls, walking two and two, each with a lighted taper in her hand, and all dressed in black with a white veil, came from behind the altar and began to descend the nave; the four first carrying a Virgin and Child upon a table. The priests and choristers arose from their knees and followed after, singing "Ave Mary" as they went. In this order they made the circuit of the cathedral, passing twice before me where I leaned against a pillar. The priest who seemed of most consequence was a strange-down-looking old man. He kept mumbling prayers with his lips; but, as he looked upon me darkling, it did not seem as if prayer were uppermost in his heart. Two others, who bore the burden of the chant, were stout, brutal, military-looking men of forty, with bold, over-fed eyes; they sang with some lustiness, and trolled forth "Ave Mary" like a garrison catch. The little girls were timid and grave. As they footed slowly up the aisle, each one took a moment's glance at the Englishman; and the big nun who played marshal fairly stared him out of countenance. As for the choristers, from first to last they misbehaved as only boys can misbehave, and cruelly marred the performance with their antics.

I understood a great deal of the spirit of what went on. Indeed, it would be difficult not to understand the *Miserere*, which I take to be the composition of an atheist. If it ever be a good thing to take such despondency to heart, the *Miserere* is the right music and a cathedral a fit scene. So far I am at one with the Catholics, — an odd name for them, after all! But why, in God's name, these holiday choristers? why these priests who steal wander-

ing looks about the congregation while they feign to be
at prayer? why this fat nun, who rudely arranges her
procession and shakes delinquent virgins by the elbow?
why this spitting, and snuffing, and forgetting of keys,
and the thousand and one little misadventures that disturb a frame of mind, laboriously edified with chants
and organings? In any play-house reverend fathers may
see what can be done with a little art, and how, to move
high sentiments, it is necessary to drill the supernumeraries
and have every stool in its proper place.

One other circumstance distressed me. I could bear
a *Miserere* myself, having had a good deal of open-air
exercise of late; but I wished the old people somewhere
else. It was neither the right sort of music nor the right
sort of divinity for men and women who have come
through most accidents by this time, and probably have
an opinion of their own upon the tragic element in life.
A person up in years can generally do his own *Miserere*
for himself; although I notice that such an one often
prefers *Jubilate Deo* for his ordinary singing. On the
whole, the most religious exercise for the aged is probably
to recall their own experience; so many friends dead, so
many hopes disappointed, so many slips and stumbles,
and withal so many bright days and smiling providences;
there is surely the matter of a very eloquent sermon in
all this.

On the whole I was greatly solemnised. In the little
pictorial map of our whole Inland Voyage, which my
fancy still preserves, and sometimes unrolls for the amusement of odd moments, Noyon cathedral figures on a most
preposterous scale, and must be nearly as large as the
department. I can still see the faces of the priests as if

they were at my elbow, and hear *Ave Maria, ora pro nobis* sounding through the church. All Noyon is blotted out for me by these superior memories; and I do not care to say more about the place. It was but a stack of brown roofs at the best, where I believe people live very reputably, in a quiet way; but the shadow of the church falls upon it when the sun is low, and the five bells are heard in all quarters, telling that the organ has begun. If ever I join the church of Rome I shall stipulate to be Bishop of Noyon on the Oise.

DOWN THE OISE

To Compiègne

THE most patient people grow weary at last with being continually wetted with rain; except, of course, in the Scotch Highlands, where there are not enough fine intervals to point the difference. That was like to be our case the day we left Noyon. I remember nothing of the voyage; it was nothing but clay banks, and willows, and rain; incessant, pitiless, beating rain; until we stopped to lunch at a little inn at Pimprez, where the canal ran very near the river. We were so sadly drenched that the landlady lit a few sticks in the chimney for our comfort; there we sat in a steam of vapour lamenting our concerns. The husband donned a game-bag and strode out to shoot; the wife sat in a far corner watching us. I think we were worth looking at. We grumbled over the misfortune of La Fère; we forecast other La Fères in the future, — although things went better with the *Cigarette* for spokesman; he had more aplomb altogether than I; and a dull, positive way of approaching a landlady that carried off the india-rubber bags. Talking of La Fère put us talking of the reservists.

"Reservery," said he, "seems a pretty mean way to spend one's autumn holiday."

"About as mean," returned I, dejectedly, "as canoeing."

"These gentlemen travel for their pleasure?" asked the landlady, with unconscious irony.

It was too much. The scales fell from our eyes. Another wet day, it was determined, and we put the boats into the train.

The weather took the hint. That was our last wetting. The afternoon faired up; grand clouds still voyaged in the sky, but now singly, and with a depth of blue around their path; and a sunset, in the daintiest rose and gold, inaugurated a thick night of stars and a month of unbroken weather. At the same time, the river began to give us a better outlook into the country. The banks were not so high, the willows disappeared from along the margin, and pleasant hills stood all along its course and marked their profile on the sky.

In a little while the canal, coming to its last lock, began to discharge its water houses on the Oise; so that we had no lack of company to fear. Here were all our old friends; the *Deo Gratias* of Condé and the *Four Sons of Aymon* journeyed cheerily down the stream along with us; we exchanged water-side pleasantries with the steersman perched among the lumber, or the driver hoarse with bawling to his horses; and the children came and looked over the side as we paddled by. We had never known all this while how much we missed them; but it gave us a fillip to see the smoke from their chimneys.

A little below this junction we made another meeting of yet more account. For there we were joined by the Aisne, already a far-travelled river and fresh out of Champagne. Here ended the adolescence of the Oise; this was his marriage day; thenceforward he had a stately, brimming march, conscious of his own dignity and sundry dams. He became a tranquil feature in the scene. The trees and towns saw themselves in him, as in a mirror.

He carried the canoes lightly on his broad breast; there
was no need to work hard against an eddy, but idleness
became the order of the day, and mere straightforward
dipping of the paddle, now on this side, now on that,
without intelligence or effort. Truly we were coming
into halcyon weather upon all accounts, and were floating
towards the sea like gentlemen.

We made Compiègne as the sun was going down: a
fine profile of a town above the river. Over the bridge a
regiment was parading to the drum. People loitered on
the quay, some fishing, some looking idly at the stream.
And as the two boats shot in along the water, we could
see them pointing them out and speaking one to another.
We landed at a floating lavatory, where the washerwomen
were still beating the clothes.

AT COMPIÈGNE

WE put up at a big, bustling hotel in Compiègne, where nobody observed our presence.

Reservery and general *militarismus* (as the Germans call it) was rampant. A camp of conical white tents without the town looked like a leaf out of a picture Bible; sword-belts decorated the walls of the *cafés*, and the streets kept sounding all day long with military music. It was not possible to be an Englishman and avoid a feeling of elation; for the men who followed the drums were small and walked shabbily. Each man inclined at his own angle, and jolted to his own convenience as he went. There was nothing of the superb gait with which a regiment of tall Highlanders moves behind its music, solemn and inevitable, like a natural phenomenon. Who, that has seen it, can forget the drum-major pacing in front, the drummers' tiger-skins, the pipers' swinging plaids, the strange, elastic rhythm of the whole regiment footing it in time, and the bang of the drum when the brasses cease, and the shrill pipes taking up the martial story in their place?

A girl at school in France began to describe one of our regiments on parade to her French schoolmates, and as she went on, she told me the recollection grew so vivid, she became so proud to be the countrywoman of such soldiers, and so sorry to be in another country, that her voice failed her and she burst into tears. I have never forgotten that girl, and I think she very nearly deserves a statue. To call her a young lady, with all its niminy associations, would be to offer her an insult. She may rest assured of one thing, although she never should marry a heroic general, never see any great or immediate result of her life, she will not have lived in vain for her native land.

But though French soldiers show to ill-advantage on parade, on the march they are gay, alert, and willing, like a troop of fox-hunters. I remember once seeing a company pass through the forest of Fontainebleau, on the Chailly road, between the Bas Bréau and the Reine Blanche. One fellow walked a little before the rest, and sang a loud, audacious marching song. The rest bestirred their feet, and even swung their muskets in time. A young officer on horseback had hard ado to keep his countenance at the words. You never saw anything so cheerful and spontaneous as their gait; school-boys do not look more eagerly at hare and hounds; and you would have thought it impossible to tire such willing marchers.

My great delight in Compiègne was the town hall. I doted upon the town hall. It is a monument of Gothic insecurity, all turreted, and gargoyled, and slashed, and bedizened with half a score of architectural fancies. Some of the niches are gilt and painted; and in a great square panel in the centre, in black relief on a gilt ground, Louis XII. rides upon a pacing horse, with hand on hip, and head thrown back. There is royal arrogance in every line of him; the stirruped foot projects insolently from the frame; the eye is hard and proud; the very horse seems to be treading with gratification over prostrate serfs, and to have the breath of the trumpet in his nos-

THE TOWN HALL AT COMPIÈGNE

trils. So rides for ever, on the front of the town hall, the good King Louis XII., the father of his people.

Over the king's head, in the tall centre turret, appears the dial of a clock; and high above that, three little mechanical figures, each one with a hammer in his hand, whose business it is to chime out the hours, and halves, and quarters for the burgesses of Compiègne. The centre figure has a gilt breastplate; the two others wear gilt trunk-hose; and they all three have elegant, flapping hats like cavaliers. As the quarter approaches they turn their heads and look knowingly one to the other; and then, *kling* go the three hammers on three little bells below. The hour follows, deep and sonorous, from the interior of the tower; and the gilded gentlemen rest from their labours with contentment.

I had a great deal of healthy pleasure from their manœuvres, and took good care to miss as few performances as possible; and I found that even the *Cigarette*, while he pretended to despise my enthusiasm, was more or less a devotee himself. There is something highly absurd in the exposition of such toys to the outrages of winter on a housetop. They would be more in keeping in a glass case before a Nürnberg clock. Above all, at night, when the children are abed, and even grown people are snoring under quilts, does it not seem impertinent to leave these gingerbread figures winking and tinkling to the stars and the rolling moon? The gargoyles may fitly enough twist their ape-like heads; fitly enough may the potentate bestride his charger, like a centurion in an old German print of the *Via Dolorosa;* but the toys should be put away in a box among some cotton, until the sun rises, and the children are abroad again to be amused.

In Compiègne post-office a great packet of letters awaited us; and the authorities were, for this occasion only, so polite as to hand them over upon application.

In some way, our journey may be said to end with this letter-bag at Compiègne. The spell was broken. We had partly come home from that moment.

No one should have any correspondence on a journey; it is bad enough to have to write; but the receipt of letters is the death of all holiday feeling.

"Out of my country and myself I go." I wish to take a dive among new conditions for awhile, as into another element. I have nothing to do with my friends or my affections for the time; when I came away, I left my heart at home in a desk, or sent it forward with port-manteau to await me at my destination. After my journey is over, I shall not fail to read your admirable letters with the attention they deserve. But I have paid all this money, look you, and paddled all these strokes, for no other purpose than to be abroad; and yet you keep me at home with your perpetual communications. You tug the string, and I feel that I am a tethered bird. You pursue me all over Europe with the little vexations that I came away to avoid. There is no discharge in the war of life, I am well aware; but shall there not be so much as a week's furlough?

We were up by six, the day we were to leave. They had taken so little note of us that I hardly thought they would have condescended on a bill. But they did, with some smart particulars, too; and we paid in a civilised manner to an uninterested clerk, and went out of that hotel, with the india-rubber bags, unremarked. No one cared to know about us. It is not possible to rise

before a village; but Compiègne was so grown a town
that it took its ease in the morning; and we were up and
away while it was still in dressing-gown and slippers.
The streets were left to people washing door-steps; nobody was in full dress but the cavaliers upon the town
hall; they were all washed with dew, spruce in their
gilding, and full of intelligence and a sense of professional
responsibility. *Kling* went they on the bells for the half-
past six, as we went by. I took it kind of them to make
me this parting compliment; they never were in better
form, not even at noon upon a Sunday.

There was no one to see us off but the early washerwomen, — early and late, — who were already beating
the linen in their floating lavatory on the river. They
were very merry and matutinal in their ways; plunged
their arms boldly in, and seemed not to feel the shock.
It would be dispiriting to me, this early beginning and
first cold dabble of a most dispiriting day's work. But I
believe they would have been as unwilling to change days
with us as we could be to change with them. They
crowded to the door to watch us paddle away into the
thin sunny mists upon the river; and shouted heartily
after us till we were through the bridge.

CHANGED TIMES

THERE is a sense in which those mists never rose from off our journey; and from that time forth they lie very densely in my note-book. As long as the Oise was a small, rural river it took us near by people's doors, and we could hold a conversation with natives in the riparian fields. But now that it had grown so wide, the life along shore passed us by at a distance. It was the same difference as between a great public highway and a country by-path that wanders in and out of cottage gardens. We now lay in towns, where nobody troubled us with questions; we had floated into civilised life, where people pass without salutation. In sparsely inhabited places we make all we can of each encounter; but when it comes to a city, we keep to ourselves, and never speak unless we have trodden on a man's toes. In these waters we were no longer strange birds, and nobody supposed we had travelled farther than from the last town. I remember, when we came into L'Isle Adam, for instance, how we met dozens of pleasure-boats outing it for the afternoon, and there was nothing to distinguish the true voyager from the amateur, except, perhaps, the filthy condition of my sail. The company in one boat actually thought they recognised me for a neighbour. Was there ever anything more wounding? All the romance had come down to that. Now, on the upper Oise, where nothing sailed, as a general thing, but fish, a pair of canoeists could not be thus vulgarly explained away; we were strange and picturesque intruders; and out of people's wonder sprang a sort of light and passing intimacy all along our route. There is nothing but tit for tat in this world, though sometimes it be a little difficult to trace: for the scores are older than we ourselves, and there has never yet been a settling-day since things were. You get entertainment pretty much in proportion as you give. As long as we were a sort of odd wanderers, to be stared at and followed like a quack doctor or a caravan, we had no want of amusement in return; but as soon as we sank into commonplace ourselves, all whom we met were similarly disenchanted. And here is one reason of a dozen why the world is dull to dull persons.

In our earlier adventures there was generally something to do, and that quickened us. Even the showers of rain had a revivifying effect, and shook up the brain from torpor. But now, when the river no longer ran in a proper sense, only glided seaward with an even, outright, but imperceptible speed, and when the sky smiled upon us day after day without variety, we began to slip into that golden doze of the mind which follows upon much exercise in the open air. I have stupefied myself in this way more than once: indeed, I dearly love the feeling; but I never had it to the same degree as when paddling down the Oise. It was the apotheosis of stupidity.

We ceased reading entirely. Sometimes, when I found a new paper, I took a particular pleasure in reading a single number of the current novel; but I never could bear more than three instalments; and even the second was a disappointment. As soon as the tale became in any way perspicuous, it lost all merit in my eyes; only a single scene, or, as is the way with these *feuilletons*, half a scene, without antecedent or consequence, like a piece of a dream, had the knack of fixing my interest. The less I saw of the novel the better I liked it : a pregnant reflection. But for the most part, as I said, we neither of us read anything in the world, and employed the very little while we were awake between bed and dinner in poring upon maps. I have always been fond of maps, and can voyage in an atlas with the greatest enjoyment. The names of places are singularly inviting; the contour of coasts and rivers is enthralling to the eye; and to hit in a map upon some place you have heard of before makes history a new possession. But we thumbed our charts, on those evenings, with the blankest unconcern. We cared not a fraction for this place or that. We stared at the sheet as children listen to their rattle, and read the names of towns or villages to forget them again at once. We had no romance in the matter; there was nobody so fancy-free. If you had taken the maps away while we were studying them most intently it is a fair bet whether we might not have continued to study the table with the same delight.

About one thing we were mightily taken up, and that was eating. I think I made a god of my belly. I remember dwelling in imagination upon this or that dish till my mouth watered; and long before we got in for the night my appetite was a clamant, instant annoyance. Sometimes we paddled alongside for awhile and whetted each other with gastronomical fancies as we went. Cake and sherry, a homely refection, but not within reach upon the Oise, trotted through my head for many a mile; and once, as we were approaching Verberie, the *Cigarette* brought my heart into my mouth by the suggestion of oyster patties and Sauterne.

I suppose none of us recognise the great part that is played in life by eating and drinking. The appetite is so imperious that we can stomach the least interesting viands, and pass off a dinner hour thankfully enough on bread and water; just as there are men who must read something, if it were only Bradshaw's Guide. But there is a romance about the matter, after all. Probably the table has more devotees than love; and I am sure that food is much more generally entertaining than scenery. Do you give in, as Walt Whitman would say, that you are any the less immortal for that? The true materialism is to be ashamed of what we are. To detect the flavour of an olive is no less a piece of human perfection than to find beauty in the colours of the sunset.

Canoeing was easy work. To dip the paddle at the proper inclination, now right, now left; to keep the head down stream; to empty the little pool that gathered in the lap of the apron; to screw up the eyes against the glittering sparkles of sun upon the water; or now and again to pass below the whistling tow-rope of the *Deo Gratias* of Condé, or *Four Sons of Aymon*, — there was not much art in that; certain silly muscles managed it between sleep and waking; and meanwhile the brain had a whole holiday, and went to sleep. We took in at a glance the larger features of the scene, and beheld, with half an eye, bloused fishers and dabbling washerwomen on the bank. Now and again we might be half wakened by some church spire, by a leaping fish, or by a trail of river grass that clung about the paddle and had to be plucked off and thrown away. But these luminous intervals were only partially luminous. A little more of us was called into action, but never the whole. The central bureau of nerves, what in some moods we call Ourselves, enjoyed its holiday without disturbance, like a Government Office. The great wheels of intelligence turned idly in the head, like fly-wheels, grinding no grist. I have gone on for half an hour at a time, counting my strokes and forgetting the hundreds. I flatter myself the beasts that perish could not underbid that, as a low form of consciousness. And what a pleasure it was! What a hearty, tolerant temper did it bring about! There is nothing captious about a man who has attained to this, the one possible apotheosis in life, the Apotheosis of Stupidity; and

There was one odd piece of practical metaphysics which accompanied what I may call the depth, if I must not call it the intensity, of my abstraction. What philosophers call *me* and *not me*, *ego* and *non ego*, preoccupied me whether I would or no. There was less *me* and more *not me* than I was accustomed to expect. I looked on upon somebody else, who managed the paddling; I was aware of somebody else's feet against the stretcher; my own body seemed to have no more intimate relation to me than the canoe, or the river, or the river banks. Nor this alone: something inside my mind, a part of my brain, a province of my proper being, had thrown off allegiance and set up for itself, or perhaps for the somebody else who did the paddling. I had dwindled into quite a little thing in a corner of myself. I was isolated in my own skull. Thoughts presented themselves unbidden; they were not my thoughts, they were plainly some one else's; and I considered them like a part of the landscape. I

take it, in short, that I was about as near Nirvana as would
be convenient in practical life; and, if this be so, I make
the Buddhists my sincere compliments; 'tis an agreeable
state, not very consistent with mental brilliancy, not
exactly profitable in a money point of view, but very calm,
golden, and incurious, and one that sets a man superior
to alarms. It may be best figured by supposing yourself
to get dead drunk, and yet keep sober to enjoy it. I have
a notion that open-air labourers must spend a large portion of their days in this ecstatic stupor, which explains
their high composure and endurance. A pity to go to
the expense of laudanum when here is a better paradise
for nothing!

This frame of mind was the great exploit of our voyage,
take it all in all. It was the farthest piece of travel accomplished. Indeed, it lies so far from beaten paths of
language that I despair of getting the reader into sympathy with the smiling, complacent idiocy of my condition; when ideas came and went like motes in a sun-
beam; when trees and church spires along the bank surged
up from time to time into my notice, like solid objects
through a rolling cloud-land; when the rhythmical swish
of boat and paddle in the water became a cradle-song to
lull my thoughts asleep; when a piece of mud on the
deck was sometimes an intolerable eyesore, and sometimes
quite a companion for me, and the object of pleased consideration; and all the time, with the river running and
the shores changing upon either hand, I kept counting my
strokes and forgetting the hundreds, the happiest animal
in France.

DOWN THE OISE

Church Interiors

WE made our first stage below Compiègne to Pont Sainte-Maxence. I was abroad a little after six the next morning. The air was biting and smelt of frost. In an open place a score of women wrangled together over the day's market; and the noise of their negotiation sounded thin and querulous, like that of sparrows on a winter's morning. The rare passengers blew into their hands, and shuffled in their wooden shoes to set the blood agog. The streets were full of icy shadow, although the chimneys were smoking overhead in golden sunshine. If you wake early enough at this season of the year, you may get up in December to break your fast in June.

I found my way to the church, for there is always something to see about a church, whether living worshippers or dead men's tombs; you find there the deadliest earnest, and the hollowest deceit; and even where it is not a piece of history, it will be certain to leak out some contemporary gossip. It was scarcely so cold in the church as it was without, but it looked colder. The white nave was positively arctic to the eye; and the tawdriness of a continental altar looked more forlorn than usual in the solitude and the bleak air. Two priests sat in the chancel reading and waiting penitents; and out in the nave one very old woman was engaged in her devotions. It was a won-

der how she was able to pass her beads when healthy
young people were breathing in their palms and slapping
their chest; but though this concerned me, I was yet
more dispirited by the nature of her exercises. She went
from chair to chair, from altar to altar, circumnavigating
the church. To each shrine she dedicated an equal
number of beads and an equal length of time. Like a
prudent capitalist with a somewhat cynical view of the
commercial prospect, she desired to place her supplica-
tions in a great variety of heavenly securities. She would
risk nothing on the credit of any single intercessor. Out
of the whole company of saints and angels, not one but
was to suppose himself her champion elect against the
Great Assizes! I could only think of it as a dull, transparent jugglery, based upon unconscious unbelief.

She was as dead an old woman as ever I saw; no more
than bone and parchment, curiously put together. Her
eyes, with which she interrogated mine, were vacant of
sense. It depends on what you call seeing, whether you
might not call her blind. Perhaps she had known love:
perhaps borne children, suckled them, and given them
pet names. But now that was all gone by, and had left
her neither happier nor wiser; and the best she could do
with her mornings was to come up here into the cold
church and juggle for a slice of heaven. It was not without a gulp that I escaped into the streets and the keen
morning air. Morning? why, how tired of it she would
be before night! and if she did not sleep, how then? It
is fortunate that not many of us are brought up publicly
to justify our lives at the bar of threescore years and
ten; fortunate that such a number are knocked oppor-
tunely on the head in what they call the flower of their

years, and go away to suffer for their follies in private somewhere else. Otherwise, between sick children and discontented old folk, we might be put out of all conceit of life.

I had need of all my cerebral hygiene during that day's paddle: the old devotee stuck in my throat sorely. But I was soon in the seventh heaven of stupidity; and knew nothing but that somebody was paddling a canoe, while I was counting his strokes and forgetting the hundreds. I used sometimes to be afraid I should remember the hundreds; which would have made a toil of a pleasure; but the terror was chimerical, they went out of my mind by enchantment, and I knew no more than the man in the moon about my only occupation.

At Creil, where we stopped to lunch, we left the canoes in another floating lavatory, which, as it was high noon, was packed with washerwomen, red-handed and loud-voiced; and they and their broad jokes are about all I remember of the place. I could look up my history books, if you were very anxious, and tell you a date or two; for it figured rather largely in the English wars. But I prefer to mention a girls' boarding-school, which had an interest for us because it was a girls' boarding-school, and because we imagined we had rather an interest for it. At least, there were the girls about the garden; and here were we on the river; and there was more than one handkerchief waved as we went by. It caused quite a stir in my heart; and yet how we should have wearied and despised each other, these girls and I, if we had been introduced at a croquet party! But this is a fashion I love: to kiss the hand or wave a handkerchief to people I shall never see again, to play with possibility, and knock in a peg for fancy to hang upon. It gives the traveller a jog, reminds him that he is not a traveller everywhere, and that his journey is no more than a siesta by the way on the real march of life.

The church at Creil was a nondescript place in the inside, splashed with gaudy lights from the windows, and picked out with medallions of the Dolorous Way. But there was one oddity, in the way of an *ex voto*, which pleased me hugely: a faithful model of a canal boat, swung from the vault, with a written aspiration that God should conduct the *Saint Nicholas* of Creil to a good haven. The thing was neatly executed, and would have made the delight of a party of boys on the water-side. But what tickled me was the gravity of the peril to be conjured. You might hang up the model of a sea-going ship, and welcome: one that is to plough a furrow round the world, and visit the tropic or the frosty poles, runs dangers that are well worth a candle and a mass. But the *Saint Nicholas* of Creil, which was to be tugged for some ten years by patient draught horses, in a weedy canal, with the poplars chattering overhead, and the skipper whistling at the tiller; which was to do all its errands in green inland places, and never got out of sight of a village belfry in all its cruising; why, you would have thought if anything could be done without the intervention of Providence, it would be that! But perhaps the skipper was a humourist: or perhaps a prophet, reminding people of the seriousness of life by this preposterous token.

At Creil, as at Noyon, St. Joseph seemed a favourite saint on the score of punctuality. Day and hour can be specified; and grateful people do not fail to specify them on a votive tablet, when prayers have been punctually and neatly answered. Whenever time is a consideration, St. Joseph is the proper intermediary. I took a sort of pleasure in observing the vogue he had in France, for the good man plays a very small part in my religion at home. Yet I could not help fearing that, where the saint is so much commended for exactitude, he will be expected to be very grateful for his tablet.

This is foolishness to us Protestants; and not of great importance anyway. Whether people's gratitude for the good gifts that come to them be wisely conceived or dutifully expressed is a secondary matter, after all, so long as they feel gratitude. The true ignorance is when a man does not know that he has received a good gift, or begins to imagine that he has got it for himself. The self-made man is the funniest windbag after all! There is a marked difference between decreeing light in chaos, and lighting the gas in a metropolitan back-parlour with a box of patent matches; and, do what we will, there is always something made to our hand, if it were only our fingers.

But there was something worse than foolishness placarded in Creil Church. The Association of the Living Rosary (of which I had never previously heard) is responsible for that. This association was founded, according to the printed advertisement, by a brief of Pope Gregory Sixteenth, on the 17th of January, 1832: according to a coloured bas-relief, it seems to have been founded, some time or other, by the Virgin giving one rosary to St. Dominic, and the Infant Saviour giving another to St. Catherine of Sienna. Pope Gregory is not so imposing, but he is nearer hand. I could not distinctly make out whether the association was entirely devotional, or had an eye to good works; at least it is highly organised: the names of fourteen matrons and misses were filled in for each week of the month as associates, with one other, generally a married woman, at the top for *Zêlatrice*, the choragus of the band. Indulgences, plenary and partial, follow on the performance of the duties of the association. "The partial indulgences are attached to the recitation of the rosary." On "the recitation of the required *dizaine*," a partial indulgence promptly follows. When people serve the kingdom of Heaven with a pass-book in their hands, I should always be afraid lest they should carry the same commercial spirit into their dealings with their fellow-men, which would make a sad and sordid business of this life.

There is one more article, however, of happier import. "All these indulgences," it appeared, "are applicable to souls in purgatory." For God's sake, ye ladies of Creil, apply them all to the souls in purgatory without delay! Burns would take no hire for his last songs, preferring to serve his country out of unmixed love. Suppose you were to imitate the excise man, Mesdames, and even if the souls in purgatory were not greatly bettered, some souls in Creil upon the Oise would find themselves none the worse either here or hereafter.

I cannot help wondering, as I transcribe these notes, whether a Protestant born and bred is in a fit state to understand these signs, and do them what justice they deserve; and I cannot help answering that he is not. They cannot look so merely ugly and mean to the faithful as they do to me. I see that as clearly as a proposition in Euclid. For these believers are neither weak nor wicked. They can put up their tablet commending St. Joseph for his despatch as if he were still a village car-

penter; they can "recite the required *dizaine*," and meta-
phorically pocket the indulgences as if they had done a
job for heaven; and then they can go out and look down
unabashed upon this wonderful river flowing by, and
up without confusion at the pin-point stars, which are
themselves great worlds full of flowing rivers greater than
the Oise. I see it as plainly, I say, as a proposition in
Euclid, that my Protestant mind has missed the point,
and that there goes with these deformities some higher
and more religious spirit than I dream.

I wonder if other people would make the same allow-
ances for me? Like the ladies of Creil, having recited
my rosary of toleration, I look for my indulgence on the
spot.

PRÉCY AND THE MARIONETTES

WE made Précy about sundown. The plain is rich with tufts of poplar. In a wide, luminous curve the Oise lay under the hillside. A faint mist began to rise and confound the different distances together. There was not a sound audible but that of the sheep-bells in some meadows by the river, and the creaking of a cart down the long road that descends the hill. The villas in their gardens, the shops along the street, all seemed to have been deserted the day before; and I felt inclined to walk discreetly as one feels in a silent forest. All of a sudden we came round a corner, and there, in a little green round the church, was a bevy of girls in Parisian costumes playing croquet. Their laughter and the hollow sound of ball and mallet made a cheery stir in the neighbourhood; and the look of these slim figures, all corseted and ribboned, produced an answerable disturbance in our hearts. We were within sniff of Paris, it seemed. And here were females of our own species playing croquet, just as if Précy had been a place in real life instead of a stage in the fairyland of travel. For, to be frank, the peasant-woman is scarcely to be counted as a woman at all, and after having passed by such a succession of people in petticoats digging, and hoeing, and making dinner, this company of coquettes under arms made quite a surprising feature in the landscape, and convinced us at once of being fallible males.

The inn at Précy is the worst inn in France. Not even in Scotland have I found worse fare. It was kept by a brother and sister, neither of whom was out of their teens. The sister, so to speak, prepared a meal for us; and the brother, who had been tippling, came in and brought with him a tipsy butcher, to entertain us as we ate. We found pieces of loo-warm pork among the salad, and pieces of unknown yielding substance in the *ragoût*. The butcher entertained us with pictures of Parisian life, with which he professed himself well acquainted; the brother sitting the while on the edge of the billiard table, toppling precariously, and sucking the stump of a cigar. In the midst of these diversions bang went a drum past the house, and a hoarse voice began issuing a proclamation. It was a man with marionettes announcing a performance for that evening.

He had set up his caravan and lighted his candles on another part of the girls' croquet green, under one of those open sheds which are so common in France to shelter markets; and he and his wife, by the time we strolled up there, were trying to keep order with the audience.

It was the most absurd contention. The show-people had set out a certain number of benches; and all who sat upon them were to pay a couple of sous for the accommodation. They were always quite full — a bumper house — as long as nothing was going forward; but let the show-woman appear with an eye to a collection, and at the first rattle of the tambourine the audience slipped off the seats and stood round on the outside, with their hands in their pockets. It certainly would have tried an angel's temper. The showman roared from the proscenium; he had been all over France, and nowhere, nowhere, "not even on the borders of Germany," had he met with such misconduct. Such thieves, and rogues, and rascals as he called them! And now and again the wife issued on another round, and added her shrill quota to the tirade. I remarked here, as elsewhere, how far more copious is the female mind in the material of insult. The audience laughed in high good-humour over the man's declamations; but they bridled and cried aloud under the woman's pungent sallies. She picked out the sore points. She had the honour of the village at her mercy. Voices answered her angrily out of the crowd, and received a smarting retort for their trouble. A couple of old ladies beside me, who had duly paid for their seats, waxed very red and indignant, and discoursed to each other audibly about the impudence of these mountebanks; but as soon as the show-woman caught a whisper of this she was down upon them with a swoop; if mesdames could persuade their neighbours to act with common honesty, the mountebanks, she assured them, would be polite enough; mesdames had probably had their bowl of soup, and, perhaps, a glass of wine that evening; the mountebanks, also, had a taste for soup, and did not choose to have their little earnings stolen from them before their eyes. Once, things came as far as a brief personal encounter between the showman and some lads, in which the former went down as readily as one of his own marionettes to a peal of jeering laughter.

I was a good deal astonished at this scene, because I am pretty well acquainted with the ways of French strollers more or less artistic; and have always found them singularly pleasing. Any stroller must be dear to the right-thinking heart; if it were only as a living protest against offices and the mercantile spirit, and as something to

remind us that life is not by necessity the kind of thing
we generally make it. Even a German band, if you see
it leaving town in the early morning for a campaign in
country places, among trees and meadows, has a romantic
flavour for the imagination. There is nobody under
thirty so dead but his heart will stir a little at sight of a
gipsies' camp. "We are not cotton-spinners all"; or,
at least, not all through. There is some life in humanity
yet; and youth will now and again find a brave word to
say in dispraise of riches, and throw up a situation to go
strolling with a knapsack.

An Englishman has always special facilities for intercourse with French gymnasts; for England is the natural
home of gymnasts. This or that fellow, in his tights and
spangles, is sure to know a word or two of English, to have
drunk English *aff-n-aff*, and, perhaps, performed in an
English music hall. He is a countryman of mine by profession. He leaps like the Belgian boating-men to the
notion that I must be an athlete myself.

But the gymnast is not my favourite; he has little or
no tincture of the artist in his composition; his soul is
small and pedestrian, for the most part, since his profession makes no call upon it, and does not accustom him to
high ideas. But if a man is only so much of an actor that
he can stumble through a farce, he is made free of a new
order of thoughts. He has something else to think about
beside the money-box. He has a pride of his own, and,
what is of far more importance, he has an aim before him
that he can never quite attain. He has gone upon a pil-
grimage that will last him his life long, because there is no
end to it short of perfection. He will better himself a
little day by day; or, even if he has given up the attempt,

he will always remember that once upon a time he had
conceived this high ideal, that once upon a time he fell in
love with a star. "'Tis better to have loved and lost."
Although the moon should have nothing to say to Endymion, although he should settle down with Audrey and
feed pigs, do you not think he would move with a better
grace and cherish higher thoughts to the end? The louts
he meets at church never had a fancy above Audrey's
snood; but there is a reminiscence in Endymion's heart
that, like a spice, keeps it fresh and haughty.

To be even one of the outskirters of art leaves a fine
stamp on a man's countenance. I remember once dining
with a party in the inn at Chateau Landon. Most of
them were unmistakable bagmen; others well-to-do
peasantry; but there was one young fellow in a blouse,
whose face stood out from among the rest surprisingly.
It looked more finished; more of the spirit looked out
through it; it had a living, expressive air, and you could
see that his eyes took things in. My companion and I
wondered greatly who and what he could be. It was
fair time in Chateau Landon, and when we went along
to the booths we had our question answered; for there
was our friend busily fiddling for the peasants to caper to.
He was a wandering violinist.

A troop of strollers once came to the inn where I was
staying, in the department of Seine et Marne. There
were a father and mother; two daughters, brazen, blowsy
hussies, who sang and acted, without an idea of how to
set about either; and a dark young man, like a tutor, a
recalcitrant house-painter, who sang and acted not amiss.
The mother was the genius of the party, so far as genius
can be spoken of with regard to such a pack of incompetent

humbugs; and her husband could not find words to express his admiration for her comic countryman. "You
should see my old woman," said he, and nodded his beery
countenance. One night they performed in the stable-
yard with flaring lamps: a wretched exhibition, coldly
looked upon by a village audience. Next night, as soon
as the lamps were lighted, there came a plump of rain,
and they had to sweep away their baggage as fast as
possible, and make off to the barn, where they harboured,
cold, wet, and supperless. In the morning a dear friend
of mine, who has as warm a heart for strollers as I have
myself, made a little collection, and sent it by my hands
to comfort them for their disappointment. I gave it to
the father; he thanked me cordially, and we drank a
cup together in the kitchen, talking of roads and audiences,
and hard times.

When I was going, up got my old stroller, and off with
his hat. "I am afraid," said he, "that Monsieur will
think me altogether a beggar; but I have another de-
mand to make upon him." I began to hate him on the
spot. "We play again to-night," he went on. "Of
course I shall refuse to accept any more money from
Monsieur and his friends, who have been already so liberal.
But our programme of to-night is something truly credit-
able; and I cling to the idea that Monsieur will honour us
with his presence." And then, with a shrug and a smile:
"Monsieur understands, — the vanity of an artist!"
Save the mark! The vanity of an artist! That is the
kind of thing that reconciles me to life: a ragged, tippling,
incompetent old rogue, with the manners of a gentleman
and the vanity of an artist, to keep up his self-respect!

But the man after my own heart is M. de Vauversin.

It is nearly two years since I saw him first, and indeed I hope I may see him often again. Here is his first programme as I found it on the breakfast-table, and have kept it ever since as a relic of bright days:

" Mesdames et Messieurs,

" Mademoiselle Ferrario et M. de Vauversin auront l'honneur de chanter ce soir les morceaux suivants.

" Mademoiselle Ferrario chantera — Mignon — Oiseaux Légers — France — Des Français dorment là — le château bleu — Où voulez-vous aller ?

" M. de Vauversin — Madame Fontaine et M. Robinet — Les plongeurs à cheval — Le Mari mécontent — Tais-toi, gamin — Mon voisin l'original — Heureux comme ça — comme on est trompé."

They made a stage at one end of the *salle-à-manger*. And what a sight it was to see M. de Vauversin, with a cigarette in his mouth, twanging a guitar, and following Mademoiselle Ferrario's eyes with the obedient, kindly look of a dog! The entertainment wound up with a tombola, or auction of lottery tickets: an admirable amusement, with all the excitement of gambling, and no hope of gain to make you ashamed of your eagerness; for there, all is loss; you make haste to be out of pocket; it is a competition who shall lose most money for the benefit of M. de Vauversin and Mademoiselle Ferrario.

M. de Vauversin is a small man, with a great head of black hair, a vivacious and engaging air, and a smile that would be delightful if he had better teeth. He was once an actor in the Chatelet; but he contracted a nervous affection from the heat and glare of the foot-lights, which unfitted him for the stage. At this crisis Mademoiselle Ferrario, otherwise Mademoiselle Rita of the Alcazar, agreed to share his wandering fortunes. "I could never forget the generosity of that lady," said he. He wears trousers so tight that it has long been a problem to all who knew him how he manages to get in and out of them. He sketches a little in water-colours, he writes verses; he is the most patient of fishermen, and spent long days at the bottom of the inn-garden fruitlessly dabbling a line in the clear river.

You should hear him recounting his experiences over a bottle of wine; such a pleasant vein of talk as he has, with a ready smile at his own mishaps, and every now and then a sudden gravity, like a man who should hear the surf roar while he was telling the perils of the deep. For it was no longer ago than last night, perhaps, that the receipts only amounted to a franc and a half to cover three francs of railway fare and two of board and lodging. The Maire, a man worth a million of money, sat in the front seat, repeatedly applauding Mademoiselle Ferrario, and yet gave no more than three sous the whole evening. Local authorities look with such an evil eye upon the strolling artist. Alas! I know it well, who have been myself taken for one, and pitilessly incarcerated on the strength of the misapprehension. Once, M. de Vauversin visited a commissary of police for permission to sing. The commissary, who was smoking at his ease, politely doffed his hat upon the singer's entrance. "Mr. Commissary," he began, "I am an artist." And on went the commissary's hat again. No courtesy for the companions of Apollo! "They are as degraded as that," said M. de Vauversin, with a sweep of his cigarette.

But what pleased me most was one outbreak of his, when we had been talking all the evening of the rubs, indignities, and pinchings of his wandering life. Some one said it would be better to have a million of money down, and Mademoiselle Ferrario admitted that she would prefer that mightily. *"Eh bien, moi non;* — not I," cried De Vauversin, striking the table with his hand. "If any one is a failure in the world, is it not I? I had an art, in which I have done things well, — as well as some, better, perhaps, than others; and now it is closed against me. I must go about the country gathering coppers and singing nonsense. Do you think I regret my life? Do you think I would rather be a fat burgess, like a calf? Not I! I have had moments when I have been applauded on the boards: I think nothing of that; but I have known in my own mind sometimes, when I had not a clap from the whole house, that I had found a true intonation, or an exact and speaking gesture; and then, messieurs, I have known what pleasure was, what it was to do a thing well, what it was to be an artist. And to know what art is, is to have an interest for ever, such as no burgess can find in his petty concerns. *Tenez, messieurs, je vais vous le dire,* — it is like a religion."

Such, making some allowance for the tricks of memory and the inaccuracies of translation, was the profession of faith of M. de Vauversin. I have given him his own name, lest any other wanderer should come across him, with his guitar and cigarette, and Mademoiselle Ferrario; for should not all the world delight to honour this unfortunate and loyal follower of the Muses? May Apollo send him rhymes hitherto undreamed of; may the river be no longer scanty of her silver fishes to his lure; may the cold not pinch him on long winter rides, nor the village jack-in-office affront him with unseemly manners: and may he never miss Mademoiselle Ferrario from his side, to follow with his dutiful eyes and accompany on the guitar!

The marionettes made a very dismal entertainment. They performed a piece called *Pyramus and Thisbe*, in five mortal acts, and all written in Alexandrines fully as long as the performers. One marionette was the king; another the wicked counsellor; a third, credited with exceptional beauty, represented Thisbe; and then there were guards, and obdurate fathers, and walking gentlemen. Nothing particular took place during the two or three acts that I sat out; but you will be pleased to learn that the unities were properly respected, and the whole piece, with one exception, moved in harmony with classical rules. That exception was the comic countryman, a lean marionette in wooden shoes, who spoke in prose and in a broad *patois* much appreciated by the audience. He took unconstitutional liberties with the person of his sovereign; kicked his fellow-marionettes in the mouth with his wooden shoes, and whenever none of the versifying suitors were about, made love to Thisbe on his own account in comic prose.

This fellow's evolutions, and the little prologue, in which the showman made a humorous eulogium of his troop, praising their indifference to applause and hisses, and their single devotion to their art, were the only circumstances in the whole affair that you could fancy would so much as raise a smile. But the villagers of Précy seemed delighted. Indeed, so long as a thing is an exhibition, and you pay to see it, it is nearly certain to amuse. If we were charged so much a head for sunsets, or if God sent round a drum before the hawthorns came in flower, what work should

we not make about their beauty! But these things, like
good companions, stupid people early cease to observe
and the Abstract Bagman tittups past in his spring gig,
and is positively not aware of the flowers along the lane,
or the scenery of the weather overhead.

BACK TO THE WORLD

Of the next two days' sail little remains in my mind, and nothing whatever in my note-book. The river streamed on steadily through pleasant river-side landscapes. Washerwomen in blue dresses, fishers in blue blouses, diversified the green banks; and the relation of the two colours was like that of the flower and the leaf in the forget-me-not. A symphony in forget-me-not; I think Théophile Gautier might thus have characterised that two days' panorama. The sky was blue and cloudless; and the sliding surface of the river held up, in smooth places, a mirror to the heaven and the shores. The washerwomen hailed us laughingly; and the noise of trees and water made an accompaniment to our dozing thoughts, as we fleeted down the stream.

The great volume, the indefatigable purpose of the river, held the mind in chain. It seemed now so sure of its end, so strong and easy in its gait, like a grown man full of determination. The surf was roaring for it on the sands of Havre. For my own part slipping along this moving thoroughfare in my fiddle-case of a canoe, I also was beginning to grow aweary for my ocean. To the civilised man there must come, sooner or later, a desire for civilisation. I was weary of dipping the paddle; I was weary of living on the skirts of life; I wished to be in the thick of it once more; I wished to get to work; I wished to meet people who understood my own speech, and could meet with me on equal terms, as a man, and no longer as a curiosity.

And so a letter at Pontoise decided us, and we drew up our keels for the last time out of that river of Oise that had faithfully piloted them, through rain and sunshine, for so long. For so many miles had this fleet and footless beast of burthen charioted our fortunes that we turned our back upon it with a sense of separation. We had a long detour out of the world, but now we were back in the familiar places, where life itself makes all the running, and we are carried to meet adventure without a stroke of the paddle. Now we were to return, like the voyager in the play, and see what rearrangements fortune had perfected the while in our surroundings; what surprises stood ready-made for us at home; and whither and how far the world had voyaged in our absence. You may paddle all day long; but it is when you come back at nightfall, and look in at the familiar room, that you find Love or Death awaiting you beside the stove; and the most beautiful adventures are not those we go to seek.

EPILOGUE TO "AN INLAND VOYAGE"

EPILOGUE TO "AN INLAND VOYAGE"

THE country where they journeyed, that green, breezy valley of the Loing, is one very attractive to cheerful and solitary people. The weather was superb; all night it thundered and lightened, and the rain fell in sheets; by day, the heavens were cloudless, the sun fervent, the air vigorous and pure. They walked separate: the *Cigarette* plodding behind with some philosophy, the lean *Arethusa* posting on ahead. Thus each enjoyed his own reflections by the way; each had perhaps time to tire of them before he met his comrade at the designated inn; and the pleasures of society and solitude combined to fill the day. The *Arethusa* carried in his knapsack the works of Charles of Orleans, and employed some of the hours of travel in the concoction of English roundels. In this path, he must thus have preceded Mr. Lang, Mr. Dobson, Mr. Henley, and all contemporary roundeleers; but for good reasons, he will be the last to publish the result. The *Cigarette* walked burthened with a volume of Michelet. And both these books, it will be seen, played a part in the subsequent adventure.

The *Arethusa* was unwisely dressed. He is no precisian in attire; but by all accounts, he was never so ill-inspired as on that tramp; having set forth indeed, upon a moment's notice, from the most unfashionable spot in Europe, Barbizon. On his head, he wore a smoking-cap of Indian work, the gold lace pitifully frayed and tarnished. A flannel shirt of an agreeable dark hue, which the satirical called black; a light tweed coat made by a good English tailor; ready-made cheap linen trousers and leathern gaiters completed his array. In person, he is exceptionally lean; and his face is not like those of happier mortals, a certificate. For years he could not pass a frontier or visit a bank without suspicion; the police everywhere but in his native city, looked askance upon him; and (though I am sure it will not be credited) he is actually denied admittance to the casino of Monte Carlo. If you will imagine him, dressed as above, stooping under his knapsack, walking nearly five miles an hour with the folds of the ready-made trousers fluttering about his spindle shanks, and still looking eagerly round him as if in terror of pursuit — the figure, when realised, is far from reassuring. When Villon journeyed (perhaps by the same pleasant valley) to his exile at Roussillon, I wonder if he had not something of the same appearance. Something of the same preoccupation he had beyond a doubt, for he too must have tinkered verses as he walked, with more success than his successor. And if he had anything like the same inspiring weather, the same nights of uproar, men in armour rolling and resounding down the stairs of heaven, the rain hissing on the village streets, the wild bull's-eye of the storm flashing all night long into the bare inn-chamber — the same sweet return of day, the same unfathomable blue of noon, the same high-coloured, halcyon eyes — and above all if he had anything like as good a comrade, anything like as keen a relish for what he saw, and what he ate, and the rivers that he bathed in, and the rubbish that he wrote, I would exchange estates to-day with the poor exile, and count myself a gainer.

But there was another point of similarity between the two journeys, for which the *Arethusa* was to pay dear: both were gone upon in days of incomplete security. It was not long after the Franco-Prussian war. Swiftly as men forget, that country-side was still alive with tale of uhlans, and outlying sentries, and hairbreadth 'scapes from the ignominious cord, and pleasant momentary friendships between invader and invaded. A year, at the most two years later, you might have tramped all that country over and not heard one anecdote. And a year or two later, you would — if you were a rather ill-looking young man in nondescript array — have gone your rounds in greater safety; for along with more interesting matter, the Prussian spy would have somewhat faded from men's imaginations.

For all that, our voyager had got beyond Château Renard before he was conscious of arousing wonder. On the road between that place and Châtillon-sur-Loing, however, he encountered a rural postman; they fell together in talk, and spoke of a variety of subjects; but through one and all, the postman was still visibly preoccupied, and his eyes were faithful to the *Arethusa's* knapsack. At last, with mysterious roguishness, he inquired what it contained, and on being answered, shook his head with kindly incredulity. "*Non*," said he, "*non, vous avez des portraits.*" And then with a languishing appeal, "Voyons, show me the portraits!" It was some little while before the *Arethusa*, with a shout of laughter, recognised his drift. By portraits he meant indecent photographs; and in the *Arethusa*, an austere and rising author, he thought to have identified a pornographic colporteur. When countryfolk in France have made up their minds as to a person's calling, argument is fruitless. Along all the rest of the way, the postman piped and fluted meltingly to get a sight of the collection; now he would upbraid, now he would reason — "*Voyons*, I will tell nobody"; then he tried corruption, and insisted on paying for a glass of wine; and, at last, when their ways separated — "*Non*," said he, "*ce n'est pas bien de votre part. O non, ce n'est pas bien.*" And shaking his head with quite a sentimental sense of injury, he departed unrefreshed.

On certain little difficulties encountered by the *Arethusa* at Châtillon-sur-Loing, I have not space to dwell; another Châtillon, of grislier memory, looms too near at hand. But the next day, in a certain hamlet called La Jussière, he stopped to drink a glass of syrup in a very poor, bare drinking-shop. The hostess, a comely woman, suckling a child, examined the traveller with kindly and pitying eyes. "You are not of this department?" she asked. The *Arethusa* told her he was English. "Ah!" she said, surprised. "We have no English. We have many Italians, however, and they do very well; they do not complain of the people of hereabouts. An Englishman may do very well also; it will be something new." Here was a dark saying, over which the *Arethusa* pondered as he drank his grenadine; but when he rose and asked what was to pay, the light came upon him in a flash. "*O, pour vous,*" replied the landlady, "a halfpenny!" *Pour vous?* By heaven, she took him for a beggar! He paid his halfpenny, feeling that it were ungracious to correct her. But when he was forth again upon the road, he became vexed in spirit. The conscience is a gentleman, he is a rabbinical fellow; and his conscience told him he had stolen the syrup.

That night the travellers slept in Gien; the next day they passed the river and set forth (severally, as their custom was) on a short stage through the green plain upon the Berry side, to Châtillon-sur-Loire. It was the first day of the shooting; and the air rang with the report of firearms and the admiring cries of sportsmen. Overhead the birds were in consternation, wheeling in clouds, settling and re-arising. And yet with all this bustle on either hand, the road itself lay solitary. The *Arethusa* smoked a pipe beside a milestone, and I remember he laid down very exactly all he was to do at Châtillon: how he was to enjoy a cold plunge, to change his shirt, and to await the *Cigarette's* arrival, in sublime inaction, by the margin of the Loire. Fired by these ideas, he pushed the more rapidly forward, and came, early in the afternoon and in a breathing heat, to the entering-in of that ill-fated town. Childe Roland to the dark tower came.

A polite gendarme threw his shadow on the path.

"*Monsieur est voyageur?*" he asked.

And the *Arethusa*, strong in his innocence, forgetful of his vile attire, replied — I had almost said with gaiety: "So it would appear."

"His papers are in order?" said the gendarme. And when the *Arethusa* with a slight change of voice, admitted he had none, he was informed (politely enough) that he must appear before the Commissary.

The Commissary sat at a table in his bedroom, stripped to the shirt and trousers, but still copiously perspiring; and when he turned upon the prisoner a large meaningless countenance, that was (like Bardolph's) "all whelks and bubuckles," the dullest might have been prepared for grief. Here was a stupid man, sleepy with the heat and fretful at the interruption, whom neither appeal nor argument could reach.

THE COMMISSARY. You have no papers?

THE ARETHUSA. Not here.

THE COMMISSARY. Why?

THE ARETHUSA. I have left them behind in my valise.

THE COMMISSARY. You know, however, that it is forbidden to circulate without papers?

THE ARETHUSA. Pardon me : I am convinced of the contrary. I am here on my rights as an English subject by international treaty.

THE COMMISSARY (*with scorn*). You call yourself an Englishman?

THE ARETHUSA. I do.

THE COMMISSARY. Humph. — What is your trade?

THE ARETHUSA. I am a Scotch Advocate.

THE COMMISSARY (*with singular annoyance*). A Scotch advocate! Do you then pretend to support yourself by that in this department?

The *Arethusa* modestly disclaimed the pretension. The Commissary had scored a point.

THE COMMISSARY. Why, then, do you travel?

THE ARETHUSA. I travel for pleasure.

THE COMMISSARY (*pointing to the knapsack, and with sublime incredulity*). *Avec ça? Voyez-vous, je suis un homme intelligent!* (With that? Look here, I am a person of intelligence!)

The culprit remaining silent under this home thrust, the Commissary relished his triumph for awhile, and then demanded (like the postman, but with what different expectations!) to see the contents of the knapsack. And here the *Arethusa*, not yet sufficiently awake to his position, fell into a grave mistake. There was little or no furniture in the room except the Commissary's chair and table; and to facilitate matters, the *Arethusa* (with all the innocence on earth) leant the knapsack on a corner of the bed. The Commissary fairly bounded from his seat; his face and neck flushed past purple, almost into blue; and he screamed to lay the desecrating object on the floor.

The knapsack proved to contain a change of shirts, of shoes, of socks, and of linen trousers, a small dressing-case, a piece of soap in one of the shoes, two volumes of the *Collection Jannet* lettered *Poésies de Charles d'Orléans*, a map, and a version book containing divers notes in prose and the remarkable English roundels of the voyager, still to this day unpublished: the Commissary of Châtillon is the only living man who has clapped an eye on these artistic trifles. He turned the assortment over with a contumelious finger; it was plain from his daintiness that he regarded the *Arethusa* and all his belongings as the very temple of infection. Still there was nothing suspicious about the map, nothing really criminal except the roundels; as for Charles of Orleans, to the ignorant mind of the prisoner, he seemed as good as a certificate; and it was supposed the farce was nearly over.

The inquisitor resumed his seat.

THE COMMISSARY (*after a pause*). *Eh bien, je vais vous dire ce que vous êtes. Vous êtes allemand et vous venez chanter à la foire.* (Well, then, I will tell you what you are. You are a German and have come to sing at the fair.)

THE ARETHUSA. Would you like to hear me sing? I believe I could convince you of the contrary.

THE COMMISSARY. *Pas de plaisanterie, monsieur!*

THE ARETHUSA. Well, sir, oblige me at least by looking at this book. Here, I open it with my eyes shut. Read one of these songs — read this one — and tell me, you who are a man of intelligence, if it would be possible to sing it at a fair?

THE COMMISSARY (*critically*). *Mais oui. Tres bien.*

THE ARETHUSA. *Comment, monsieur!* What! But you do not observe it is antique. It is difficult to understand, even for you and me; but for the audience at a fair, it would be meaningless.

THE COMMISSARY (*taking a pen*). *Enfin, il faut en finir.* What is your name?

THE ARETHUSA (*speaking with the swallowing vivacity of the English*). Robert-Louis-Stev'ns'n.

THE COMMISSARY (*aghast*). *Hé! Quoi!*

THE ARETHUSA (*perceiving and improving his advantage*). Rob'rt-Lou's-Stev'ns'n.

THE COMMISSARY (*after several conflicts with his pen*). *Eh bien, il faut se passer du nom. Ça ne s'écrit pas.* (Well, we must do without the name: it is unspellable.)

The above is a rough summary of this momentous conversation, in which I have been chiefly careful to preserve the plums of the Commissary; but the remainder of the scene, perhaps because of his rising anger, has left but little definite in the memory of the *Arethusa*. The Commissary was not, I think, a practised literary man; no sooner, at least, had he taken pen in hand and embarked on the composition of the *procès-verbal*, than he became distinctly more uncivil and began to show a predilection for that simplest of all forms of repartee: "You lie!" Several times the *Arethusa* let it pass, and then suddenly flared up, refused to accept more insults or to answer further questions, defied the Commissary to do his worst, and promised him, if he did, that he should bitterly repent it. Perhaps if he had worn this proud front from the first, instead of beginning with a sense of entertainment and then going on to argue, the thing might have turned otherwise; for even at this eleventh hour the Commissary was visibly staggered. But it was too late; he had been challenged; the *procès-verbal* was begun; and he again squared his elbows over his writing, and the *Arethusa* was led forth a prisoner.

A step or two down the hot road stood the gendarmerie. Thither was our unfortunate conducted, and there he was bidden to empty forth the contents of his pockets. A handkerchief, a pen, a pencil, a pipe and tobacco, matches, and some ten francs of change: that was all. Not a file, not a cipher, not a scrap of writing whether to identify or to condemn. The very gendarme was appalled before such destitution.

"I regret," he said, "that I arrest you, for I see that you are no *voyou*." And he promised him every indulgence.

The *Arethusa*, thus encouraged, asked for his pipe. That he was told was impossible, but if he chewed, he might have some tobacco. He did not chew, however, and asked instead to have his handkerchief.

"*Non*," said the gendarme. "*Nous avons eu des histoires de gens qui se sont pendus.*" (No, we have had histories of people who hanged themselves.)

"What," cried the *Arethusa*. "And is it for that you refuse me my handkerchief? But see how much more easily I could hang myself in my trousers!"

The man was struck by the novelty of the idea; but he stuck to his colours, and only continued to repeat vague offers of service.

"At least," said the *Arethusa*, "be sure that you arrest my comrade; he will follow me erelong on the same road, and you can tell him by the sack upon his shoulders."

This promised, the prisoner was led round into the back court of the building, a cellar door was opened, he was motioned down the stair, and bolts grated and chains clanged behind his descending person.

The philosophic and still more the imaginative mind is apt to suppose itself prepared for any mortal accident. Prison, among other ills, was one that had been often faced by the undaunted *Arethusa*. Even as he went down the stairs, he was telling himself that here was a famous occasion for a roundel, and that like the committed linnets of the tuneful cavalier, he too would make his prison musical. I will tell the truth at once: the roundel was never written, or it should be printed in this place, to raise a smile. Two reasons interfered: the first moral, the second physical.

It is one of the curiosities of human nature, that although all men are liars, they can none of them bear to be told so of themselves. To get and take the lie with equanimity is a stretch beyond the stoic; and the *Arethusa*, who had been surfeited upon that insult, was blazing inwardly with a white heat of smothered wrath. But the physical had also its part. The cellar in which he was confined was some feet underground, and it was only lighted by an unglazed, narrow aperture high up in the wall and smothered in the leaves of a green vine. The walls were of naked masonry, the floor of bare earth; by way of furniture there was an earthenware basin, a water-jug, and a wooden bedstead with a blue-grey cloak for bedding. To be taken from the hot air of a summer's afternoon, the reverberation of the road and the stir of rapid exercise, and plunged into the gloom and damp of this receptacle for vagabonds, struck an instant chill upon the *Arethusa's* blood. Now see in how small a matter a hardship may consist: the floor was exceedingly uneven underfoot, with the very spade-marks, I suppose, of the labourers who dug the foundations of the barrack; and what with the poor twilight and the irregular surface, walking was impossible. The caged author resisted for a good while; but the chill of the place struck deeper and deeper; and at length, with such reluctance as you may fancy, he was driven to climb upon the bed and wrap himself in the public covering. There, then, he lay upon the verge of shivering, plunged in semi-darkness, wound in a garment whose touch he dreaded like the plague, and (in a spirit far removed from resignation) telling the roll of the insults he had just received. These are not circumstances favourable to the muse.

Meantime (to look at the upper surface where the sun was still shining and the guns of sportsmen were still noisy through the tufted plain) the *Cigarette* was drawing near at his more philosophic pace. In those days of liberty and health he was the constant partner of the *Arethusa,* and had ample opportunity to share in that gentleman's disfavour with the police. Many a bitter bowl had he partaken of with that disastrous comrade. He was himself a man born to float easily through life, his face and manner artfully recommending him to all. There was but one suspicious circumstance he could not carry off, and that was his companion. He will not readily forget the Commissary in what is ironically called the free town of Frankfort-on-the-Main; nor the Franco-Belgian frontier; nor the inn at La Fère; last, but not least, he is pretty certain to remember Châtillon-sur-Loire.

At the town entry, the gendarme culled him like a wayside flower; and a moment later, two persons, in a high state of surprise, were confronted in the Commissary's office. For if the *Cigarette* was surprised to be arrested, the Commissary was no less taken aback by the appearance and appointments of his captive. Here was a man about whom there could be no mistake: a man of an unquestionable and unassailable manner, in apple-pie order, dressed not with neatness merely but elegance, ready with his passport, at a word, and well supplied with money: a man the Commissary would have doffed his hat to on chance upon the highways; and this *beau cavalier* unblushingly claimed the *Arethusa* for his comrade! The conclusion of the interview was foregone; of its humours, I remember only one. "Baronet?" demanded the magistrate, glancing up from the passport. "*Alors, monsieur, vous êtes le fils d'un baron?*" And when the *Cigarette* (his one mistake throughout the interview) denied the soft impeachment, "Alors," from the Commissary, "*ce n'est pas votre passeport!*" But these were ineffectual thunders; he never dreamed of laying hands upon the *Cigarette;* presently he fell into a mood of unrestrained admiration, gloating over the contents of the knapsack, commending our friend's tailor. Ah, what an honoured guest was the Commissary entertaining! what suitable clothes he wore for the warm weather! what beautiful maps, what an attractive work of history he carried in his knapsack! You are to understand there was now but one point of difference between them: what was to be done with the *Arethusa*? the *Cigarette* demanding his release, the Commissary still claiming him as the dungeon's own. Now it chanced that the *Cigarette* had passed some years of his life in Egypt, where he had made acquaintance with two very bad things, cholera morbus and pashas; and in the eye of the Commissary, as he fingered the volume of Michelet, it seemed to our traveller there was something Turkish. I pass over this lightly; it is highly possible there was some misunderstanding, highly possible that the Commissary (charmed with his visitor) supposed the attraction to be mutual and took for an act of growing friendship what the *Cigarette* himself regarded as a bribe. And at any rate, was there ever a bribe more singular than an odd volume of Michelet's history? The work was promised him for the morrow, before our departure; and presently after, either because he had his price, or to show that he was not the man to be behind in friendly offices — "*Eh bien*," he said, "*je suppose qu'il faut lacher votre camarade.*" And he tore up that feast of humour, the unfinished *procès-verbal*. Ah, if he had only torn up instead the *Arethusa's* roundels! There were many works burnt at Alexandria, there are many treasured in the British Museum, that I could better spare than the *procès-verbal* of Châtillon. Poor bu-buckled Commissary! I begin to be sorry that he never had his Michelet: perceiving in him fine human traits, a broad-based stupidity, a gusto in his magisterial functions, a taste for letters, a ready admiration for the admirable. And if he did not admire the *Arethusa*, he was not alone in that.

To the imprisoned one, shivering under the public covering, there came suddenly a noise of bolts and chains. He sprang to his feet, ready to welcome a companion in calamity; and instead of that, the door was flung wide, the friendly gendarme appeared above in the strong daylight, and with a magnificent gesture (being probably a student of the drama) — "*Vous êtes libre!*" he said. None too soon for the *Arethusa*. I doubt if he had been half an hour imprisoned; but by the watch in a man's brain (which was the only watch he carried) he should have been eight times longer; and he passed forth with ecstasy up the cellar stairs into the healing warmth of the afternoon sun; and the breath of the earth came as sweet as a cow's into his nostril; and he heard again (and could have laughed for pleasure) the concord of delicate noises that we call the hum of life.

And here it might be thought that my history ended; but not so, this was an act-drop and not the curtain. Upon what followed in front of the barrack, since there was a lady in the case, I scruple to expatiate. The wife of the Maréchal-des-logis was a handsome woman, and yet the *Arethusa* was not sorry to be gone from her society. Something of her image, cool as a peach on that hot afternoon, still lingers in his memory: yet more of her conversation. "You have there a very fine parlour," said the poor gentleman. — "Ah," said Madame la Maréchale (*des-logis*), "you are very well acquainted with such parlours!" And you should have seen with what a hard and scornful eye she measured the vagabond before her! I do not think he ever hated the Commissary; but before that interview was at an end, he hated Madame la Maréchale. His passion (as I am led to understand by one who was present) stood confessed in a burning eye, a pale cheek, and a trembling utterance; Madame meanwhile tasting the joys of the matador, goading him with barbed words and staring him coldly down.

It was certainly good to be away from this lady, and better still to sit down to an excellent dinner in the inn. Here, too, the despised travellers scraped acquaintance with their next neighbour, a gentleman of these parts, returned from the day's sport, who had the good taste to find pleasure in their society. The dinner at an end, the gentleman proposed the acquaintance should be ripened in the *café*.

The *café* was crowded with sportsmen conclamantly explaining to each other and the world the smallness of their bags. About the centre of the room, the *Cigarette* and the *Arethusa* sat with their new acquaintance; a trio very well pleased, for the travellers (after their late experience) were greedy of consideration, and their sportsman rejoiced in a pair of patient listeners. Suddenly the glass door flew open with a crash; the Maréchal-des-logis appeared in the interval, gorgeously belted and befrogged, entered without salutation, strode up the room with a clang of spurs and weapons, and disappeared through a door at the far end. Close at his heels followed the *Arethusa's* gendarme of the afternoon, imitating, with a nice shade of difference, the imperial bearing of his chief; only, as he passed, he struck lightly with his open hand on the shoulder of his late captive, and with that ringing, dramatic utterance of which he had the secret — "*Suivez!*" said he.

The arrest of the members, the oath of the Tennis Court, the signing of the Declaration of Independence,

Mark Antony's oration, all the brave scenes of history, I conceive as having been not unlike that evening in the *café* at Châtillon. Terror breathed upon the assembly. A moment later, when the *Arethusa* had followed his re-captors into the farther part of the house, the *Cigarette* found himself alone with his coffee in a ring of empty chairs and tables, all the lusty sportsmen huddled into corners, all their clamorous voices hushed in whispering, all their eyes shooting at him furtively as at a leper.

And the *Arethusa?* Well, he had a long, sometimes a trying, interview in the back kitchen. The Maréchal-des-logis, who was a very handsome man, and I believe both intelligent and honest, had no clear opinion on the case. He thought the Commissary had done wrong, but he did not wish to get his subordinates into trouble; and he proposed this, that, and the other, to all of which the *Arethusa* (with a growing sense of his position) demurred.

"In short," suggested the *Arethusa*, "you want to wash your hands of further responsibility? Well, then, let me go to Paris."

The Maréchal-des-logis looked at his watch.

"You may leave," said he, "by the ten o'clock train for Paris."

And at noon the next day the travellers were telling their misadventure in the dining-room at Siron's.

NOTES

PAGE xxxi. **Sir Walter Grindlay Simpson, Bart.** : A close friend of Stevenson's during their student days at Edinburgh. See Balfour's *Life of Stevenson*, Vol. I, p. 107. **Burgee** : A pennant bearing the name of the ship; used in the merchant marine. **Eleven thousand Virgins of Cologne** : these virgins, according to legend, were massacred by the Huns at Cologne. **Tricolor** : the Belgian flag.

PAGE xxxiv. **Caleb and Joshua brought back from Palestine a formidable bunch of grapes.** See *Numbers*, xiii, 23.

PAGE 1. **stevedore** : one who loads and unloads vessels. **Cigarette** : used throughout the narrative to designate the canoe and also the companion in it. **Arethusa** : used likewise to designate Stevenson's canoe and himself. **sheet** : the rope which is fastened to the lower edge of the sail.

PAGE 2. **heady** : "exciting," "thrilling."

PAGE 3. **bagman** : commercial traveller. The word connotes contempt.

PAGE 4. **barnacled** : wearing spectacles. **Miss Howe, Miss Harlowe** : leading characters in Samuel Richardson's novel, *Clarissa Harlowe* (1748). Cf. Stevenson's estimate of the book in *Correspondence*, edited by Colvin, p. 141. **huntress** : Diana. **Anthony** : St. Anthony (251–356), an early saint who retired to the desert and founded what is thought to be the first monastic community. **gymnosophist** : a member of an ancient sect of Hindu philosophers who retired to a life of solitary contemplation in the woods.

PAGE 6. **Willebroek Canal** : connects Brussels with the Rupel and the Scheldt. "**C'est vite, mais c'est long**" : equivalent to, "You are going fast but you have a long journey." **dingy** : a small boat.

PAGE 8. **Etna cooking apparatus** : a vessel in which water may be heated by means of an attached alcohol burner.   **à la papier**: "in paper."

PAGE **9**.   **loo-warm**: "luke-warm," "tepid."

PAGE **10**.   **sterlings**: piles set closely together.   **trepanned**: a surgical operation in which parts of the bones of the skull are removed.

PAGE **12**.   **Laeken**: the northeast suburb of Brussels.   **Allée Verte**: "green lane."   A double avenue of limes extending along the canal to Laeken.   **estaminet**: "a public tavern."

PAGE **13**.   **Royal Sport Nautique**: "Royal Nautical Sport."   **French Huguenots**: the Protestants of France from 15 o until their extinction as a religious sect in 1685.   **out of great tribulation**: cf. *Revelation*, vii, 14.

PAGE **14**.   **entre frères!** "between brothers."   **En Angleterre, vous employez des sliding-seats, n'est-ce pas?**" "In England you use sliding seats, do you not?"   "**voyez-vous, nous sommes sérieux**": "You see, we are serious."

PAGE **15**.   **Mammon, the least erected spirit that fell**
              From Heaven:
quoted from Milton's *Paradise Lost*, I, 679–680.

PAGE **17**.   **drive the coursers of the sun against Apollo**: cf. the fable of Phaeton in Greek mythology.   Gayley's *Classic Myths*, pp. 121–125.   **The great billows had gone over our head**: cf. *Psalms*, xlii, 7.

PAGE **18**.   **Charleroi**: a manufacturing town thirty miles south of Brussels.   **He is, somehow or other, a marked man for the official eye**: for a further description of Stevenson's personal appearance cf. pp. 135–150 of this volume, and Colvin's Introduction to *Letters of R. L. S.*, p. xxxix, and Mrs. Stevenson's note in Biographical Edition, *Prince Otto*, Preface, pp. vii–x.   **Murray**: a guide book issued by the publisher, John Murray.

PAGE **19**.   **knolled to church and sat at good men's feasts**: cf. Shakespeare's *As You Like It*, II, vii, 113–115.   **Grand Cerf**: "Great Stag."

PAGE **20**.   **cœnacula**: "a supping room."   The upper room in which Christ and his disciples ate the last supper; hence, "secret meeting place."

PAGE **21**.   **Drake**: Sir Francis Drake (1540(?)–1596), the first Englishman to see the Pacific and to circumnavigate the globe.

PAGE **28.** **amphora**: originally a large jar with two handles and a pointed base, used by the ancients as a wine container; hence, "a big vase."

PAGE **29.** **Bluebeards**: the nickname of the imaginary Chevalier Raoul, who was celebrated for his cruelty. **beknived**: "furnished with knives." **Jove**: in classic mythology, the gods in disguise often sought adventure among men.

PAGE **30.** **hold**: "stronghold," "fortress."

PAGE **31.** **auberge**: "inn."

PAGE **32.** **Hainaulters**: residents of Hainault, a frontier province in Belgium through which Stevenson and his friend were now passing. **bread-berry**: prepared by pouring boiling water over toast and then flavoring it with sugar. **swipes**: "weak beer."

PAGE **34.** **Lucretian maxim**: Lucretius, the Roman poet (96(?) B.C.–55 B.C.). The maxim is as follows: "'Tis sweet, when the seas are roughened by violent winds, to view on land the toils of others, not that there is pleasure in seeing others in distress, but because man is glad to know himself secure."

PAGE **35.** **Landau**: a four-wheeled carriage, first made in Landau, Germany.

PAGE **36.** **Molière's farce**: cf. Molière's farce, *Les Precieuses Ridicules*, scene xiv (1659). **képi**: a military cap with flat top and horizontal visor.

PAGE **37.** **galette**: a thin cake.

PAGE **41.** **Landrecies**: a fortress on the Sombre. "**Voilà de l'eau pour vous débarbouiller**": "There is water for washing your faces." **Waterloo crackers**: "fire crackers." In memory of Napoleon's victory over the combined forces of Russia and Austria at Austerlitz, in 1805. **Waterloo Bridge**: a bridge in London over the Thames, opened on the anniversary of the battle.

PAGE **42.** **Mormal, a sinister name**: sinister because of its association with *mort*, "death," and *mal*, "evil."

PAGE **43.** **Heine**: Heinrich Heine (1797–1856), the German poet and critic. **Merlin**: the magician of King Arthur, who was left spellbound forever in a hollow oak in the forest of Broceliande. Cf. Tennyson's *Merlin and Vivien*.

PAGE **44.** **jeremiads**: from Jeremiah, the Hebrew prophet, the writer of *Lamentations*. Applied to utterances of woe or distress.

PAGE 46. bedlamite: wild like a madman. From Bedlam, a hospital for the insane, in London. Marshal Clarke: Henri Jacques Guillaume Clarke (1765–1818), a native of Landrecies, but of Irish descent. He was closely associated with Napoleon, and was appointed Marshal of France in 1807.

PAGE 47. Lyonnese costermongers: hawkers of fruit in Lyons. presumptuous Hebrew prophets: cf. *Numbers*, xxii, 21–25. heights of Alma: a small river which flows into the Black Sea near Sebastopol. Here, in 1854, the Russians were defeated by the British, the French, and the Turks. Spicheren: a village in Lorraine. Here in 1870 the Germans defeated the French. tuck: "beat or flourish."

PAGE 48. bastinadoing: "cudgeling." Juge de Paix: "justice of the peace." Scotch Sheriff Substitute: an assistant to the sheriff, who in Scotland is the chief local judge of a county.

PAGE 51. Archangel tar: wood-tar made at Archangel, Russia. Loch Caron: an inlet, east of the Isle of Skye, on the west coast of Scotland. Just before starting on the voyage here described, Stevenson visited a friend near this loch.

PAGE 54. Hollandais: a canary bird, bred and trained in Holland.

PAGE 55. canaletti: Italian for "little canals"; used here for "those who dwell in the barges." "Cependant": "Yet," "however."

PAGE 57. colza: "coleseed," cultivated for its oily seeds. shivering of the reeds: cf. the myth of the nymph Syrinx, Gayley's *Classic Myths*, pp. 93–94. Pan: the Greek god of shepherds and goatherds.

PAGE 58. Centaur: a mythical creature, half horse, half man.

PAGE 59. like a toy Burns who had just ploughed up the Mountain Daisy: cf. Burns's poem, *To a Mountain Daisy*.

PAGE 60. "Come away, Death": cf. Shakespeare's *Twelfth Night*, II, iv, for the song. The scene is laid in Illyria. heritors: in Scotland, a landowner in a parish. Birmingham-hearted substitutes: bells manufactured in Birmingham, England.

PAGE 63. queasy: "uncomfortable."

PAGE 65. "O France, mes amours": "O France, my love." Alsace: the war of 1870, which ended in the giving of Alsace and Lorraine to Germany. "Les malheurs de la France": "The misfortunes of France."

Notes

PAGE **66.** **Empire:** the Second Empire, the government of France under Napoleon III. **Farmer George:** George III of England, who was king at the time the United States gained its independence. **Caudine Forks:** two mountain passes in ancient Samnium, Italy. Here the Samnites defeated the Russians in 321 B.C. **Conscrits Français:** "French conscripts." **Fletcher:** Andrew Fletcher (1653–1716), a Scotch patriot who remarked: "If a man were permitted to make all the ballads, he need not care who should make the laws of the nation."

PAGE **67.** **Paul Déroulède:** a French author and politician. See *Chants du Soldat*, 1872–1875.

PAGE **68.** **Othello over again:** Othello won the heart of Desdemona through the story of his perilous adventures. Cf. Shakespeare's *Othello*, I, iii, 128–170.

PAGE **70.** **St. Quentin:** a French town eight miles east from Origny.

PAGE **72.** **his hair flourishing like Samson's:** cf. *Book of Judges*, xiii–xvi; also, Milton's *Samson Agonistes*. **"Tristes têtes de Danois!"** "Sad Danish heads." **Gaston Lafenestre:** Gaston Ernest Lafenestre, a contemporary French genre painter, a pupil of Jacques.

PAGE **73.** **Jacques:** Charles Emile Jacques (1813–1894), a French painter and engraver. **National Gallery:** founded in 1824; situated on the north side of Trafalgar Square, London. **Psalms:** cf. *Psalms*, cxvi, 15.

PAGE **74.** **Barbizon:** a village near the forest of Fontainebleau, a favorite haunt of artists. Stevenson frequently visited the place. See Stevenson's essay, *Fontainebleau*. **proletarian:** a person who is obliged to earn his daily living.

PAGE **75.** **Reasons are as plentiful as blackberries:** cf. Shakespeare's *Henry IV*, Part I, Act II, iv, 265. **pro indiviso:** "all together," "in common."

PAGE **76.** **"Eh bien, quoi, c'est magnifique, ça!"** "Well, now, that is magnificent!"

PAGE **77.** **the Inquisition:** a court of the Roman Catholic Church, established in the thirteenth century, for the purpose of suppressing heresy. **Poe's horrid story:** see Edgar Allan Poe's *The Pit and the Pendulum*. **Tristram Shandy:** see Laurence Sterne's *Tristram Shandy*, Book I, Chap. xvii.

PAGE **78.** **Nanty Ewart**: a character in Scott's *Red Gauntlet*. See Chap. xv for the remark.   **Communist**: one who believes in holding everything in common, in abolishing private ownership. **Communard**: one who believes in community or corporation control.

PAGE **82.**   **Paris Bourse**: the Stock Exchange.

PAGE **83.**   **La Fère**: a fortified town which was taken by the Germans in 1870.   **Nürnberg figures**: busts, statuettes, and toy figures from Nuremberg, Germany.   " **C'est bon, n'est-ce pas?** " " It is good, is it not? "

PAGE **87.**   **temple of Diana**: the temple of Diana at Ephesus, one of the Seven Wonders of the world, which was set afire by Herostratus, for the sake of immortalizing his name.   **Timon**: Timon of Athens, " hater of mankind." See Shakespeare's *Timon of Athens*.

PAGE **88.**   " **Bazin, aubergiste, loge a pied** ": " Bazin, innkeeper, lodging for pedestrians."   " **À la Croix de Malte** ": " At the Maltese Cross."   **Zola's**: Émile Zola (1840–1902). See his novel, *L'Assommoir*, Chap. iii.

PAGE **92.**   **Hôtel de Ville**: " Town hall."   " **Put off thy shoes from off thy feet, for the place whereon thou standest is holy ground** ": see *Exodus*, iii, 5.   **The Hotel du Nord**: " Hotel of the North."

PAGE **93.**   **Sacristan**: an officer of the church who has charge of the furnishings of the altar and of the sacred vessels.

PAGE **94.**   **Miserere**: the liturgical rendering of the fifty-first Psalm in the Roman Catholic Church. The opening words are " *Miserere mei, Domine*," " Have mercy upon me, O Lord."

PAGE **95.**   **darkling**: " in the dark." See Shakespeare's *King Lear*, I, iv, 237.   " **Ave Mary** ": a hymn to the Virgin Mary. " *Ave Maria, ora pro nobis*," " Hail Mary, pray for us."   **garrison catch**: a round composed as a continuous melody. An example may be seen in Shakespeare's *Twelfth Night*, II, iii.

PAGE **96.**   **Jubilate Deo**: " Make a joyful noise unto the Lord." See *Psalms*, lxvi and c.   **department**: one of the eighty-seven parts into which France is divided in its civil administration. The size of these departments varies from two to three thousand square miles.

PAGE **99.**   **water houses**: " canal-boats."   **Deo Gratias**: " Thanks to God." The name of a canal boat, which had come all the way from Normandy. **Four Sons of Aymon**: these were Heroes of a mediæval romance.

PAGE **101**. **Compiègne**: an old French province which bordered upon Lorraine and Belgium. It was noted for its wine.

PAGE **102**. **niminy:** "affectedly delicate." **Chailly road**: an avenue near Barbizon. **Gothic**: Gothic is applied to the pointed styles of architecture which developed in northern Europe between the thirteenth and sixteenth centuries. **gargoyled**: a gargoyle is usually a projecting water-spout grotesquely carved to represent the neck and head of an animal or a man. **Louis XII**: King of France from 1498 to 1515.

PAGE **103**. **Via Dolorosa**: " Dolorous Way," the path in Jerusalem which Christ traversed on His way to Calvary.

PAGE **104**. **" Out of my country and myself I go "**: ascribed by Stevenson to an old poet.

PAGE **106**. **L'Isle Adam**: a town fifteen miles northwest of Paris.

PAGE **108**. **feuilletons**: the lower section of the front page of a French newspaper which is devoted to light literature, serials, and criticism.

PAGE **109**. **Bradshaw's Guide**: a railway guide originated by George Bradshaw, a printer in Manchester, in 1839. **Walt Whitman**: an American poet (1819–1892). For his influence on Stevenson, see his essay on Whitman in *Familiar Studies of Men and Books*.

PAGE **111**. **Nirvana**: the state of complete happiness — according to Buddhism — in which, after death, the soul reposes and its individuality is absorbed by the absolute union with the infinite. **Buddhists**: followers of Buddha, a teacher and philosopher of India, who lived in the fifth century B.C.

PAGE **113**. **Great Assizes**: " the final judgment."

PAGE **114**. **English wars**: the wars between France and England from the twelfth to the fourteenth centuries.

PAGE **115**. **ex voto**: " as a votive offering." **St. Joseph**: the husband of the Virgin Mary.

PAGE **116**. **St. Dominic**: (1170–1221). The founder of the Dominican order of monks. According to tradition, he instituted the Rosary. **St. Catherine**: (1347–1380). A Dominican, noted for having had the impressions of the wounds of the crucified Christ miraculously reproduced on her hands, feet, and heart.   **Pope Gregory**: he was pope from 1831–1846.

PAGE **117**. **Zélatrice**: a zealous nun who usually had charge of the correspondence and finance of the convent.   **dizaine**: " ten prayers."   **Euclid**: a text-book in geometry based upon the Greek geometer, Euclid, who lived about 300 B.C.

PAGE **120**. **marionettes**: puppets.   **performance**: a puppet show.

PAGE **122**. " We are not cotton-spinners all ": see Tennyson's poem, *The Third of February*, stanza viii, l. 3.   **aff-n-aff**: " half and half," a mixture of malt liquors.

PAGE **123**. " 'T is better to have loved and lost ": see Tennyson's *In Memoriam*, xxvii and lxxxv.   **Endymion**: in Greek mythology, Endymion, a beautiful youth, was loved by Diana, the goddess of the moon, who charmed him into eternal sleep, and descended nightly from among the stars to kiss him. See Keats's poem, *Endymion*.   **Audrey**: see Shakespeare's *As You Like It*, III, iii.

PAGE **125**. " Mesdames et Messieurs,

" Mademoiselle Ferrario et M. de Vauversin auront l'honneur de chanter ce soir les morceaux suivants.

" Mademoiselle Ferrario chantera — Mignon — Oiseaux Légers — France — Des Français dorment là — le château bleu — Où voulez-vous aller ?

" M. de Vauversin — Madame Fontaine et M. Robinet — Les plongeurs à cheval — Le Mari mécontent — Tais-toi, gamin — Mon voisin l'original — Heureux comme ça — comme on est trompé."

" Ladies and gentlemen, Miss Ferrario and Mr. de Vauversin will have the honor of singing this evening the following pieces : Miss Ferrario will sing ' Mignon,' ' Birds lightly on the Wing,' ' France,' ' Frenchmen Sleep There,' ' The Blue Château,' ' Where are You Going ? '; Mr. de Vauversin, Madame Fontaine, and Mr. Robinet : ' The Divers on Horseback,' ' The Discontented Husband,' ' Be Quiet, Boy,' ' My Queer Neighbor,' ' Happy like That,' ' How We are Deceived.' "

salle-a-manger: " dining room."   **Châtelet**: a prominent theatre in Paris.   **Alcazar**: a music-hall in Paris.

PAGE **126**. **Maire**: " the mayor,"

Notes 159

PAGE **127**. **Tenez, messieurs, je vais vous le dire**: " Now then, gentlemen, I will tell you what it is." **the Muses**: the nine daughters of Zeus and Mnemosyne, who presided over science, art, music, and poetry.

PAGE **128**. **Pyramus and Thisbe**: a tragical story of two lovers of Ancient Babylon, as related in Ovid's *Metamorphoses*, Book IV. **Alexandrines**: verses of six iambic feet. **unities**: the classical unities of time, place, and action. **patois**: a local, rustic dialect.

PAGE **130**. **Théophile Gautier**: a French poet, critic, and novelist (1811–1872). Stevenson's allusion is to the poet's delicate perception of color.

PAGE **135**. **Charles of Orleans**: a French poet (1391–1465), who gave a distinct form to the roundel. **Mr. Lang**: Andrew Lang (1844–   ), Scotch critic, essayist, and poet. A friend of Stevenson. **Mr. Dobson**: Austin Dobson (1840–   ). A poet and biographer. A friend of Stevenson. **Mr. Henley**: William E. Henley (1849–1903), a poet and critic. An intimate friend of Stevenson. **Michelet**: Jules Michelet (1798–1874). A French historian.

PAGE **136**. **Villon**: François Villon (1431(?)–1484). A French poet.

PAGE **137**. **Franco-Prussian**: the war of 1870–1871.

PAGE **139**. **Childe Roland to the dark tower came**: see Shakespeare's *King Lear*, III, iv, 187; also Browning's *Childe Roland*. "**Monsieur est voyageur?**" " Monsieur is a traveller? " **Bardolph's**: a character in Shakespeare's *Henry IV*, Parts I and II.

PAGE **142**. **Pas de plaisanterie, monsieur!** " No joking, monsieur." **Mais oui. Très bien**: " Yes, very well." **Comment, monsieur!** " How, monsieur! " **Enfin, il faut en finir**: " It is necessary to make an end." **Quoi?** " Blackguard."

PAGE **146**. " **Alors, monsieur, vous êtes le fils d'un baron?** " " Then, monsieur, you are the son of a baron? " " **ce n'est pas votre passeport!** " " Then this is not your passport."

PAGE **147**. " **Eh bien, je suppose qu'il faut lâcher votre camarade** ": " I suppose that it is necessary to release your companion." **procès-verbal**: " official report." **Alexandria**: the Saracens burned the famous library at Alexandria in 640 A.D. **British Museum**: in London, founded in 1753.

PAGE **149.** " Suivez! " " Follow."   **members**: the members of the House of Commons who favored treating with King Charles were arrested, Dec. 6, 1648.   **Tennis Court**: the French deputies to the States General, when they found themselves unable to enter their own hall because of a royal decree suspending their sittings, went to the Tennis Court, a large building in Versailles, and swore never to separate until they had drawn up a constitution for France. This occurred on June 20, 1789.   **Declaration of Independence**: July 4, 1776.

PAGE **150.** **Mark Antony's oration**: see Shakespeare's *Julius Cæsar*, III, ii, 78.   **Siron's**: an inn at Barbizon. See note 1, p. 74; see also the Introduction.

TRAVELS WITH A DONKEY

BY

ROBERT LOUIS STEVENSON

EDITED FOR SCHOOL USE, WITH INTRODUCTION AND NOTES

JAMES CLOYD BOWMAN, M.A.
ASSOCIATE PROFESSOR OF ENGLISH IN
THE IOWA STATE COLLEGE

———o◦o✜o◦o———

ALLYN AND BACON
Boston   New York   Chicago

CONTENTS

MY DEAR SIDNEY COLVIN,

The journey which this little book is to describe was very agreeable and fortunate for me. After an uncouth beginning, I had the best of luck to the end. But we are all travellers in what John Bunyan calls the wilderness of this world, — all, too, travellers with a donkey; and the best that we find in our travels is an honest friend. He is a fortunate voyager who finds many. We travel, indeed, to find them. They are the end and the reward of life. They keep us worthy of ourselves; and, when we are alone, we are only nearer to the absent.

Every book is, in an intimate sense, a circular letter to the friends of him who writes it. They alone take his meaning; they find private messages, assurances of love, and expressions of gratitude dropped for them in every corner. The public is but a generous patron who defrays the postage. Yet, though the letter is directed to all, we have an old and kindly custom of addressing it on the outside to one. Of what shall a man be proud, if he is not proud of his friends? And so, my dear Sidney Colvin, it is with pride that I sign myself affectionately yours,

R. L. S.

VELAY

> *"Many are the mighty things, and nought is more mighty than man. . . . He masters by his devices the tenant of the fields."* — ANTIGONE.

> *"Who hath loosed the bands of the wild ass?"* — JOB.

SCALE OF MILES

0   10   20   30   40   50

St. Etienne

Mts. du Puy Velay

St. Julien
Lausonne
Le Monastier
Goudet
Pradelles
Le Puy
Bouchet
St. Nicholas
Langogne
Luc
La Bastide
Chasserades
Mende
Bleyma
Florac
St. Germain
de Calberte
St. Jean
du Gard
Cheylard
Mt. La Goulet
Villefort
Pont de Montvert
Alais

Mt. Mezenc

Valence

Montélimar

Orange

Avignon

Nimes

Montpellier

Cette

Arles

Marseille

Allier R.

Loire R.

Loire R.

Chassezac R.

Ardèche R.

Cèze R.

Rhône R.

Durance R.

Gardon R.

Tarn R.

GEVAUDAN

44°

44°

4°

4°

GULF   OF   LYONS

MAP OF *Travels with a Donkey*

started when

TRAVELS WITH A DONKEY

VELAY

The Donkey, the Pack, and the Pack-Saddle

IN a little place called Le Monastier, in a pleasant highland valley fifteen miles from Le Puy, I spent about a month of fine days. Monastier is notable for the making of lace, for drunkenness, for freedom of language, and for unparalleled political dissension. There are adherents of each of the four French parties — Legitimists, Orleanists, Imperialists, and Republicans — in this little mountain-town; and they all hate, loathe, decry, and calumniate each other. Except for business purposes, or to give each other the lie in a tavern brawl, they have laid aside even the civility of speech. 'Tis a mere mountain Poland. In the midst of this Babylon I found myself a rallying-point; every one was anxious to be kind and helpful to the stranger. This was not merely from the natural hospitality of mountain people, nor even from the surprise with which I was regarded as a man living of his own free will in Monastier, when he might just as well have lived anywhere else in this big world; it arose a good deal from my projected excursion southward through the Cévennes. A traveller of my sort was a thing hitherto

I

unheard of in that district.   I was looked upon with contempt, like a man who should project a journey to the
moon, but yet with a respectful interest, like one setting
forth for the inclement Pole.   All were ready to help in my
preparations ; a crowd of sympathisers supported me at the
critical moment of a bargain ; not a step was taken but
was heralded by glasses round and celebrated by a dinner
or a breakfast.

It was already hard upon October before I was ready
to set forth, and at the high altitudes over which my road
lay there was no Indian summer to be looked for.   I was
determined, if not to camp out, at least to have the means
of camping out in my possession ; for there is nothing more
harassing to an easy mind than the necessity of reaching
shelter by dusk, and the hospitality of a village inn is not
always to be reckoned sure by those who trudge on foot.
A tent, above all for a solitary traveller, is troublesome to
pitch, and troublesome to strike again ; and even on the
march it forms a conspicuous feature in your baggage.
A sleeping-sack, on the other hand, is always ready —
you have only to get into it ; it serves a double purpose
— a bed by night, a portmanteau by day ; and it does
not advertise your intention of camping out to every
curious passer-by.   This is a huge point.   If the camp is
not secret, it is but a troubled resting-place ; you become
a public character ; the convivial rustic visits your bedside
after an early supper ; and you must sleep with one eye
open, and be up before the day.   I decided on a sleeping-
sack ; and after repeated visits to Le Puy, and a deal of
high living for myself and my advisers, a sleeping-sack
was designed, constructed, and triumphally brought
home.

This child of my invention was nearly six feet square, exclusive of two triangular flaps to serve as a pillow by night and as the top and bottom of the sack by day. I call it "the sack," but it was never a sack by more than courtesy : only a sort of long roll or sausage, green waterproof cart cloth without and blue sheep's fur within. It was commodious as a valise, warm and dry for a bed. There was luxurious turning-room for one ; and at a pinch

GENERAL VIEW OF LE PUY

the thing might serve for two. I could bury myself in it up to the neck ; for my head I trusted to a fur cap, with a hood to fold down over my ears and a band to pass under my nose like a respirator ; and in case of heavy rain I proposed to make myself a little tent, or tentlet, with my waterproof coat, three stones, and a bent branch.

It will readily be conceived that I could not carry this huge package on my own, merely human, shoulders. It remained to choose a beast of burthen. Now, a horse is a fine lady among animals, flighty, timid, delicate in eating, of tender health; he is too valuable and too restive to be left alone, so that you are chained to your brute as to a fellow galley-slave; a dangerous road puts him out of his wits; in short, he's an uncertain and exacting ally, and adds thirty-fold to the troubles of the voyager. What I required was something cheap and small and hardy, and of a stolid and peaceful temper; and all these requisites pointed to a donkey.

There dwelt an old man in Monastier, of rather unsound intellect according to some, much followed by street-boys, and known to fame as Father Adam. Father Adam had a cart, and to draw the cart a diminutive she-ass, not much bigger than a dog, the colour of a mouse, with a kindly eye and a determined under-jaw. There was something neat and high-bred, a quakerish elegance, about the rogue that hit my fancy on the spot. Our first interview was in Monastier market-place. To prove her good temper, one child after another was set upon her back to ride, and one after another went head over heels into the air; until a want of confidence began to reign in youthful bosoms, and the experiment was discontinued from a dearth of subjects. I was already backed by a deputation of my friends; but as if this were not enough, all the buyers and sellers came round and helped me in the bargain; and the ass and I and Father Adam were the centre of a hubbub for near half an hour. At length she passed into my service for the consideration of sixty-five francs and a glass of brandy. The sack had already cost eighty francs and two glasses of beer; so that Modestine, as I instantly baptised her, was upon all accounts the cheaper article. Indeed, that was as it should be; for she was only an appurtenance of my mattress, or self-acting bedstead on four castors.

I had a last interview with Father Adam in a billiard room at the witching hour of dawn, when I administered the brandy. He professed himself greatly touched by the separation, and declared he had often bought white bread for the donkey when he had been content with black bread for himself; but this, according to the best authorities, must have been a flight of fancy. He had a name in the village for brutally misusing the ass; yet it is certain that he shed a tear, and the tear made a clean mark down one cheek.

By the advice of a fallacious local saddler, a leather pad was made for me with rings to fasten on my bundle; and I thoughtfully completed my kit and arranged my toilette. By way of armoury and utensils, I took a revolver, a little spirit-lamp and pan, a lantern and some halfpenny candles, a jack-knife and a large leather flask. The main cargo consisted of two entire changes of warm clothing — besides my travelling' wear of country velveteen, pilot-coat, and knitted spencer — some books, and my railway-rug, which, being also in the form of a bag, made me a double castle for cold nights. The permanent larder was represented by cakes of chocolate and tins of Bologna sausage. All this, except what I carried about my person, was easily stowed into the sheepskin bag; and by good fortune I threw in my empty knapsack, rather for convenience of carriage than from any thought that I should want it on my journey. For more immediate needs, I took a leg of cold mutton, a bottle of Beaujolais, an empty bottle to carry milk, an egg-beater, and a considerable quantity of black bread and white, like Father Adam, for myself and donkey, only in my scheme of things the destinations were reversed.

Monastrians, of all shades of thought in politics, had agreed in threatening me with many ludicrous misadventures and with sudden death in many surprising forms. Cold, wolves, robbers, above all the nocturnal practical joker were daily and eloquently forced on my attention. Yet in these vaticinations, the true, patent danger was left out. Like Christian, it was from my pack I suffered by the way. Before telling my own mishaps, let me, in two words, relate the lesson of my experience. If the pack is well strapped at the ends, and hung at full length — not doubled, for your life — across the pack-saddle the traveller is safe. The saddle will certainly not fit, such is the imperfection of our transitory life; it will assuredly topple and tend to overset; but there are stones on every roadside, and a man soon learns the art of correcting any tendency to overbalance with a well-adjusted stone.

On the day of my departure I was up a little after five; by six, we began to load the donkey; and ten minutes after, my hopes were in the dust. The pad would not stay on Modestine's back for half a moment. I returned it to its maker, with whom I had so contumelious a passage that the street outside was crowded from wall to wall with gossips looking on and listening. The pad changed hands with much vivacity; perhaps it would be more descriptive to say that we threw it at each other's heads; and, at any rate, we were very warm and unfriendly, and spoke with a deal of freedom.

I had a common donkey pack-saddle — a *barde*, as

they call it — fitted upon Modestine; and once more loaded her with my effects. The double sack, my pilot-coat (for it was warm, and I was to walk in my waist-coat), a great bar of black bread, and an open basket containing the white bread, the mutton, and the bottles, were all corded together in a very elaborate system of knots, and I looked on the result with fatuous content. In such a monstrous deck-cargo, all poised above the donkey's shoulders, with nothing below to balance, on a brand-new pack-saddle that had not yet been worn to fit the animal, and fastened with brand-new girths that might be expected to stretch and slacken by the way, even a very careless traveller should have seen disaster brewing. That elaborate system of knots, again, was the work of too many sympathisers to be very artfully designed. It is true they tightened the cords with a will; as many as three at a time would have a foot against Modestine's quarters, and be hauling with clenched teeth; but I learned afterwards that one thoughtful person, without any exercise of force, can make a more solid job than half-a-dozen heated and enthusiastic grooms. I was then but a novice; even after the mis-adventure of the pad nothing could disturb my security, and I went forth from the stable-door as an ox goeth to the slaughter.

The Green Donkey-driver

THE bell of Monastier was just striking nine as I got quit of these preliminary troubles and descended the hill through the common. As long as I was within sight of the windows, a secret shame and the fear of some laughable defeat withheld me from tampering with Modestine. She tripped along upon her four small hoofs with a sober daintiness of gait; from time to time she shook her ears or her tail; and she looked so small under the bundle that my mind misgave me. We got across the ford without difficulty — there was no doubt about the matter, she was docility itself — and once on the other bank, where the road begins to mount through pinewoods, I took in my right hand the unhallowed staff, and with a quaking spirit applied it to the donkey. Modestine brisked up her pace for perhaps three steps, and then relapsed into her former minuet. Another application had the same effect, and so with the third. I am worthy the name of an Englishman, and it goes against my conscience to lay my hand rudely on a female. I desisted, and looked her all over from head to foot; the poor brute's knees were trembling and her breathing was distressed; it was plain that she could go no faster on a hill. God forbid, thought I, that I should brutalise this innocent creature; let her go at her own pace, and let me patiently follow.

What that pace was, there is no word mean enough to describe; it was something as much slower than a walk

as a walk is slower than a run; it kept me hanging on each
foot for an incredible length of time; in five minutes it
exhausted the spirit and set up a fever in all the muscles
of the leg. And yet I had to keep close at hand and
measure my advance exactly upon hers; for if I dropped
a few yards into the rear, or went on a few yards ahead,
Modestine came instantly to a halt and began to browse.
The thought that this was to last from here to Alais nearly
broke my heart. Of all conceivable journeys, this promised
to be the most tedious. I tried to tell myself it was a
lovely day; I tried to charm my foreboding spirit with
tobacco; but I had a vision ever present to me of the long,
long roads, up hill and down dale, and a pair of figures
ever infinitesimally moving, foot by foot, a yard to the
minute, and, like things enchanted in a nightmare, approaching no nearer to the goal.

In the meantime there came up behind us a tall peasant,
perhaps forty years of age, of an ironical snuffy countenance, and arrayed in the green tailcoat of the country.
He overtook us hand over hand, and stopped to consider
our pitiful advance.

"Your donkey," says he, "is very old?"

I told him, I believed not.

Then, he supposed, we had come far.

I told him, we had but newly left Monastier.

"*Et vous marchez comme ça!*" cried he; and throwing
back his head, he laughed long and heartily. I watched
him, half prepared to feel offended, until he had satisfied
his mirth; and then, "You must have no pity on these
animals," said he; and, plucking a switch out of a thicket,
he began to lace Modestine about the stern-works, utter-
ing a cry. The rogue pricked up her ears and broke into

a good round pace, which she kept up without flagging, and without exhibiting the least symptom of distress, as long as the peasant kept beside us. Her former panting and shaking had been, I regret to say, a piece of comedy.

My *deus ex machina*, before he left me, supplied some excellent, if inhumane, advice; presented me with the switch, which he declared she would feel more tenderly than my cane; and finally taught me the true cry or masonic word of donkey-drivers, "Proot!" All the time, he regarded me with a comical incredulous air, which was embarrassing to confront; and smiled over my donkey-driving, as I might have smiled over his orthography, or his green tail-coat. But it was not my turn for the moment.

I was proud of my new lore, and thought I had learned the art to perfection. And certainly Modestine did wonders for the rest of the forenoon, and I had a breathing space to look about me. It was Sabbath; the mountain-fields were all vacant in the sunshine; and as we came down through St. Martin de Frugères, the church was crowded to the door, there were people kneeling without upon the steps, and the sound of the priest's chanting came forth out of the dim interior. It gave me a home feeling on the spot; for I am a countryman of the Sabbath, so to speak, and all Sabbath observances, like a Scotch accent, strike in me mixed feelings, grateful and the reverse. It is only a traveller, hurrying by like a person from another planet, who can rightly enjoy the peace and beauty of the great ascetic feast. The sight of the resting country does his spirit good. There is something better than music in the wide unusual silence;

and it disposes him to amiable thoughts, like the sound of a little river or the warmth of sunlight.

In this pleasant humour I came down the hill to where Goudet stands in the green end of a valley, with Château Beaufort opposite upon a rocky steep, and the stream, as clear as crystal, lying in a deep pool between them. Above and below, you may hear it wimpling over the stones, an amiable stripling of a river, which it seems absurd to call the Loire. On all sides, Goudet is shut in by mountains; rocky foot-paths, practicable at best for donkeys, join it to the outer world of France; and the men and women drink and swear, in their green corner, or look up at the snow-clad peaks in winter from the threshold of their homes, in an isolation, you would think, like that of Homer's Cyclops. But it is not so; the postman reaches Goudet with the letter-bag; the aspiring youth of Goudet are within a day's walk of the railway at Le Puy; and here in the inn you may find an engraved portrait of the host's nephew, Régis Senac, "Professor of Fencing and Champion of the two Americas," a distinction gained by him, along with the sum of five hundred dollars, at Tammany Hall, New York, on the 10th April, 1876.

I hurried over my midday meal, and was early forth again. But, alas, as we climbed the interminable hill upon the other side, "Proot!" seemed to have lost its virtue. I prooted like a lion, I prooted mellifluously like a sucking-dove; but Modestine would be neither softened nor intimidated. She held doggedly to her pace; nothing but a blow would move her, and that only for a second. I must follow at her heels, incessantly belabouring. A moment's pause in this ignoble toil, and she relapsed into her own private gait. I think I never heard of any one in as mean a situation. I must reach the lake of Bouchet, where I meant to camp, before sundown, and, to have even a hope of this, I must instantly maltreat this uncomplaining animal. The sound of my own blows sickened me. Once, when I looked at her, she had a faint resemblance to a lady of my acquaintance who formerly loaded me with kindness; and this increased my horror of my cruelty.

To make matters worse, we encountered another donkey, ranging at will upon the roadside; and this other donkey chanced to be a gentleman. He and Modestine met nickering for joy, and I had to separate the pair and beat down their young romance with a renewed and feverish bastinado. If the other donkey had had the heart of a male under his hide, he would have fallen upon me tooth and hoof; and this was a kind of consolation — he was plainly unworthy of Modestine's affection. But the incident saddened me, as did everything that spoke of my donkey's sex.

It was blazing hot up the valley, windless, with vehement sun upon my shoulders; and I had to labour so consistently with my stick that the sweat ran into my eyes. Every five minutes, too, the pack, the basket, and the pilot-coat would take an ugly slew to one side or the other; and I had to stop Modestine, just when I had got her to a tolerable pace of about two miles an hour, to tug, push, shoulder, and readjust the load. And at last, in the village of Ussel, saddle and all, the whole hypothec turned round and grovelled in the dust below the donkey's belly. She, none better pleased, incontinently drew up and seemed to smile; and a party of one man, two women, and two children came up, and, standing round me in a half-circle, encouraged her by their example.

I had the devil's own trouble to get the thing righted; and the instant I had done so, without hesitation, it toppled and fell down upon the other side. Judge if I was hot! And yet not a hand was offered to assist me. The man, indeed, told me I ought to have a package of a different shape. I suggested, if he knew nothing better to the point in my predicament, he might hold his tongue. And the good-natured dog agreed with me smilingly. It was the most despicable fix. I must plainly content myself with the pack for Modestine, and take the following items for my own share of the portage: a cane, a quart flask, a pilot-jacket heavily weighted in the pockets, two pounds of black bread, and an open basket full of meats and bottles. I believe I may say I am not devoid of greatness of soul; for I did not recoil from this infamous burthen. I disposed it, Heaven knows how, so as to be mildly portable, and then proceeded to steer Modestine through the village. She tried, as was indeed her invariable habit, to enter every house and every court-yard in the whole length; and, encumbered as I was, without a hand to help myself, no words can render an idea of my difficulties. A priest, with six or seven others, was examining a church in process of repair, and he and his acolytes laughed loudly as they saw my plight. I remembered having laughed myself when I had seen good men struggling with adversity in the person of a jackass, and the recollection filled me with penitence. That was in my old light days, before this trouble came upon me. God knows at least that I shall never laugh again, thought I. But O, what a cruel thing is a farce to those engaged in it!

A little out of the village, Modestine, filled with the demon, set her heart upon a by-road, and positively refused to leave it. I dropped all my bundles, and, I am ashamed to say, struck the poor sinner twice across the face. It was pitiful to see her lift up her head with shut eyes, as if waiting for another blow. I came very near crying; but I did a wiser thing than that, and sat squarely down by the roadside to consider my situation under the cheerful influence of tobacco and a nip of brandy. Modestine, in the meanwhile, munched some black bread with a contrite hypocritical air. It was plain that I must make a sacrifice to the gods of shipwreck. I threw away the empty bottle destined to carry milk; I threw away my own white bread, and, disdaining to act by general average, kept the black bread for Modestine; lastly, I threw away the cold leg of mutton and the egg-whisk, although this last was dear to my heart. Thus I found room for everything in the basket, and even stowed the boating-coat on the top. By means of an end of cord I slung it under one arm; and although the cord cut my shoulder, and the jacket hung almost to the ground, it was with a heart greatly lightened that I set forth again.

I had now an arm free to thrash Modestine, and cruelly I chastised her. If I were to reach the lakeside before dark, she must bestir her little shanks to some tune. Already the sun had gone down into a windy-looking mist; and although there were still a few streaks of gold far off to the east on the hills and the black fir-woods, all was cold and grey about our onward path. An infinity of little country by-roads led hither and thither among the fields. It was the most pointless labyrinth. I could see my destination overhead, or rather the peak that dominates it; but choose as I pleased, the roads always ended by turning away from it, and sneaking back towards the valley, or northward along the margin of the hills. The failing light, the waning colour, the naked, unhomely, stony country through which I was travelling, threw me into some despondency. I promise you, the stick was not idle; I think every decent step that Modestine took must have cost me at least two emphatic blows. There was not another sound in the neighbourhood but that of my unwearying bastinado.

Suddenly, in the midst of my toils, the load once more bit the dust, and, as by enchantment, all the cords were simultaneously loosened, and the road scattered with my dear possessions. The packing was to begin again from the beginning; and as I had to invent a new and better system, I do not doubt but I lost half an hour. It began to be dusk in earnest as I reached a wilderness of turf and stones. It had the air of being a road which should lead everywhere at the same time; and I was falling into something not unlike despair when I saw two figures stalking towards me over the stones. They walked one behind the other like tramps, but their pace was remarkable. The son led the way, a tall, ill-made, sombre, Scotch-looking man; the mother followed, all in her Sunday's best, with an elegantly-embroidered ribbon to her cap, and a new felt hat atop, and proffering, as she strode along with kilted petticoats, a string of obscene and blasphemous oaths.

I hailed the son and asked him my direction. He pointed loosely west and north-west, muttered an inaudible comment, and, without slacking his pace for an instant, stalked on, as he was going, right athwart my path. The mother followed without so much as raising her head. I shouted and shouted after them, but they continued to scale the hillside, and turned a deaf ear to my outcries. At last, leaving Modestine by herself, I was constrained to run after them, hailing the while. They stopped as I drew near, the mother still cursing; and I could see she was a handsome, motherly, respectable-looking woman. The son once more answered me roughly and inaudibly, and was for setting out again. But this time I simply collared the mother, who was nearest me, and, apologising for my violence, declared that I could not let them go until they had put me on my road. They were neither of them offended — rather mollified than otherwise; told me I had only to follow them; and then the mother asked me what I wanted by the lake at such an hour. I replied, in the Scotch manner, by inquiring if she had far to go herself. She told me, with another oath, that she had an hour and a half's road before her. And then, without salutation, the pair strode forward again up the hillside in the gathering dusk.

I returned for Modestine, pushed her briskly forward, and, after a sharp ascent of twenty minutes, reached the edge of a plateau. The view, looking back on my day's journey, was both wild and sad. Mount Mézenc and the peaks beyond St. Julien stood out in trenchant gloom against a cold glitter in the east; and the intervening field of hills had fallen together into one broad wash of shadow, except here and there the outline of a wooded sugar-loaf in black, here and there a white irregular patch to represent a cultivated farm, and here and there a blot where the Loire, the Gazeille, or the Lausonne wandered in a gorge.

Soon we were on a highroad, and surprise seized on my mind as I beheld a village of some magnitude close at hand; for I had been told that the neighbourhood of the lake was uninhabited except by trout. The road smoked in the twilight with children driving home cattle from the fields; and a pair of mounted stride-legged women, hat and cap and all, dashed past me at a hammering trot from the canton where they had been to church and market. I asked one of the children where I was. At Bouchet St. Nicolas, he told me. Thither, about a mile south of my destination, and on the other side of a respectable summit, had these confused roads and treacherous peasantry conducted me. My shoulder was cut, so that it hurt sharply; my arm ached like toothache from perpetual beating; I gave up the lake and my design to camp, and asked for the *auberge*.

I Have a Goad

THE *auberge* of Bouchet St. Nicolas was among the least pretentious I have ever visited; but I saw many more of the like upon my journey. Indeed, it was typical of these French highlands. Imagine a cottage of two stories, with a bench before the door; the stable and kitchen in a suite, so that Modestine and I could hear each other dining; furniture of the plainest, earthen floors, a single bed-chamber for travellers, and that without any convenience but beds. In the kitchen cooking and eating go forward side by side, and the family sleep at night. Any one who has a fancy to wash must do so in public at the common table. The food is sometimes spare; hard fish and omelette have been my portion more than once; the wine is of the smallest, the brandy abominable to man; and the visit of a fat sow grunting under the table and rubbing against your legs, is no impossible accompaniment to dinner.

But the people of the inn, in nine cases out of ten, show themselves friendly and considerate. As soon as you cross the doors you cease to be a stranger; and although this peasantry are rude and forbidding on the highway, they show a tincture of kind breeding when you share their hearth. At Bouchet, for instance, I uncorked my bottle of Beaujolais, and asked the host to join me. He would take but little.

"I am an amateur of such wine, do you see?" he said, "and I am capable of leaving you not enough."

In these hedge-inns the traveller is expected to eat with his own knife; unless he ask, no other will be supplied: with a glass, a whang of bread, and an iron fork, the table is completely laid. My knife was cordially admired by the landlord of Bouchet, and the spring filled him with wonder.

"I should never have guessed that," he said. "I would bet," he added, weighing it in his hand, "that this cost you not less than five francs."

When I told him it had cost me twenty, his jaw dropped.

He was a mild, handsome, sensible, friendly old man, astonishingly ignorant. His wife, who was not so pleasant in her manners, knew how to read, although I do not suppose she ever did so. She had a share of brains and spoke with a cutting emphasis, like one who ruled the roast.

"My man knows nothing," she said, with an angry nod; "he is like the beasts."

And the old gentleman signified acquiescence with his head. There was no contempt on her part, and no shame on his; the facts were accepted loyally, and no more about the matter.

I was tightly cross-examined about my journey; and the lady understood in a moment, and sketched out what I should put into my book when I got home. "Whether people harvest or not in such or such a place; if there were forests; studies of manners; what, for example, I and the master of the house say to you; the beauties of Nature, and all that." And she interrogated me with a look.

"It is just that," said I.

"You see," she added to her husband, "I understood that."

They were both much interested by the story of my misadventures.

"In the morning," said the husband, "I will make you something better than your cane. Such a beast as that feels nothing; it is in the proverb — *dur comme un âne;* you might beat her insensible with a cudgel, and yet you would arrive nowhere."

Something better! I little knew what he was offering.

The sleeping-room was furnished with two beds. I had one; and I will own I was a little abashed to find a young man and his wife and child in the act of mounting into the other. This was my first experience of the sort; and if I am always to feel equally silly and extraneous, I pray God it be my last as well. I kept my eyes to myself, and know nothing of the woman except that she had beautiful arms, and seemed no whit abashed by my appearance. As a matter of fact, the situation was more trying to me than to the pair. A pair keep each other in countenance; it is the single gentleman who has to blush. But I could not help attributing my sentiments to the husband, and sought to conciliate his tolerance with a cup of brandy from my flask. He told me that he was a cooper of Alais travelling to St. Etienne in search of work, and that in his spare moments he followed the fatal calling of a maker of matches. Me he readily enough divined to be a brandy merchant.

I was up first in the morning (Monday, September 23d), and hastened my toilette guiltily, so as to leave a clear field for madam, the cooper's wife. I drank a bowl of milk, and set off to explore the neighbourhood of Bouchet. It was perishing cold, a grey, windy, wintry morning; misty clouds flew fast and low; the wind piped over the naked platform; and the only speck of colour was away behind Mount Mézenc and the eastern hills, where the sky still wore the orange of the dawn.

It was five in the morning, and four thousand feet above the sea; and I had to bury my hands in my pockets and trot. People were trooping out to the labours of the field by twos and threes, and all turned round to stare upon the stranger. I had seen them coming back last night, I saw them going afield again; and there was the life of Bouchet in a nutshell.

When I came back to the inn for a bit of breakfast the landlady was in the kitchen combing out her daughter's hair; and I made her my compliments upon its beauty.

"O no," said the mother; "it is not so beautiful as it ought to be. Look, it is too fine."

Thus does a wise peasantry console itself under adverse physical circumstances, and, by a startling democratic process, the defects of the majority decide the type of beauty.

"And where," said I, "is monsieur?"

"The master of the house is up-stairs," she answered, "making you a goad."

Blessed be the man who invented goads! Blessed the innkeeper of Bouchet St. Nicolas, who introduced me to their use! This plain wand, with an eighth of an inch of pin, was indeed a sceptre when he put it in my hands. Thenceforward Modestine was my slave. A prick, and she passed the most inviting stable-door. A prick, and

she broke forth into a gallant little trotlet that devoured
the miles. It was not a remarkable speed, when all was
said; and we took four hours to cover ten miles at the
best of it. But what a heavenly change since yesterday!
No more wielding of the ugly cudgel; no more flailing
with an aching arm; no more broadsword exercise, but a
discreet and gentlemanly fence. And what although now
and then a drop of blood should appear on Modestine's
mouse-coloured wedge-like rump? I should have preferred it otherwise, indeed; but yesterday's exploits had
purged my heart of all humanity. The perverse little
devil, since she would not be taken with kindness, must
even go with pricking.

It was bleak and bitter cold, and, except a cavalcade
of stride-legged ladies and a pair of postrunners, the road
was dead solitary all the way to Pradelles. I scarce remember an incident but one. A handsome foal with a
bell about his neck came charging up to us upon a stretch
of common, sniffed the air martially as one about to do
great deeds, and, suddenly thinking otherwise in his
green young heart, put about and galloped off as he had
come, the bell tinkling in the wind. For a long while
afterwards I saw his noble attitude as he drew up, and
heard the note of his bell; and when I struck the highroad, the song of the telegraph-wires seemed to continue
the same music.

Pradelles stands on a hillside, high above the Allier,
surrounded by rich meadows. They were cutting after-
math on all sides, which gave the neighbourhood, this
gusty autumn morning, an untimely smell of hay. On
the opposite bank of the Allier the land kept mounting
for miles to the horizon: a tanned and sallow autumn

THE ABBEY OF MOUNT ST. MICHAEL AT LE PUY

landscape, with black blots of fir-wood and white roads
wandering through the hills. Over all this the clouds
shed a uniform and purplish shadow, sad and somewhat
menacing, exaggerating height and distance, and throwing into still higher relief the twisted ribbons of the highway. It was a cheerless prospect, but one stimulating to
a traveller. For I was now upon the limit of Velay, and
all that I beheld lay in another county — wild Gévaudan,
mountainous, uncultivated, and but recently disforested
from terror of the wolves.

Wolves, alas, like bandits, seem to flee the traveller's
advance; and you may trudge through all our comfortable Europe, and not meet with an adventure worth the
name. But here, if anywhere, a man was on the frontiers
of hope. For this was the land of the ever-memorable
BEAST, the *Napoléon Buonaparte* of wolves. What a
career was his! He lived ten months at free quarters in
Gévaudan and Vivarais; he ate women and children and
"shepherdesses celebrated for their beauty"; he pursued
armed horsemen; he has been seen at broad noonday
chasing a postchaise and outrider along the king's highroad, and chaise and outrider fleeing before him at the
gallop. He was placarded like a political offender, and
ten thousand francs were offered for his head. And yet,
when he was shot and sent to Versailles, behold! a common wolf, and even small for that. "Though I could
reach from pole to pole," sang Alexander Pope; the little
corporal shook Europe; and if all wolves had been as
this wolf, they would have changed the history of man.
M. Elie Berthet has made him the hero of a novel, which
I have read, and do not wish to read again.

I hurried over my lunch, and was proof against the

landlady's desire that I should visit our Lady of Pradelles, "who performed many miracles, although she was of wood"; and before three quarters of an hour I was goading Modestine down the steep descent that leads to Langogne on the Allier. On both sides of the road, in big dusty fields, farmers were preparing for next spring. Every fifty yards a yoke of great-necked stolid oxen were patiently haling at the plough. I saw one of these mild, formidable servants of the glebe, who took a sudden interest in Modestine and me. The furrow down which he was journeying lay at an angle to the road, and his head was solidly fixed to the yoke like those of caryatides below a ponderous cornice; but he screwed round his big honest eyes and followed us with a ruminating look, until his master bade him turn the plough and proceed to reascend the field. From all these furrowing ploughshares, from the feet of oxen, from a labourer here and there who was breaking the dry clods with a hoe, the wind carried away a thin dust like so much smoke. It was a fine, busy, breathing, rustic landscape; and as I continued to descend, the highlands of Gévaudan kept mounting in front of me against the sky.

I had crossed the Loire the day before; now I was to cross the Allier; so near are these two confluents in their youth. Just at the bridge of Langogne, as the long-promised rain was beginning to fall, a lassie of some seven or eight addressed me in the sacramental phrase, "*D'où'st que vous venez?*" She did it with so high an air that she set me laughing; and this cut her to the quick. She was evidently one who reckoned on respect, and stood looking after me in silent dudgeon, as I crossed the bridge and entered the county of Gévaudan.

UPPER GÉVAUDAN

*"The way also here was very weari-
some through dirt and slabbi-
ness; nor was there on all this
ground so much as one inn or
victualling-house wherein to re-
fresh the feebler sort."* — Pilgrim's Progress.

UPPER GÉVAUDAN

A Camp in the Dark

THE next day (Tuesday, September 24th), it was two o'clock in the afternoon before I got my journal written up and my knapsack repaired, for I was determined to carry my knapsack in the future and have no more ado with baskets; and half an hour afterwards I set out for Le Cheylard l'Evêque, a place on the borders of the forest of Mercoire. A man, I was told, should walk there in an hour and a half; and I thought it scarce too ambitious to suppose that a man encumbered with a donkey might cover the same distance in four hours.

All the way up the long hill from Langogne it rained and hailed alternately; the wind kept freshening steadily, although slowly; plentiful hurrying clouds — some dragging veils of straight rainshower, others massed and luminous, as though promising snow — careered out of the north and followed me along my way. I was soon out of the cultivated basin of the Allier, and away from the ploughing oxen, and such-like sights of the country. Moor, heathery marsh, tracts of rock and pines, woods of birch all jewelled with the autumn yellow, here and there a few naked cottages and bleak fields, — these were the characters of the country. Hill and valley followed valley and hill; the little green and stony cattle-tracks wandered in and out of one another, split into three or four, died away in marshy hollows, and began again sporadically on hillsides or at the borders of a wood.

There was no direct road to Cheylard, and it was no easy affair to make a passage in this uneven country and through this intermittent labyrinth of tracks. It must have been about four when I struck Sagnerousse, and went on my way rejoicing in a sure point of departure. Two hours afterwards, the dusk rapidly falling, in a lull of the wind, I issued from a fir-wood where I had long been wandering, and found, not the looked-for village, but another marish bottom among rough-and-tumble hills. For some time past I had heard the ringing of cattle-bells ahead; and now, as I came out of the skirts of the wood, I saw near upon a dozen cows and perhaps as many more black figures, which I conjectured to be children, although the mist had almost unrecognisably exaggerated their forms. These were all silently following each other round and round in a circle, now taking hands, now breaking up with chains and reverences. A dance of children appeals to very innocent and lively thoughts; but, at nightfall on the marshes, the thing was eerie and fantastic to behold. Even I, who am well enough read in Herbert Spencer, felt a sort of silence fall for an instant on my mind. The next, I was pricking Modestine forward, and guiding her like an unruly ship through the open. In a path, she went doggedly ahead of her own accord, as before a fair wind; but once on the turf or among heather, and the brute became demented. The tendency of lost travellers to go round in a circle was developed in her to the degree of passion, and it took all the steering I had in me to keep even a decently straight course through a single field.

While I was thus desperately tacking through the bog, children and cattle began to disperse, until only a pair of girls remained behind. From these I sought direction on my path. The peasantry in general were but little disposed to counsel a wayfarer. One old devil simply retired into his house, and barricaded the door on my approach; and I might beat and shout myself hoarse, he turned a deaf ear. Another, having given me a direction which, as I found afterwards, I had misunderstood, complacently watched me going wrong without adding a sign. He did not care a stalk of parsley if I wandered all night upon the hills! As for these two girls, they were a pair of impudent sly sluts, with not a thought but mischief. One put out her tongue at me, the other bade me follow the cows; and they both giggled and jogged each other's elbows. The Beast of Gévaudan ate about a hundred children of this district; I began to think of him with sympathy.

Leaving the girls, I pushed on through the bog, and got into another wood and upon a well-marked road. It grew darker and darker. Modestine, suddenly beginning to smell mischief, bettered the pace of her own accord, and from that time forward gave me no trouble. It was the first sign of intelligence I had occasion to remark in her. At the same time, the wind freshened into half a gale, and another heavy discharge of rain came flying up out of the north. At the other side of the wood I sighted some red windows in the dusk. This was the hamlet of Fouzilhic; three houses on a hillside, near a wood of birches. Here I found a delightful old man, who came a little way with me in the rain to put me safely on the road for Cheylard. He would hear of no

reward; but shook his hands above his head almost
as if in menace, and refused volubly and shrilly, in
unmitigated *patois*.

All seemed right at last. My thoughts began to turn
upon dinner and a fireside, and my heart was agreeably
softened in my bosom. Alas, and I was on the brink of
new and greater miseries! Suddenly, at a single swoop,
the night fell. I have been abroad in many a black night,
but never in a blacker. A glimmer of rocks, a glimmer of
the track where it was well beaten, a certain fleecy dens-
ity, or night within night, for a tree, — this was all that
I could discriminate. The sky was simply darkness overhead; even the flying clouds pursued their way invisibly
to human eyesight. I could not distinguish my hand at
arm's length from the track, nor my goad, at the same
distance, from the meadows or the sky.

Soon the road that I was following split, after the
fashion of the country, into three or four in a piece of
rocky meadow. Since Modestine had shown such a fancy
for beaten roads, I tried her instinct in this predicament.
But the instinct of an ass is what might be expected from
the name; in half a minute she was clambering round and
round among some boulders, as lost a donkey as you
would wish to see. I should have camped long before
had I been properly provided; but as this was to be so
short a stage, I had brought no wine, no bread for myself,
and a little over a pound for my lady-friend. Add to
this, that I and Modestine were both handsomely wetted
by the showers. But now, if I could have found some
water, I should have camped at once in spite of all. Water,
however, being entirely absent, except in the form of rain,
I determined to return to Fouzilhic, and ask a guide a

little further on my way — "a little farther lend thy
guiding hand."

The thing was easy to decide, hard to accomplish. In
this sensible roaring blackness I was sure of nothing but
the direction of the wind. To this I set my face; the
road had disappeared, and I went across country, now in
marshy opens, now baffled by walls unscalable to Modestine, until I came once more in sight of some red windows.
This time they were differently disposed. It was not
Fouzilhic, but Fouzilhac, a hamlet little distant from the
other in space, but worlds away in the spirit of its inhabitants. I tied Modestine to a gate, and groped forward, stumbling among rocks, plunging mid-leg in bog,
until I gained the entrance of the village. In the first
lighted house there was a woman who would not open to
me. She could do nothing, she cried to me through the
door, being alone and lame; but if I would apply at the
next house, there was a man who could help me if he had
a mind.

They came to the next door in force, a man, two women,
and a girl, and brought a pair of lanterns to examine the
wayfarer. The man was not ill-looking, but had a shifty
smile. He leaned against the door-post, and heard me
state my case. All I asked was a guide as far as Cheylard.

"C'est que, voyez-vous, il fait noir," said he.

I told him that was just my reason for requiring help.

"I understand that," said he, looking uncomfortable;
"mais — c'est — de la peine."

I was willing to pay, I said. He shook his head. I
rose as high as ten francs; but he continued to shake his
head. "Name your own price, then," said I.

"Ce n'est pas ça," he said at length, and with evident

difficulty; "but I am not going to cross the door — *mais je ne sortirai pas de la porte.*"

I grew a little warm, and asked him what he proposed that I should do.

"Where are you going beyond Cheylard?" he asked by way of answer.

"That is no affair of yours," I returned, for I was not going to indulge his bestial curiosity; "it changes nothing in my present predicament."

"*C'est vrai, ça,*" he acknowledged, with a laugh; "*oui, c'est vrai. Et d'où venez-vous?*"

A better man than I might have felt nettled.

"O," said I, "I am not going to answer any of your questions, so you may spare yourself the trouble of putting them. I am late enough already; I want help. If you will not guide me yourself, at least help me to find some one else who will."

"Hold on," he cried suddenly. "Was it not you who passed in the meadow while it was still day?"

"Yes, yes," said the girl, whom I had not hitherto recognised; "it was monsieur; I told him to follow the cow."

"As for you, mademoiselle," said I, "you are a *farceuse.*"

"And," added the man, "what the devil have you done to be still here?"

What the devil, indeed! But there I was. "The great thing," said I, "is to make an end of it"; and once more proposed that he should help me to find a guide.

"*C'est que,*" he said again, "*c'est que — il fait noir.*"

"Very well," said I; "take one of your lanterns."

"No," he cried, drawing a thought backward, and

again intrenching himself behind one of his former phrases; "I will not cross the door."

I looked at him. I saw unaffected terror struggling on his face with unaffected shame; he was smiling pitifully and wetting his lip with his tongue, like a detected school-boy. I drew a brief picture of my state, and asked him what I was to do.

"I don't know," he said; "I will not cross the door." Here was the Beast of Gévaudan, and no mistake.

"Sir," said I, with my most commanding manners, "you are a coward."

And with that I turned my back upon the family party, who hastened to retire within their fortifications; and the famous door was closed again, but not till I had overheard the sound of laughter. *Filia barbara pater barbarior.* Let me say it in the plural: the Beasts of Gévaudan.

The lanterns had somewhat dazzled me, and I ploughed distressfully among stones and rubbish-heaps. All the other houses in the village were both dark and silent; and though I knocked at here and there a door, my knocking was unanswered. It was a bad business; I gave up Fouzilhac with my curses. The rain had stopped, and the wind, which still kept rising, began to dry my coat and trousers. "Very well," thought I, "water or no water, I must camp." But the first thing was to return to Modestine. I am pretty sure I was twenty minutes groping for my lady in the dark; and if it had not been for the unkindly services of the bog, into which I once more stumbled, I might have still been groping for her at the dawn. My next business was to gain the shelter of a wood, for the wind was cold as well as boisterous.

How, in this well-wooded district, I should have been so long in finding one, is another of the insoluble mysteries of this day's adventures; but I will take my oath that I put near an hour to the discovery.

At last black trees began to show upon my left, and, suddenly crossing the road, made a cave of unmitigated blackness right in front. I call it a cave without exaggeration; to pass below that arch of leaves was like entering a dungeon. I felt about until my hand encountered a stout branch, and to this I tied Modestine, a haggard, drenched, desponding donkey. Then I lowered my pack, laid it along the wall on the margin of the road, and unbuckled the straps. I knew well enough where the lantern was; but where were the candles? I groped and groped among the tumbled articles, and, while I was thus groping, suddenly I touched the spirit-lamp. Salvation! This would serve my turn as well. The wind roared unwearyingly among the trees; I could hear the boughs tossing and the leaves churning through half a mile of forest; yet the scene of my encampment was not only as black as the pit, but admirably sheltered. At the second match the wick caught flame. The light was both livid and shifting; but it cut me off from the universe, and doubled the darkness of the surrounding night.

I tied Modestine more conveniently for herself, and broke up half the black bread for her supper, reserving the other half against the morning. Then I gathered what I should want within reach, took off my wet boots and gaiters, which I wrapped in my waterproof, arranged my knapsack for a pillow under the flap of my sleeping-bag, insinuated my limbs into the interior, and buckled myself in like a *bambino*. I opened a tin of Bologna sausage and broke a cake of chocolate, and that was all I had to eat. It may sound offensive, but I ate them together, bite by bite, by way of bread and meat. All I had to wash down this revolting mixture was neat brandy; a revolting beverage in itself. But I was rare and hungry; ate well, and smoked one of the best cigarettes in my experience. Then I put a stone in my straw hat, pulled the flap of my fur cap over my neck and eyes, put my revolver ready to my hand, and snuggled well down among the sheepskins.

I questioned at first if I were sleepy, for I felt my heart beating faster than usual, as if with an agreeable excitement to which my mind remained a stranger. But as soon as my eyelids touched, that subtle glue leaped between them, and they would no more come separate.

The wind among the trees was my lullaby. Sometimes it sounded for minutes together with a steady even rush, not rising nor abating; and again it would swell and burst like a great crashing breaker, and the trees would patter me all over with big drops from the rain of the afternoon. Night after night, in my own bedroom in the country, I have given ear to this perturbing concert of the wind among the woods; but whether it was a difference in the trees, or the lie of the ground, or because I was myself outside and in the midst of it, the fact remains that the wind sang to a different tune among these woods of Gévaudan. I hearkened and hearkened; and meanwhile sleep took gradual possession of my body and subdued my thoughts and senses; but still my last waking effort was to listen and distinguish, and my last conscious state was one of wonder at the foreign clamour in my ears.

Twice in the course of the dark hours — once when a

stone galled me underneath the sack, and again when the poor patient Modestine, growing angry, pawed and stamped upon the road — I was recalled for a brief while to consciousness, and saw a star or two overhead, and the lace-like edge of the foliage against the sky. When I awoke for the third time (Wednesday, September 25th), the world was flooded with a blue light, the mother of the dawn. I saw the leaves labouring in the wind and the ribbon of the road; and, on turning my head, there was Modestine tied to a beech, and standing half across the path in an attitude of inimitable patience. I closed my eyes again, and set to thinking over the experience of the night. I was surprised to find how easy and pleasant it had been, even in this tempestuous weather. The stone which annoyed me would not have been there, had I not been forced to camp blindfold in the opaque night; and I had felt no other inconvenience, except when my feet encountered the lantern or the second volume of Peyrat's *Pastors of the Desert* among the mixed contents of my sleeping-bag; nay more, I had felt not a touch of cold, and awakened with unusually lightsome and clear sensations.

With that, I shook myself, got once more into my boots and gaiters, and, breaking up the rest of the bread for Modestine, strolled about to see in what part of the world I had awakened. Ulysses, left on Ithaca, and with a mind unsettled by the goddess, was not more pleasantly astray. I have been after an adventure all my life, a pure dispassionate adventure, such as befell early and heroic voyagers; and thus to be found by morning in a random woodside nook in Gévaudan — not knowing north from south, as strange to my surroundings as the first man upon the earth, an inland castaway — was to find a fraction of my day-dreams realised. I was on the skirts of a little wood of birch, sprinkled with a few beeches; behind, it adjoined another wood of fir; and in front, it broke up and went down in open order into a shallow and meadowy dale. All around there were bare hill-tops, some near, some far away, as the perspective closed or opened, but none apparently much higher than the rest. The wind huddled the trees. The golden specks of autumn in the birches tossed shiveringly. Overhead the sky was full of strings and shreds of vapour, flying, vanishing, reappearing, and turning about an axis like tumblers, as the wind hounded them through heaven. It was wild weather and famishing cold. I ate some chocolate, swallowed a mouthful of brandy, and smoked a cigarette before the cold should have time to disable my fingers. And by the time I had got all this done, and had made my pack and bound it on the pack-saddle, the day was tiptoe on the threshold of the east. We had not gone many steps along the lane, before the sun, still invisible to me, sent a glow of gold over some cloud mountains that lay ranged along the eastern sky.

The wind had us on the stern, and hurried us bitingly forward. I buttoned myself into my coat, and walked on in a pleasant frame of mind with all men, when suddenly at a corner, there was Fouzilhic once more in front of me. Nor only that, but there was the old gentleman who had escorted me so far the night before, running out of his house at sight of me, with hands upraised in horror.

"My poor boy!" he cried, "what does this mean?"

I told him what had happened. He beat his old hands like clappers in a mill, to think how lightly he had let me go; but when he heard of the man of Fouzilhac, anger and depression seized upon his mind.

"This time, at least," said he, "there shall be no mistake."

And he limped along, for he was very rheumatic, for about half a mile, and until I was almost within sight of Cheylard, the destination I had hunted for so long.

Cheylard and Luc

CANDIDLY, it seemed little worthy of all this searching. A few broken ends of village, with no particular street, but a succession of open places heaped with logs and fagots; a couple of tilted crosses, a shrine to our Lady of all Graces on the summit of a little hill; and all this, upon a rattling highland river, in the corner of a naked valley. What went ye out for to see? thought I to myself. But the place had a life of its own. I found a board commemorating the liberalities of Cheylard for the past year, hung up, like a banner, in the diminutive and tottering church. In 1877, it appeared, the inhabitants subscribed forty-eight francs ten centimes for the "Work of the Propagation of the Faith." Some of this, I could not help hoping, would be applied to my native land. Cheylard scrapes together halfpence for the darkened souls in Edinburgh; while Balquidder and Dunrossness bemoan the ignorance of Rome. Thus, to the high entertainment of the angels, do we pelt each other with evangelists, like school-boys bickering in the snow.

The inn was again singularly unpretentious. The whole furniture of a not ill-to-do family was in the kitchen: the beds, the cradle, the clothes, the plate-rack, the meal-chest, and the photograph of the parish priest. There were five children, one of whom was set to its morning prayers at the stair-foot soon after my arrival, and a sixth would erelong be forthcoming. I was kindly received by these good folk. They were much interested in my misadventure. The wood in which I had slept belonged to them; the man of Fouzilhac they thought a monster of iniquity, and counselled me warmly to summon him at law — "because I might have died." The good wife was horror-stricken to see me drink over a pint of uncreamed milk.

"You will do yourself an evil," she said. "Permit me to boil it for you."

After I had begun the morning on this delightful liquor, she having an infinity of things to arrange, I was permitted, nay requested, to make a bowl of chocolate for myself. My boots and gaiters were hung up to dry, and, seeing me trying to write my journal on my knee, the eldest daughter let down a hinged table in the chimney-corner for my convenience. Here I wrote, drank my chocolate, and finally ate an omelette before I left. The table was thick with dust; for, as they explained, it was not used except in winter weather. I had a clear look up the vent, through brown agglomerations of soot and blue vapour, to the sky; and whenever a handful of twigs was thrown on to the fire, my legs were scorched by the blaze.

The husband had begun life as a muleteer, and when I came to charge Modestine showed himself full of the prudence of his art. "You will have to change this package," said he; "it ought to be in two parts, and then you might have double the weight."

I explained that I wanted no more weight; and for no donkey hitherto created would I cut my sleeping-bag in two.

"It fatigues her, however," said the inn-keeper; "it fatigues her greatly on the march. Look."

Alas, there were her two forelegs no better than raw beef on the inside, and blood was running from under her tail. They told me when I left, and I was ready to believe it, that before a few days I should come to love Modestine like a dog. Three days had passed, we had shared some misadventures, and my heart was still as cold as a potato towards my beast of burthen. She was pretty enough to look at; but then she had given proof of dead stupidity, redeemed indeed by patience, but aggravated by flashes of sorry and ill-judged light-heartedness. And I own this new discovery seemed another point against her. What the devil was the good of a she-ass if she could not carry a sleeping-bag and a few necessaries? I saw the end of the fable rapidly approaching, when I should have to carry Modestine. Æsop was the man to know the world! I assure you I set out with heavy thoughts upon my short day's march.

It was not only heavy thoughts about Modestine that weighted me upon the way; it was a leaden business altogether. For first, the wind blew so rudely that I had to hold on the pack with one hand from Cheylard to Luc and second, my road lay through one of the most beggarly countries in the world. It was like the worst of the Scotch Highlands, only worse; cold, naked, and ignoble, scant of wood, scant of heather, scant of life. A road and some fences broke the unvarying waste, and the line of the road was marked by upright pillars, to serve in time of snow.

Why any one should desire to visit either Luc or Cheylard is more than my much-inventing spirit can suppose.

For my part, I travel not to go anywhere, but to go. I travel for travel's sake. The great affair is to move; to feel the needs and hitches of our life more nearly; to come down off this feather-bed of civilisation, and find the globe granite underfoot and strewn with cutting flints. Alas, as we get up in life, and are more preoccupied with our affairs, even a holiday is a thing that must be worked for. To hold a pack upon a pack-saddle against a gale out of the freezing north is no high industry, but it is one that serves to occupy and compose the mind. And when the present is so exacting, who can annoy himself about the future?

I came out at length above the Allier. A more unsightly prospect at this season of the year it would be hard to fancy. Shelving hills rose round it on all sides, here dabbled with wood and fields, there rising to peaks alternately naked and hairy with pines. The colour throughout was black or ashen, and came to a point in the ruins of the castle of Luc, which pricked up impudently from below my feet, carrying on a pinnacle a tall white statue of our Lady, which, I heard with interest, weighed fifty quintals, and was to be dedicated on the 6th of October. Through this sorry landscape trickled the Allier and a tributary of nearly equal size, which came down to join it through a broad nude valley in Vivarais. The weather had somewhat lightened, and the clouds massed in squadron; but the fierce wind still hunted them through heaven, and cast great ungainly splashes of shadow and sunlight over the scene.

Luc itself was a straggling double file of houses wedged between hill and river. It had no beauty, nor was there any notable feature, save the old castle overhead with its fifty quintals of brand-new Madonna. But the inn was clean and large. The kitchen, with its two box-beds hung with clean check curtains, with its wide stone chimney, its chimney-shelf four yards long and garnished with lanterns and religious statuettes, its array of chests and pair of ticking clocks, was the very model of what a kitchen ought to be; a melodrama kitchen, suitable for bandits or noblemen in disguise. Nor was the scene disgraced by the landlady, a handsome, silent, dark old woman, clothed and hooded in black like a nun. Even the public bedroom had a character of its own, with the long deal tables and benches, where fifty might have dined, set out as for a harvest-home, and the three box-beds along the wall. In one of these, lying on straw and covered with a pair of table-napkins, did I do penance all night long in goose-flesh and chattering teeth, and sigh from time to time as I awakened for my sheepskin sack and the lee of some great wood.

OUR LADY OF THE SNOWS

"*I behold*
The House, the Brotherhood austere —
And what am I, that I am here?"
— MATTHEW ARNOLD.

OUR LADY OF THE SNOWS

Father Apollinaris

NEXT morning (Thursday, 26th September) I took the
road in a new order. The sack was no longer doubled,
but hung at full length across the saddle, a green sausage
six feet long with a tuft of blue wool hanging out of either
end. It was more picturesque, it spared the donkey, and,
as I began to see, it would insure stability, blow high,
blow low. But it was not without a pang that I had so
decided. For although I had purchased a new cord, and
made all as fast as I was able, I was yet jealously uneasy
lest the flaps should tumble out and scatter my effects
along the line of march.

My way lay up the bald valley of the river, along the
march of Vivarais and Gévaudan. The hills of Gévaudan
on the right were a little more naked, if anything, than
those of Vivarais upon the left, and the former had a
monopoly of a low dotty underwood that grew thickly in
the gorges and died out in solitary burrs upon the shoulder
and the summits. Black bricks of fir-wood were plastered
here and there upon both sides, and here and there were
cultivated fields. A railway ran beside the river; the
only bit of railway in Gévaudan, although there are many
proposals afoot and surveys being made, and even, as
they tell me, a station standing ready-built in Mende.
A year or two hence and this may be another world.

47

The desert is beleaguered. Now may some Languedocian Wordsworth turn the sonnet into *patois:* "Mountains and vales and floods, heard YE that whistle?"

At a place called La Bastide I was directed to leave the river, and follow a road that mounted on the left among the hills of Vivarais, the modern Ardeche; for I was now come within a little way of my strange destination, the Trappist monastery of our Lady of the Snows. The sun came out as I left the shelter of a pine-wood, and I beheld suddenly a fine wild landscape to the south. High rocky hills, as blue as sapphire, closed the view, and between these lay ridge upon ridge, heathery, craggy, the sun glittering on veins of rock, the underwood clambering in the hollows, as rude as God made them at the first. There was not a sign of man's hand in all the prospect; and indeed not a trace of his passage, save where generation after generation had walked in twisted foot-paths, in and out among the beeches, and up and down upon the channelled slopes. The mists, which had hitherto beset me, were now broken into clouds, and fled swiftly and shone brightly in the sun. I drew a long breath. It was grateful to come, after so long, upon a scene of some attraction for the human heart. I own I like definite form in what my eyes are to rest upon; and if landscapes were sold, like the sheets of characters of my boyhood, one penny plain and twopence coloured, I should go the length of twopence every day of my life.

But if things had grown better to the south, it was still desolate and inclement near at hand. A spidery cross on every hill-top marked the neighbourhood of a religious house; and a quarter of a mile beyond, the outlook southward opening out and growing bolder with every step, a white statue of the Virgin at the corner of a young plantation directed the traveller to our Lady of the Snows. Here, then, I struck leftward, and pursued my way, driving my secular donkey before me, and creaking in my secular boots and gaiters, towards the asylum of silence.

I had not gone very far ere the wind brought to me the clanging of a bell, and somehow, I can scarce tell why, my heart sank within me at the sound. I have rarely approached anything with more unaffected terror than the monastery of our Lady of the Snows. This it is to have had a Protestant education. And suddenly, on turning a corner, fear took hold on me from head to foot — slavish superstitious fear; and though I did not stop in my advance, yet I went on slowly, like a man who should have passed a bourne unnoticed, and strayed into the country of the dead. For there upon the narrow new-made road, between the stripling pines, was a mediæval friar, fighting with a barrowful of turfs. Every Sunday of my childhood I used to study the *Hermits* of Marco Sadeler — enchanting prints, full of wood and field and mediæval landscapes, as large as a county, for the imagination to go a-travelling in; and here, sure enough, was one of Marco Sadeler's heroes. He was robed in white like any spectre, and the hood falling back, in the instancy of his contention with the barrow, disclosed a pate as bald and yellow as a skull. He might have been buried any time these thousand years, and all the lively parts of him resolved into earth and broken up with the farmer's harrow.

I was troubled besides in my mind as to etiquette. Durst I address a person who was under a vow of silence? Clearly not. But drawing near, I doffed my cap to him with a far-away superstitious reverence. He nodded back, and cheerfully addressed me. Was I going to the monastery? Who was I? An Englishman? Ah, an Irishman, then?

"No," I said, "a Scotsman."

A Scotsman? Ah, he had never seen a Scotsman before. And he looked me all over, his good, honest, brawny countenance shining with interest, as a boy might look upon a lion or an alligator. From him I learned with disgust that I could not be received at our Lady of the Snows; I might get a meal, perhaps, but that was all. And then, as our talk ran on, and it turned out that I was not a pedlar, but a literary man, who drew landscapes and was going to write a book, he changed his manner of thinking as to my reception (for I fear they respect persons even in a Trappist monastery), and told me I must be sure to ask for the Father Prior, and state my case to him in full. On second thoughts he determined to go down with me himself; he thought he could manage for me better. Might he say that I was a geographer?

No; I thought, in the interests of truth, he positively might not.

"Very well, then" (with disappointment), "an author."

It appeared he had been in a seminary with six young Irishmen, all priests long since, who had received newspapers and kept him informed of the state of ecclesiastical affairs in England. And he asked me eagerly after Dr. Pusey, for whose conversion the good man had continued ever since to pray night and morning.

"I thought he was very near the truth," he said; "and he will reach it yet; there is so much virtue in prayer."

He must be a stiff ungodly Protestant who can take anything but pleasure in this kind and hopeful story. While he was thus near the subject, the good father asked me if I were a Christian; and when he found I was not, or not after his way, he glossed it over with great good-will.

The road which we were following, and which this stalwart father had made with his own two hands within the space of a year, came to a corner, and showed us some white buildings a little further on beyond the wood. At the same time, the bell once more sounded abroad. We were hard upon the monastery. Father Apollinaris (for that was my companion's name) stopped me.

"I must not speak to you down there," he said. "Ask for the Brother Porter, and all will be well. But try to see me as you go out again through the wood, where I may speak to you. I am charmed to have made your acquaintance."

And then suddenly raising his arms, flapping his fingers, and crying out twice, "I must not speak, I must not speak!" he ran away in front of me, and disappeared into the monastery-door.

I own this somewhat ghastly eccentricity went a good way to revive my terrors. But where one was so good and simple, why should not all be alike? I took heart of grace, and went forward to the gate as fast as Modestine, who seemed to have a disaffection for monasteries, would permit. It was the first door, in my acquaintance of her, which she had not shown in indecent haste to enter. I summoned the place in form, though with a quaking heart. Father Michael, the Father Hospitaller, and a pair of brown-robed brothers came to the

gate and spoke with me awhile. I think my sack was the
great attraction; it had already beguiled the heart of
poor Apollinaris, who had charged me on my life to show
it to the Father Prior. But whether it was my address,
or the sack, or the idea speedily published among that
part of the brotherhood who attend on strangers that I
was not a pedlar after all, I found no difficulty as to my
reception. Modestine was led away by a layman to the
stables, and I and my pack were received into our Lady
of the Snows.

The Monks

FATHER MICHAEL, a pleasant, fresh-faced, smiling man perhaps of thirty-five, took me to the pantry, and gave me a glass of liqueur to stay me until dinner. We had some talk, or rather I should say he listened to my prattle indulgently enough, but with an abstracted air, like a spirit with a thing of clay. And truly when I remember that I descanted principally on my appetite, and that it must have been by that time more than eighteen hours since Father Michael had so much as broken bread, I can well understand that he would find an earthly savour in my conversation. But his manner, though superior, was exquisitely gracious; and I find I have a lurking curiosity as to Father Michael's past.

The whet administered, I was left alone for a little in the monastery garden. This is no more than the main court, laid out in sandy paths and beds of party-coloured dahlias, and with a fountain and a black statue of the Virgin in the centre. The buildings stand around it four-square, bleak, as yet unseasoned by the years and weather, and with no other features than a belfry and a pair of slated gables. Brothers in white, brothers in brown, passed silently along the sanded alleys; and when I first came out, three hooded monks were kneeling on the terrace at their prayers. A naked hill commands the monastery upon one side, and the wood commands it on the other. It lies exposed to wind; the snow falls off and on from October to May, and sometimes lies six weeks on end; but if they stood in Eden, with a climate like heaven's, the buildings themselves would offer the same wintry and cheerless aspect; and for my part, on this wild September day, before I was called to dinner, I felt chilly in and out.

When I had eaten well and heartily, Brother Ambrose, a hearty conversable Frenchman (for all those who wait on strangers have the liberty to speak), led me to a little room in that part of the building which is set apart for *MM. les retraitants*. It was clean and whitewashed, and furnished with strict necessaries, a crucifix, a bust of the late Pope, the *Imitation* in French, a book of religious meditations, and the *Life of Elizabeth Seton*, evangelist, it would appear, of North America and of New England in particular. As far as my experience goes, there is a fair field for some more evangelisation in these quarters; but think of Cotton Mather! I should like to give him a reading of this little work in heaven, where I hope he dwells; but perhaps he knows all that already, and much more; and perhaps he and Mrs. Seton are the dearest friends, and gladly unite their voices in the everlasting psalm. Over the table, to conclude the inventory of the room, hung a set of regulations for *MM. les retraitants:* what services they should attend, when they were to tell their beads or meditate, and when they were to rise and go to rest. At the foot was a notable N. B.: "*Le temps libre est employé à l'examen de conscience, à la confession, à faire de bonnes résolutions,*" etc. To make good resolutions, indeed! You might talk as fruitfully of making the hair grow on your head.

I had scarce explored my niche when Brother Ambrose

returned. An English boarder, it appeared, would like to speak with me. I professed my willingness, and the friar ushered in a fresh, young little Irishman of fifty, a deacon of the Church, arrayed in strict canonicals, and wearing on his head what, in default of knowledge, I can only call the ecclesiastical shako. He had lived seven years in retreat at a convent of nuns in Belgium, and now

MOUNT ST. MICHAEL AT LE PUY

five at our Lady of the Snows; he never saw an English newspaper; he spoke French imperfectly, and had he spoken it like a native, there was not much chance of conversation where he dwelt. With this, he was a man eminently sociable, greedy of news, and simple-minded like a child. If I was pleased to have a guide about the monastery, he was no less delighted to see an English face and hear an English tongue.

He showed me his own room, where he passed his time among breviaries, Hebrew bibles, and the Waverley novels. Thence he led me to the cloisters, into the chapter-house, through the vestry, where the brothers' gowns and broad straw hats were hanging up, each with his religious name upon a board, — names full of legendary suavity and interest, such as Basil, Hilarion, Raphael, or Pacifique; into the library, where were all the works of Veuillot and Chateaubriand, and the *Odes et Ballades*, if you please, and even Molière, to say nothing of innumerable fathers and a great variety of local and general historians. Thence my good Irishman took me round the workshops, where brothers bake bread, and make cart-wheels, and take photographs; where one superintends a collection of curiosities, and another a gallery of rabbits. For in a Trappist monastery each monk has an occupation of his own choice, apart from his religious duties and the general labours of the house. Each must sing in the choir, if he has a voice and ear, and join in the haymaking if he has a hand to stir; but in his private hours, although he must be occupied, he may be occupied on what he likes. Thus I was told that one brother was engaged with literature; while Father Apollinaris busies himself in making roads, and the Abbot employs himself in binding books. It is not so long since this Abbot was consecrated, by the way; and on that occasion, by a special grace, his mother was permitted to enter the chapel and witness the ceremony of consecration. A proud day for her to have a son a mitred abbot; it makes you glad to think they let her in.

In all these journeyings to and fro, many silent fathers and brethren fell in our way. Usually they paid no more regard to our passage than if we had been a cloud; but sometimes the good deacon had a permission to ask of them, and it was granted by a peculiar movement of the hands, almost like that of a dog's paws in swimming, or refused by the usual negative signs, and in either case with lowered eyelids and a certain air of contrition, as of a man who was steering very close to evil.

The monks, by special grace of their Abbot, were still taking two meals a day; but it was already time for their grand fast, which begins somewhere in September and lasts till Easter, and during which they eat but once in the twenty-four hours, and that at two in the afternoon, twelve hours after they have begun the toil and vigil of the day. Their meals are scanty, but even of these they eat sparingly; and though each is allowed a small carafe of wine, many refrain from this indulgence. Without doubt, the most of mankind grossly overeat themselves; our meals serve not only for support, but as a hearty and natural diversion from the labour of life. Although excess may be hurtful, I should have thought this Trappist regimen defective. And I am astonished, as I look back, at the freshness of face and cheerfulness of manner of all whom I beheld. A happier nor a healthier company I should scarce suppose that I have ever seen. As a matter of fact, on this bleak upland, and with the incessant occupation of the monks, life is of an uncertain tenure, and death no infrequent visitor, at our Lady of the Snows. This, at least, was what was told me. But if they die easily, they must live healthily in the meantime, for they seemed all firm of flesh and high in colour; and the only morbid sign that I could observe, an unusual brilliancy of eye, was one that served rather to increase the general impression of vivacity and strength.

Those with whom I spoke were singularly sweet-tempered, with what I can only call a holy cheerfulness in air and conversation. There is a note, in the direction to visitors, telling them not to be offended at the curt speech of those who wait upon them, since it is proper to monks to speak little. The note might have been spared; to a man the hospitallers were all brimming with innocent talk, and, in my experience of the monastery, it was easier to begin than to break off a conversation. With the exception of Father Michael, who was a man of the world, they showed themselves full of kind and healthy interest in all sorts of subjects — in politics, in voyages, in my sleeping-sack — and not without a certain pleasure in the sound of their own voices.

As for those who are restricted to silence, I can only wonder how they bear their solemn and cheerless isolation. And yet, apart from any view of mortification, I can see a certain policy, not only in the exclusion of women, but in this vow of silence. I have had some experience of lay phalansteries, of an artistic, not to say a bacchanalian, character; and seen more than one association easily formed, and yet more easily dispersed. With a Cistercian rule, perhaps they might have lasted longer. In the neighbourhood of women it is but a touch-and-go association that can be formed among defenceless men; the stronger electricity is sure to triumph; the dreams of boyhood, the schemes of youth, are abandoned after an interview of ten minutes, and the arts and sciences, and professional male jollity, deserted at once for two sweet eyes and a caressing accent. And next after this, the tongue is the great divider.

I am almost ashamed to pursue this worldly criticism

of a religious rule; but there is yet another point in which
the Trappist order appeals to me as a model of wisdom.
By two in the morning the clapper goes upon the bell,
and so on, hour by hour, and sometimes quarter by
quarter, till eight, the hour of rest; so infinitesimally is
the day divided among different occupations. The man
who keeps rabbits, for example, hurries from his hutches
to the chapel, the chapter-room, or the refectory, all day
long: every hour he has an office to sing, a duty to perform; from two, when he rises in the dark, till eight,
when he returns to receive the comfortable gift of sleep,
he is upon his feet and occupied with manifold and changing business. I know many persons, worth several thou-
sands in the year, who are not so fortunate in the dis-
posal of their lives. Into how many houses would not
the note of the monastery-bell, dividing the day into
manageable portions, bring peace of mind and healthful
activity of body? We speak of hardships, but the true
hardship is to be a dull fool, and permitted to mismanage
life in our own dull and foolish manner.

From this point of view, we may perhaps better understand the monk's existence. A long novitiate, and every
proof of constancy of mind and strength of body is required before admission to the order; but I could not
find that many were discouraged. In the photographer's
studio, which figures so strangely among the outbuildings,
my eye was attracted by the portrait of a young fellow
in the uniform of a private of foot. This was one of the
novices, who came of the age for service, and marched and
drilled and mounted guard for the proper time among the
garrison of Algiers. Here was a man who had surely
seen both sides of life before deciding; yet as soon as

he was set free from service he returned to finish his
novitiate.

This austere rule entitles a man to heaven as by right.
When the Trappist sickens, he quits not his habit ; he lies
in the bed of death as he has prayed and laboured in his
frugal and silent existence ; and when the Liberator comes,
at the very moment, even before they have carried him
in his robe to lie his little last in the chapel among continual chantings, joy-bells break forth, as if for a marriage, from the slated belfry, and proclaim throughout
the neighbourhood that another soul has gone to God.

At night, under the conduct of my kind Irishman, I
took my place in the gallery to hear compline and *Salve
Regina*, with which the Cistercians bring every day to a
conclusion.   There were none of those circumstances
which strike the Protestant as childish or as tawdry in
the public offices of Rome.   A stern simplicity, heightened
by the romance of the surroundings, spoke directly to the
heart.   I recall the whitewashed chapel, the hooded figures
in the choir, the lights alternately occluded and revealed,
the strong manly singing, the silence that ensued, the sight
of cowled heads bowed in prayer, and then the clear
trenchant beating of the bell, breaking in to show that
the last office was over and the hour of sleep had come ;
and when I remember, I am not surprised that I made
my escape into the court with somewhat whirling fancies,
and stood like a man bewildered in the windy starry night.

But I was weary ; and when I had quieted my spirits
with Elizabeth Seton's memoirs — a dull work — the cold
and the raving of the wind among the pines — for my
room was on that side of the monastery which adjoins
the woods — disposed me readily to slumber.   I was

wakened at black midnight, as it seemed, though it was really two in the morning, by the first stroke upon the bell. All the brothers were then hurrying to the chapel; the dead in life, at this untimely hour, were already beginning the uncomforted labours of their day. The dead in life — there was a chill reflection. And the words of a French song came back into my memory, telling of the best of our mixed existence:

> "Que t'as de belles filles,
>   Giroflé!
>   Girofla!
>   Que t'as de belles filles,
>   *L'Amour les comptera!*"

And I blessed God that I was free to wander, free to hope, and free to love.

The Boarders

But there was another side to my residence at our Lady of the Snows. At this late season there were not many boarders; and yet I was not alone in the public part of the monastery. This itself is hard by the gate, with a small dining-room on the ground floor, and a whole corridor of cells similar to mine up-stairs. I have stupidly forgotten the board for a regular *retraitant;* but it was somewhere between three and five francs a day, and I think most probably the first. Chance visitors like myself might give what they chose as a free-will offering, but nothing was demanded. I may mention that when I was going away, Father Michael refused twenty francs as excessive. I explained the reasoning which led me to offer him so much; but even then, from a curious point of honour, he would not accept it with his own hand. "I have no right to refuse for the monastery," he explained, "but I should prefer if you would give it to one of the brothers."

I had dined alone, because I arrived late; but at supper I found two other guests. One was a country parish priest, who had walked over that morning from the seat of his cure near Mende to enjoy four days of solitude and prayer. He was a grenadier in person, with the hale colour and circular wrinkles of a peasant; and as he complained much of how he had been impeded by his skirts upon the march, I have a vivid fancy portrait of him, striding along, upright, big-boned, with kilted cassock, through the bleak hills of Gévaudan. The other was a short, grizzling, thick-set man, from forty-five to fifty, dressed in tweed with a knitted spencer, and the red ribbon of a decoration in his buttonhole. This last was a hard person to classify. He was an old soldier, who had seen service and risen to the rank of commandant; and he retained some of the brisk decisive manners of the camp. On the other hand, as soon as his resignation was accepted, he had come to our Lady of the Snows as a boarder, and after a brief experience of its ways, had decided to remain as a novice. Already the new life was beginning to modify his appearance; already he had acquired somewhat of the quiet and smiling air of the brethren; and he was as yet neither an officer nor a Trappist, but partook of the character of each. And certainly here was a man in an interesting nick of life. Out of the noise of cannon and trumpets, he was in the act of passing into this still country bordering on the grave, where men sleep nightly in their graveclothes, and, like phantoms, communicate by signs.

At supper we talked politics. I make it my business, when I am in France, to preach political good-will and moderation, and to dwell on the example of Poland, much as some alarmists in England dwell on the example of Carthage. The priest and the Commandant assured me of their sympathy with all I said, and made a heavy sighing over the bitterness of contemporary feeling.

"Why, you cannot say anything to a man with which he does not absolutely agree," said I, "but he flies up at you in a temper."

They both declared that such a state of things was antichristian.

While we were thus agreeing, what should my tongue stumble upon but a word in praise of Gambetta's moderation. The old soldier's countenance was instantly suffused with blood; with the palms of his hands he beat the table like a naughty child.

"*Comment, monsieur?*" he shouted. "*Comment?* Gambetta moderate? Will you dare to justify these words?"

But the priest had not forgotten the tenor of our talk. And suddenly, in the height of his fury, the old soldier found a warning look directed on his face; the absurdity of his behaviour was brought home to him in a flash; and the storm came to an abrupt end, without another word.

It was only in the morning, over our coffee (Friday, September 27th), that this couple found out I was a heretic. I suppose I had misled them by some admiring expressions as to the monastic life around us; and it was only by a point-blank question that the truth came out. I had been tolerantly used, both by simple Father Apollinaris and astute Father Michael; and the good Irish deacon, when he heard of my religious weakness, had only patted me upon the shoulder and said, "You must be a Catholic and come to heaven." But I was now among a different sect of orthodox. These two men were bitter and up-right and narrow, like the worst of Scotsmen, and indeed, upon my heart, I fancy they were worse. The priest snorted aloud like a battle-horse.

"*Et vous prétendez mourir dans cette espèce de croyance?*" he demanded; and there is no type used by mortal printers large enough to qualify his accent.

I humbly indicated that I had no design of changing.

But he could not away with such a monstrous attitude. "No, no," he cried; "you must change. You have come here, God has led you here, and you must embrace the opportunity."

I made a slip in policy; I appealed to the family affections, though I was speaking to a priest and a soldier, two classes of men circumstantially divorced from the kind and homely ties of life.

"Your father and mother?" cried the priest. "Very well; you will convert them in their turn when you go home."

I think I see my father's face! I would rather tackle the Gætulian lion in his den than embark on such an enterprise against the family theologian.

But now the hunt was up; priest and soldier were in full cry for my conversion; and the Work of the Propagation of the Faith, for which the people of Cheylard subscribed forty-eight francs ten centimes during 1877, was being gallantly pursued against myself. It was an odd but most effective proselytising. They never sought to convince me in argument, where I might have attempted some defence; but took it for granted that I was both ashamed and terrified at my position, and urged me solely on the point of time. Now, they said, when God had led me to our Lady of the Snows, now was the appointed hour.

"Do not be withheld by false shame," observed the priest, for my encouragement.

For one who feels very similarly to all sects of religion, and who has never been able, even for a moment, to weigh seriously the merit of this or that creed on the eternal side of things, however much he may see to praise or blame upon the secular and temporal side, the situation thus created was both unfair and painful. I committed my second fault in tact, and tried to plead that it was all the same thing in the end, and we were all drawing near by different sides to the same kind and undiscriminating Friend and Father. That, as it seems to lay-spirits, would be the only gospel worthy of the name. But different men think differently; and this revolutionary aspiration brought down the priest with all the terrors of the law. He launched into harrowing details of hell. The damned, he said — on the authority of a little book which he had read not a week before, and which, to add conviction to conviction, he had fully intended to bring along with him in his pocket — were to occupy the same attitude through all eternity in the midst of dismal tortures. And as he thus expatiated, he grew in nobility of aspect with his enthusiasm.

As a result the pair concluded that I should seek out the Prior, since the Abbot was from home, and lay my case immediately before him.

"*C'est mon conseil comme ancien militaire,*" observed the Commandant; "*et celui de monsieur comme prêtre.*"

"*Oui,*" added the curé, sententiously nodding; "*comme ancien militaire — et comme prêtre.*"

At this moment, whilst I was somewhat embarrassed how to answer, in came one of the monks, a little brown fellow, as lively as a grig, and with an Italian accent, who threw himself at once into the contention, but in a milder and more persuasive vein, as befitted one of these pleasant brethren. Look at him, he said. The rule was very hard; he would have dearly liked to stay in his own country, Italy — it was well known how beautiful it was, the beautiful Italy; but then there were no Trappists in Italy; and he had a soul to save; and here he was.

I am afraid I must be at bottom, what a cheerful Indian critic has dubbed me, "a faddling hedonist"; for this description of the brother's motives gave me somewhat of a shock. I should have preferred to think he had chosen the life for its own sake, and not for ulterior purposes; and this shows how profoundly I was out of sympathy with these good Trappists, even when I was doing my best to sympathise. But to the *curé* the argument seemed decisive.

"Hear that!" he cried. "And I have seen a marquis here, a marquis, a marquis" — he repeated the holy word three times over — "and other persons high in society; and generals. And here, at your side, is this gentleman, who has been so many years in armies — decorated, an old warrior. And here he is, ready to dedicate himself to God."

I was by this time so thoroughly embarrassed that I pleaded cold feet, and made my escape from the apartment. It was a furious windy morning, with a sky much cleared, and long and potent intervals of sunshine; and I wandered until dinner in the wild country towards the east, sorely staggered and beaten upon by the gale, but rewarded with some striking views.

At dinner the Work of the Propagation of the Faith was recommenced, and on this occasion still more distastefully to me. The priest asked me many questions as to the contemptible faith of my fathers, and received my replies with a kind of ecclesiastical titter.

"Your sect," he said once; "for I think you will admit it would be doing it too much honour to call it a religion."

"As you please, monsieur," said I. *"La parole est à vous."*

At length I grew annoyed beyond endurance; and although he was on his own ground, and, what is more to the purpose, an old man, and so holding a claim upon my toleration, I could not avoid a protest against this uncivil usage. He was sadly discountenanced.

"I assure you," he said, "I have no inclination to laugh in my heart. I have no other feeling but interest in your soul."

And there ended my conversion. Honest man! He was no dangerous deceiver; but a country parson, full of zeal and faith. Long may he tread Gévaudan with his kilted skirts — a man strong to walk and strong to comfort his parishioners in death! I dare say he would beat bravely through a snow-storm where his duty called him; and it is not always the most faithful believer who makes the cunningest apostle.

UPPER GÉVAUDAN

(continued)

"The bed was made, the room was fit,
By punctual eve the stars were lit;
The air was sweet, the water ran;
No need was there for maid or man,
When we put up, my ass and I,
At God's green caravanserai."
—Old Play.

Across the Goulet

THE wind fell during dinner, and the sky remained clear; so it was under better auspices that I loaded Modestine before the monastery-gate. My Irish friend accompanied me so far on the way. As we came through the wood, there was Père Apollinaire hauling his barrow; and he too quitted his labours to go with me for perhaps a hundred yards, holding my hand between both of his in front of him. I parted first from one and then from the other with unfeigned regret, but yet with the glee of the traveller who shakes off the dust of one stage before hurrying forth upon another. Then Modestine and I mounted the course of the Allier, which here led us back into Gévaudan towards its sources in the forest of Mercoire. It was but an inconsiderable burn before we left its guidance. Thence, over a hill, our way lay through a naked plateau, until we reached Chasseradés at sundown.

The company in the inn-kitchen that night were all men employed in survey for one of the projected railways. They were intelligent and conversable, and we decided the future of France over hot wine, until the state of the clock frightened us to rest. There were four beds in the little up-stairs room; and we slept six. But I had a bed to myself, and persuaded them to leave the window open.

"*Hê, bourgeois; il est cinq heures!*" was the cry that wakened me in the morning (Saturday, September 28th). The room was full of a transparent darkness, which dimly

showed me the other three beds and the five different
nightcaps on the pillows. But out of the window the
dawn was growing ruddy in a long belt over the hill-tops
and day was about to flood the plateau. The hour was
inspiring; and there seemed a promise of calm weather,
which was perfectly fulfilled. I was soon under way
with Modestine. The road lay for awhile over the
plateau, and then descended through a precipitous village
into the valley of the Chassezac. This stream ran among
green meadows, well hidden from the world by its steep
banks; the broom was in flower, and here and there was
a hamlet sending up its smoke.

At last the path crossed the Chassezac upon a bridge,
and, forsaking this deep hollow, set itself to cross the
mountain of La Goulet. It wound up through Lestampes
by upland fields and woods of beech and birch, and with
every corner brought me into an acquaintance with some
new interest. Even in the gully of the Chassezac my ear
had been struck by a noise like that of a great bass bell
ringing at the distance of many miles; but this, as I continued to mount and draw nearer to it, seemed to change
in character, and I found at length that it came from
some one leading flocks afield to the note of a rural horn.
The narrow street of Lestampes stood full of sheep, from
wall to wall — black sheep and white, bleating like the
birds in spring, and each one accompanying himself upon
the sheep-bell round his neck. It made a pathetic concert, all in treble. A little higher, and I passed a pair of
men in a tree with pruning-hooks, and one of them was
singing the music of a *bourrée*. Still further, and when I
was already threading the birches, the crowing of cocks
came cheerfully up to my ears, and along with that the

voice of a flute discoursing a deliberate and plaintive air from one of the upland villages. I pictured to myself some grizzled, apple-cheeked, country schoolmaster fluting in his bit of a garden in the clear autumn sunshine. All these beautiful and interesting sounds filled my heart with an unwonted expectation; and it appeared to me that, once past this range which I was mounting, I should descend into the garden of the world. Nor was I deceived, for I was now done with rains and winds and a bleak country. The first part of my journey ended here; and this was like an induction of sweet sounds into the other and more beautiful.

There are other degrees of *feyness*, as of punishment, besides the capital; and I was now led by my good spirits into an adventure which I relate in the interest of future donkey-drivers. The road zigzagged so widely on the hillside that I chose a short cut by map and compass, and struck through the dwarf woods to catch the road again upon a higher level. It was my one serious conflict with Modestine. She would none of my short cut; she turned in my face, she backed, she reared; she, whom I had hitherto imagined to be dumb, actually brayed with a loud hoarse flourish, like a cock crowing for the dawn. I plied the goad with one hand; with the other, so steep was the ascent, I had to hold on the pack-saddle. Half-a-dozen times she was nearly over backwards on the top of me; half-a-dozen times, from sheer weariness of spirit, I was nearly giving it up, and leading her down again to follow the road. But I took the thing as a wager, and fought it through. I was surprised, as I went on my way again, by what appeared to be chill rain-drops falling on my hand, and more than once looked up in wonder at the cloudless sky. But it was only sweat which came dropping from my brow.

Over the summit of the Goulet there was no marked road — only upright stones posted from space to space to guide the drovers. The turf underfoot was springy and well scented. I had no company but a lark or two, and met but one bullock-cart between Lestampes and Bleymard. In front of me I saw a shallow valley, and beyond that the range of the Lozère, sparsely wooded and well enough modelled in the flanks, but straight and dull in outline. There was scarce a sign of culture; only about Bleymard, the white highroad from Villefort to Mende traversed a range of meadows, set with spiry poplars, and sounding from side to side with the bells of flocks and herds.

A Night Among the Pines

FROM Bleymard after dinner, although it was already late, I set out to scale a portion of the Lozère. An ill-marked stony drove-road guided me forward; and I met nearly half-a-dozen bullock-carts descending from the woods, each laden with a whole pine-tree for the winter's firing. At the top of the woods, which do not climb very high upon this cold ridge, I struck leftward by a path among the pines, until I hit on a dell of green turf, where a streamlet made a little spout over some stones to serve me for a water-tap. "In a more sacred or sequestered bower — nor nymph nor faunus haunted." The trees were not old, but they grew thickly round the glade: there was no outlook, except northeastward upon distant hill-tops, or straight upward to the sky; and the encampment felt secure and private like a room. By the time I had made my arrangements and fed Modestine, the day was already beginning to decline. I buckled myself to the knees into my sack and made a hearty meal; and as soon as the sun went down, I pulled my cap over my eyes and fell asleep.

Night is a dead monotonous period under a roof; but in the open world it passes lightly, with its stars and dews and perfumes, and the hours are marked by changes in the face of Nature. What seems a kind of temporal death to people choked between walls and curtains, is only a light and living slumber to the man who sleeps afield. All night long he can hear Nature breathing deeply and freely; even as she takes her rest she turns and smiles; and there is one stirring hour unknown to those who dwell in houses, when a wakeful influence goes abroad over the sleeping hemisphere, and all the outdoor world are on their feet. It is then that the cock first crows, not this time to announce the dawn, but like a cheerful watchman speeding the course of night. Cattle awake on the meadows; sheep break their fast on dewy hillsides, and change to a new lair among the ferns; and houseless men, who have lain down with the fowls, open their dim eyes and behold the beauty of the night.

At what inaudible summons, at what gentle touch of Nature, are all these sleepers thus recalled in the same hour to life? Do the stars rain down an influence, or do we share some thrill of mother earth below our resting bodies? Even shepherds and old countryfolk, who are the deepest read in these arcana, have not a guess as to the means or purpose of this nightly resurrection. Towards two in the morning they declare the thing takes place; and neither know nor inquire further. And at least it is a pleasant incident. We are disturbed in our slumber only, like the luxurious Montaigne, "that we may the better and more sensibly relish it." We have a moment to look upon the stars, and there is a special pleasure for some minds in the reflection that we share the impulse with all outdoor creatures in our neighbourhood, that we have escaped out of the Bastille of civilisation, and are become, for the time being, a mere kindly animal and a sheep of Nature's flock.

When that hour came to me among the pines, I wakened thirsty. My tin was standing by me half full of water.

I emptied it at a draught; and feeling broad awake after this internal cold aspersion, sat upright to make a cigarette.

THE REFECTORY AT THE ABBEY OF MOUNT ST. MICHAEL, LE PUY

The stars were clear, coloured, and jewel-like, but not frosty. A faint silvery vapour stood for the Milky Way.

All around me the black fir-points stood upright and stock-still. By the whiteness of the pack-saddle, I could see Modestine walking round and round at the length of her tether; I could hear her steadily munching at the sward; but there was not another sound, save the indescribable quiet talk of the runnel over the stones. I lay lazily smoking and studying the colour of the sky, as we call the void of space, from where it showed a reddish grey behind the pines to where it showed a glossy blue-black between the stars. As if to be more like a pedlar, I wear a silver ring. This I could see faintly shining as I raised or lowered the cigarette; and at each whiff the inside of my hand was illuminated, and became for a second the highest light in the landscape.

A faint wind, more like a moving coolness than a stream of air, passed down the glade from time to time; so that even in my great chamber the air was being renewed all night long. I thought with horror of the inn at Chasserades and the congregated nightcaps; with horror of the nocturnal prowesses of clerks and students, of hot theatres and pass-keys and close rooms. I have not often enjoyed a more serene possession of myself, nor felt more independent of material aids. The outer world, from which we cower into our houses, seemed after all a gentle habitable place; and night after night a man's bed, it seemed, was laid and waiting for him in the fields, where God keeps an open house. I thought I had re-discovered one of those truths which are revealed to savages and hid from political economists: at the least, I had discovered a new pleasure for myself. And yet even while I was exulting in my solitude I became aware of a strange lack. I wished a companion to lie near me in the starlight, silent and not moving, but ever within touch. For there is a fellowship more quiet even than solitude, and which, rightly understood, is solitude made perfect. And to live out of doors with the woman a man loves is of all lives the most complete and free.

As I thus lay, between content and longing, a faint noise stole towards me through the pines. I thought, at first, it was the crowing of cocks or the barking of dogs at some very distant farm ; but steadily and gradually it took articulate shape in my ears, until I became aware that a passenger was going by upon the highroad in the valley, and singing loudly as he went. There was more of good-will than grace in his performance ; but he trolled with ample lungs ; and the sound of his voice took hold upon the hillside and set the air shaking in the leafy glens. I have heard people passing by night in sleeping cities ; some of them sang ; one, I remember, played loudly on the bagpipes. I have heard the rattle of a cart or carriage spring up suddenly after hours of stillness, and pass, for some minutes, within the range of my hearing as I lay abed. There is a romance about all who are abroad in the black hours, and with something of a thrill we try to guess their business. But here the romance was double : first, this glad passenger, lit internally with wine, who sent up his voice in music through the night ; and then I, on the other hand, buckled into my sack, and smoking alone in the pine-woods between four and five thousand feet towards the stars.

When I awoke again (Sunday, 29th September), many of the stars had disappeared ; only the stronger companions of the night still burned visibly overhead ; and away towards the east I saw a faint haze of light upon the horizon, such as had been the Milky Way when I was last awake. Day was at hand. I lit my lantern, and by its glow-worm light put on my boots and gaiters; then I broke up some bread for Modestine, filled my can at the water-tap, and lit my spirit-lamp to boil myself some chocolate. The blue darkness lay long in the glade where I had so sweetly slumbered; but soon there was a broad streak of orange melting into gold along the mountain-tops of Vivarais. A solemn glee possessed my mind at this gradual and lovely coming in of day. I heard the runnel with delight; I looked round me for something beautiful and unexpected; but the still black pine-trees, the hollow glade, the munching ass, remained unchanged in figure. Nothing had altered but the light, and that, indeed, shed over all a spirit of life and of breathing peace, and moved me to a strange exhilaration.

I drank my water chocolate, which was hot if it was not rich, and strolled here and there, and up and down about the glade. While I was thus delaying, a gush of steady wind, as long as a heavy sigh, poured direct out of the quarter of the morning. It was cold, and set me sneezing. The trees near at hand tossed their black plumes in its passage; and I could see the thin distant spires of pine along the edge of the hill rock slightly to and fro against the golden east. Ten minutes after, the sunlight spread at a gallop along the hillside, scattering shadows and sparkles, and the day had come completely.

I hastened to prepare my pack, and tackle the steep ascent that lay before me; but I had something on my mind. It was only a fancy; yet a fancy will sometimes be importunate. I had been most hospitably received and punctually served in my green caravanserai. The room was airy, the water excellent, and the dawn had called me to a moment. I say nothing of the tapestries or the inimitable ceiling, nor yet of the view which I commanded from the windows; but I felt I was in some one's debt for all this liberal entertainment. And so it pleased me, in a half-laughing way, to leave pieces of money on the turf as I went along, until I had left enough for my night's lodging. I trust they did not fall to some rich and churlish drover.

THE COUNTRY OF THE CAMISARDS

"We travelled in the print of olden wars;
Yet all the land was green;
And love we found, and peace,
Where fire and war had been.
They pass and smile, the children of the sword —
No more the sword they wield;
And O, how deep the corn
Along the battle-field!"
— W. P. BANNATYNE.

THE COUNTRY OF THE CAMISARDS

Across the Lozère

THE track that I had followed in the evening soon died out, and I continued to follow over a bald turf ascent a row of stone pillars, such as had conducted me across the Goulet. It was already warm. I tied my jacket on the pack, and walked in my knitted waistcoat. Modestine herself was in high spirits, and broke of her own accord, for the first time in my experience, into a jolting trot that sent the oats swashing in the pocket of my coat. The view, back upon the northern Gévaudan, extended with every step; scarce a tree, scarce a house, appeared upon the fields of wild hill that ran north, east, and west, all blue and gold in the haze and sunlight of the morning. A multitude of little birds kept sweeping and twittering about my path; they perched on the stone pillars, they pecked and strutted on the turf, and I saw them circle in volleys in the blue air, and show, from time to time, translucent flickering wings between the sun and me.

Almost from the first moment of my march, a faint large noise, like a distant surf, had filled my ears. Sometimes I was tempted to think it the voice of a neighbouring waterfall, and sometimes a subjective result of the utter stillness of the hill. But as I continued to advance, the noise increased and became like the hissing of an enormous tearm, and at the same time breaths of cool air

began to reach me from the direction of the summit.   At
length I understood.   It was blowing stiffly from the
south upon the other slope of the Lozère, and every step
that I took I was drawing nearer to the wind.

Although it had been long desired, it was quite un-
expectedly at last that my eyes rose above the summit.
A step that seemed no way more decisive than many
other steps that had preceded it — and, "like stout Cortez
when, with eagle eyes, he stared on the Pacific," I took
possession, in my own name, of a new quarter of the
world.   For behold, instead of the gross turf rampart I
had been mounting for so long, a view into the hazy air
of heaven, and a land of intricate blue hills below my feet.

The Lozère lies nearly east and west, cutting Gévaudan
into two unequal parts; its highest point, this Pic de
Finiels, on which I was then standing, rises upwards of
five thousand six hundred feet above the sea, and in clear
weather commands a view over all lower Languedoc to
the Mediterranean Sea.   I have spoken with people who
either pretended or believed that they had seen, from the
Pic de Finiels, white ships sailing by Montpellier and
Cette.   Behind was the upland northern country through
which my way had lain, peopled by a dull race, without
wood, without much grandeur of hill-form and famous in
the past for little beside wolves.   But in front of me, half
veiled in sunny haze, lay a new Gévaudan, rich, picturesque, illustrious for stirring events.   Speaking largely, I
was in the Cévennes at Monastier, and during all my
journey; but there is a strict and local sense in which
only this confused and shaggy country at my feet has any
title to the name, and in this sense the peasantry employ
the word.   These are the Cévennes with an emphasis:

the Cévennes of the Cévennes. In that undeciph... labyrinth of hills, a war of bandits, a war of wild beasts, raged for two years between the Grand Monarch with all his troops and marshals on the one hand, and a few thousand Protestant mountaineers upon the other. A hundred and eighty years ago, the Camisards held a station even on the Lozère, where I stood; they had an organisation, arsenals, a military and religious hierarchy; their affairs were "the discourse of every coffee-house" in London; England sent fleets in their support; their leaders prophesied and murdered; with colours and drums, and the singing of old French psalms, their bands sometimes affronted daylight, marched before walled cities, and dispersed the generals of the king; and sometimes at night, or in masquerade, possessed themselves of strong castles, and avenged treachery upon their allies and cruelty upon their foes. There, a hundred and eighty years ago, was the chivalrous Roland, "Count and Lord Roland, generalissimo of the Protestants in France," grave, silent, imperious, pock-marked ex-dragoon, whom a lady followed in his wanderings out of love. There was Cavalier, a baker's apprentice with a genius for war, elected brigadier of Camisards at seventeen, to die at fifty-five the English governor of Jersey. There again was Castanet, a partisan leader in a voluminous peruke and with a taste for controversial divinity. Strange generals, who moved apart to take counsel with the God of Hosts, and fled or offered battle, set sentinels or slept in an unguarded camp, as the Spirit whispered to their hearts! And there, to follow these and other leaders, was the rank and file of prophets and disciples, bold, patient, indefatigable, hardy to run upon the mountains, cheering their rough life with psalms,

eager to fight, eager to pray, listening devoutly to the
oracles of brain-sick children, and mystically putting a
grain of wheat among the pewter balls with which they
charged their muskets.

I had travelled hitherto through a dull district, and in
the track of nothing more notable than the child-eating
Beast of Gévaudan, the Napoléon Buonaparte of wolves.
But now I was to go down into the scene of a romantic
chapter — or, better, a romantic foot-note — in the history of the world. What was left of all this by-gone dust
and heroism? I was told that Protestantism still sur-
vived in this head seat of Protestant resistance; so much
the priest himself had told me in the monastery parlour.
But I had yet to learn if it were a bare survival, or a lively
and generous tradition.   Again, if in the northern Cévennes
the people are narrow in religious judgments, and more
filled with zeal than charity, what was I to look for in
this land of persecution and reprisal — in a land where
the tyranny of the Church produced the Camisard rebel-
lion, and the terror of the Camisards threw the Catholic
peasantry into legalised revolt upon the other side, so
that Camisard and Florentin skulked for each other's
lives among the mountains?

Just on the brow of the hill, where I paused to look
before me, the series of stone pillars came abruptly to an
end; and only a little below, a sort of track appeared and
began to go down a breakneck slope, turning like a cork-
screw as it went.   It led into a valley between falling hills,
stubbly with rocks like a reaped field of corn, and floored
further down with green meadows. I followed the track
with precipitation; the steepness of the slope, the continual agile turning of the line of descent, and the old un-

wearied hope of finding something new in a new country, all conspired to lend me wings. Yet a little lower and a stream began, collecting itself together out of many fountains, and soon making a glad noise among the hills. Sometimes it would cross the track in a bit of waterfall, with a pool, in which Modestine refreshed her feet.

The whole descent is like a dream to me, so rapidly was it accomplished. I had scarcely left the summit ere the valley had closed round my path, and the sun beat upon me, walking in a stagnant lowland atmosphere. The track became a road, and went up and down in easy undulations. I passed cabin after cabin, but all seemed deserted; and I saw not a human creature, nor heard any sound except that of the stream. I was, however, in a different country from the day before. The stony skeleton of the world was here vigorously displayed to sun and air. The slopes were steep and changeful. Oak-trees clung along the hills, well grown, wealthy in leaf, and touched by the autumn with strong and luminous colours. Here and there another stream would fall in from the right or the left, down a gorge of snow-white and tumultuary boulders. The river in the bottom (for it was rapidly growing a river, collecting on all hands as it trotted on its way) here foamed awhile in desperate rapids, and there lay in pools of the most enchanting sea-green shot with watery browns. As far as I have gone, I have never seen a river of so changeful and delicate a hue; crystal was not more clear, the meadows were not by half so green; and at every pool I saw I felt a thrill of longing to be out of these hot, dusty, and material garments, and bathe my naked body in the mountain air and water. All the time as I went on I never forgot it was the Sabbath;

the stillness was a perpetual reminder; and I heard in spirit the church-bells clamouring all over Europe, and the psalms of a thousand churches.

At length a human sound struck upon my ear — a cry strangely modulated between pathos and derision; and looking across the valley, I saw a little urchin sitting in a meadow, with his hands about his knees, and dwarfed to almost comical smallness by the distance. But the rogue had picked me out as I went down the road, from oak-wood on to oak-wood, driving Modestine; and he made me the compliments of the new country in this tremulous high-pitched salutation. And as all noises are lovely and natural at a sufficient distance, this also, coming through so much clean hill air and crossing all the green valley, sounded pleasant to my ear, and seemed a thing rustic, like the oaks or the river.

A little after, the stream that I was following fell into the Tarn, at Pont de Montvert of bloody memory.

Pont de Montvert

ONE of the first things I encountered in Pont de Montvert was, if I remember rightly, the Protestant temple; but this was but the type of other novelties. A subtle atmosphere distinguishes a town in England from a town in France, or even in Scotland. At Carlisle you can see you are in one country; at Dumfries, thirty miles away, you are as sure that you are in the other. I should find it difficult to tell in what particulars Pont de Montvert differed from Monastier or Langogne, or even Bleymard; but the difference existed, and spoke eloquently to the eyes. The place, with its houses, its lanes, its glaring river-bed, wore an indescribable air of the South.

All was Sunday bustle in the streets and in the public-house, as all had been Sabbath peace among the mountains. There must have been near a score of us at dinner by eleven before noon; and after I had eaten and drunken, and sat writing up my journal, I suppose as many more came dropping in one after another, or by twos and threes. In crossing the Lozère I had not only come among new natural features, but moved into the territory of a different race. These people, as they hurriedly despatched their viands in an intricate sword-play of knives, questioned and answered me with a degree of intelligence which excelled all that I had met, except among the railway folk at Chasserades. They had open telling faces, and were lively both in speech and manner. They not only entered thoroughly into the spirit of my little trip,

but more than one declared, if he were rich enough, he
would like to set forth on such another.

Even physically there was a pleasant change. I had
not seen a pretty woman since I left Monastier, and
there but one. Now of the three who sat down with me
to dinner, one was certainly not beautiful — a poor timid
thing of forty, quite troubled at this roaring *table d'hote*,
whom I squired and helped to wine, and pledged and tried
generally to encourage, with quite a contrary effect; but
the other two, both married, were both more handsome
than the average of women. And Clarisse? What shall
I say of Clarisse? She waited the table with a heavy
placable nonchalance, like a performing cow; her great
grey eyes were steeped in amorous languor; her features,
although fleshy, were of an original and accurate design;
her mouth had a curl; her nostril spoke of dainty pride;
her cheek fell, into strange and interesting lines. It was a
face capable of strong emotion, and, with training, it
offered the promise of delicate sentiment. It seemed pitiful to see so good a model left to country admirers and a
country way of thought. Beauty should at least have
touched society, then, in a moment, it throws off a weight
that lay upon it, it becomes conscious of itself, it puts on
an elegance, learns a gait and a carriage of the head, and,
in a moment, *patet dea*. Before I left I assured Clarisse
of my hearty admiration. She took it like milk, without
embarrassment or wonder, merely looking at me steadily
with her great eyes; and I own the result upon myself
was some confusion. If Clarisse could read English, I
should not dare to add that her figure was unworthy of
her face. Hers was a case for stays; but that may perhaps grow better as she gets up in years.

Pont de Montvert, or Greenhill Bridge, as we might say at home, is a place memorable in the story of the Camisards. It was here that the war broke out; here that those southern Covenanters slew their Archbishop Sharpe. The persecution on the one hand, the febrile enthusiasm on the other, are almost equally difficult to understand in these quiet modern days, and with our easy modern beliefs and disbeliefs. The Protestants were one and all beside their right minds with zeal and sorrow. They were all prophets and prophetesses. Children at the breast would exhort their parents to good works. "A child of fifteen months at Quissac spoke from its mother's arms, agitated and sobbing, distinctly and with a loud voice."   Marshal Villars has seen a town where all the women "seemed possessed by the devil," and had trembling fits, and uttered prophecies publicly upon the streets. A prophetess of Vivarais was hanged at Montpellier because blood flowed from her eyes and nose, and she declared that she was weeping tears of blood for the misfortunes of the Protestants. And it was not only women and children. Stalwart dangerous fellows, used to swing the sickle or to wield the forest axe, were likewise shaken with strange paroxysms, and spoke oracles with sobs and streaming tears. A persecution unsurpassed in violence had lasted near a score of years, and this was the result upon the persecuted; hanging, burning, breaking on the wheel, had been vain; the dragoons had left their hoof-marks over all the country-side; there were men rowing in the galleys, and women pining in the prisons of the Church; and not a thought was changed in the heart of any upright Protestant.

Now the head and forefront of the persecution — after

Lamoignon de Bavile — François de Langlade du Chayla (pronounced Chéïla), Archpriest of the Cévennes and Inspector of Missions in the same country, had a house in which he sometimes dwelt in the town of Pont de Montvert. He was a conscientious person, who seems to have been intended by nature for a pirate, and now fifty-five, an age by which a man has learned all the moderation of which he is capable. A missionary in his youth in China, he there suffered martyrdom, was left for dead, and only succoured and brought back to life by the charity of a pariah. We must suppose the pariah devoid of second sight, and not purposely malicious in this act. Such an experience, it might be thought, would have cured a man of the desire to persecute; but the human spirit is a thing strangely put together; and, having been a Christian martyr, Du Chayla became a Christian persecutor. The Work of the Propagation of the Faith went roundly forward in his hands. His house in Pont de Montvert served him as a prison. There he plucked out the hairs of the beard, and closed the hands of his prisoners upon live coals, to convince them that they were deceived in their opinions. And yet had not he himself tried and proved the inefficacy of these carnal arguments among the Buddhists in China?

Not only was life made intolerable in Languedoc, but flight was rigidly forbidden. One Massip, a muleteer, and well acquainted with the mountain-paths, had already guided several troops of fugitives in safety to Geneva; and on him, with another convoy, consisting mostly of women dressed as men, Du Chayla, in an evil hour for himself, laid his hands. The Sunday following, there was a conventicle of Protestants in the woods of Altefage upon

Mont Bougès; where there stood up one Séguier — Spirit Séguier, as his companions called him — a wool-carder, tall, black-faced, and toothless, but a man full of prophecy. He declared, in the name of God, that the time for submission had gone by, and they must betake themselves to arms for the deliverance of their brethren and the destruction of the priests.

The next night, 24th July, 1702, a sound disturbed the Inspector of Missions as he sat in his prison-house at Pont de Montvert; the voices of many men upraised in psalmody drew nearer and nearer through the town. It was ten at night; he had his court about him, priests, soldiers, and servants, to the number of twelve or fifteen; and now dreading the insolence of a conventicle below his very windows, he ordered forth his soldiers to report. But the psalm-singers were already at his door, fifty strong, led by the inspired Séguier, and breathing death. To their summons, the arch-priest made answer like a stout old persecutor, and bade his garrison fire upon the mob. One Camisard (for, according to some, it was in this night's work that they came by the name) fell at this discharge; his comrades burst in the door with hatchets and a beam of wood, overran the lower story of the house, set free the prisoners, and finding one of them in the *vine*, a sort of Scavenger's Daughter of the place and period, redoubled in fury against Du Chayla, and sought by repeated assaults to carry the upper floors. But he, on his side, had given absolution to his men, and they bravely held the staircase.

"Children of God," cried the prophet, "hold your hands. Let us burn the house, with the priest and the satellites of Baal."

The fire caught readily. Out of an upper window Du Chayla and his men lowered themselves into the garden by means of knotted sheets; some escaped across the river under the bullets of the insurgents; but the arch-priest himself fell, broke his thigh, and could only crawl into the hedge. What were his reflections as this second martyrdom drew near? A poor, brave, besotted, hateful man, who had done his duty resolutely according to his light both in the Cévennes and China. He found at least one telling word to say in his defence; for when the roof fell in and the upbursting flames discovered his retreat, and they came and dragged him to the public place of the town, raging and calling him damned — "If I be damned," said he, "why should you also damn yourselves?"

Here was a good reason for the last; but in the course of his inspectorship he had given many stronger which all told in a contrary direction; and these he was now to hear. One by one, Séguier first, the Camisards drew near and stabbed him. "This," they said, "is for my father broken on the wheel. This for my brother in the galleys. That for my mother or my sister imprisoned in your cursed convents." Each gave his blow and his reason; and then all kneeled and sang psalms around the body till the dawn. With the dawn, still singing, they defiled away towards Frugères, further up the Tarn, to pursue the work of vengeance, leaving Du Chayla's prison-house in ruins, and his body pierced with two-and-fifty wounds upon the public place.

'Tis a wild night's work, with its accompaniment of psalms; and it seems as if a psalm must always have a sound of threatening in that town upon the Tarn. But the story does not end, even so far as concerns Pont de

Montvert, with the departure of the Camisards. The career of Séguier was brief and bloody. Two more priests and a whole family at Ladevèze, from the father to the servants, fell by his hand or by his orders; and yet he was but a day or two at large, and restrained all the time by the presence of the soldiery. Taken at length by a famous soldier of fortune, Captain Poul, he appeared unmoved before his judges.

"Your name?" they asked.

"Pierre Séguier."

"Why are you called Spirit?"

"Because the Spirit of the Lord is with me."

"Your domicile?"

"Lately in the desert, and soon in heaven."

"Have you no remorse for your crimes?"

"I have committed none. *My soul is like a garden full of shelter and of fountains.*"

At Pont de Montvert, on the 12th of August, he had his right hand stricken from his body, and was burned alive. And his soul was like a garden? So perhaps was the soul of Du Chayla, the Christian martyr. And perhaps if you could read in my soul, or I could read in yours, our own composure might seem little less surprising.

Du Chayla's house still stands, with a new roof, beside one of the bridges of the town; and if you are curious you may see the terrace-garden into which he dropped.

In the Valley of the Tarn

A NEW road leads from Pont de Montvert to Florac by the valley of the Tarn; a smooth sandy ledge, it runs about half-way between the summit of the cliffs and the river in the bottom of the valley; and I went in and out, as I followed it, from bays of shadow into promontories of afternoon sun. This was a pass like that of Killie-crankie; a deep turning gully in the hills, with the Tarn making a wonderful hoarse uproar far below, and craggy summits standing in the sunshine high above. A thin fringe of ash-trees ran about the hill-tops, like ivy on a ruin; but on the lower slopes and far up every glen the Spanish chestnut-trees stood each four-square to heaven under its tented foliage. Some were planted each on its own terrace, no larger than a bed; some, trusting in their roots, found strength to grow and prosper and be straight and large upon the rapid slopes of the valley; others, where there was a margin to the river, stood marshalled in a line and mighty like cedars of Lebanon. Yet even where they grew most thickly they were not to be thought of as a wood, but as a herd of stalwart individuals; and the dome of each tree stood forth separate and large, and as it were a little hill, from among the domes of its companions. They gave forth a faint sweet perfume which pervaded the air of the afternoon; autumn had put tints of gold and tarnish in the green; and the sun so shone through and kindled the broad foliage, that each chestnut was relieved against another, not in shadow, but in light. A humble sketcher here laid down his pencil in despair.

I wish I could convey a notion of the growth of these noble trees; of how they strike out boughs like the oak, and trail sprays of drooping foliage like the willow; of how they stand on upright fluted columns like the pillars of a church; or like the olive, from the most shattered bole can put out smooth and youthful shoots, and begin a new life upon the ruins of the old. Thus they partake of the nature of many different trees; and even their prickly top-knots, seen near at hand against the sky, have a certain palm-like air that impresses the imagination. But their individuality, although compounded of so many elements, is but the richer and the more original. And to look down upon a level filled with these knolls of foliage, or to see a clan of old unconquerable chestnuts cluster "like herded elephants" upon the spur of a mountain, is to rise to higher thoughts of the powers that are in Nature.

Between Modestine's laggard humour and the beauty of the scene, we made little progress all that afternoon; and at last finding the sun, although still far from setting, was already beginning to desert the narrow valley of the Tarn, I began to cast about for a place to camp in. This was not easy to find; the terraces were too narrow, and the ground, where it was unterraced, was usually too steep for a man to lie upon. I should have slipped all night, and awakened towards morning with my feet or my head in the river.

After perhaps a mile, I saw, some sixty feet above the road, a little plateau large enough to hold my sack, and securely parapeted by the trunk of an aged and enormous chestnut. Thither, with infinite trouble I goaded and kicked the reluctant Modestine and there I hastened to unload her. There was only room for myself upon the plateau, and I had to go nearly as high again before I found so much as standing room for the ass. It was on a heap of rolling stones, on an artificial terrace, certainly not five feet square in all. Here I tied her to a chestnut, and having given her corn and bread and made a pile of chestnut-leaves, of which I found her greedy, I descended once more to my own encampment.

The position was unpleasantly exposed. One or two carts went by upon the road; and as long as daylight lasted I concealed myself, for all the world like a hunted Camisard, behind my fortification of vast chestnut trunk; for I was passionately afraid of discovery and the visit of jocular persons in the night. Moreover, I saw that I must be early awake; for these chestnut gardens had been the scene of industry no farther gone than on the day before. The slope was strewn with lopped branches, and here and there a great package of leaves was propped against a trunk; for even the leaves are serviceable, and the peasants use them in winter by way of fodder for their animals. I picked a meal in fear and trembling, half lying down to hide myself from the road; and I dare say I was as much concerned as if I had been a scout from Joani's band above upon the Lozère or from Salomon's across the Tarn in the old times of psalm-singing and blood. Or, indeed, perhaps more; for the Camisards had a remarkable confidence in God; and a tale comes back into my memory of how the Count of Gévaudan, riding with a party of dragoons and a notary at his saddle-bow to enforce the oath of fidelity in all the country ham-

lets, entered a valley in the woods, and found Cavalier
and his men at dinner, gaily seated on the grass, and
their hats crowned with box-tree garlands, while fifteen
women washed their linen in the stream. Such was a
field festival in 1703; at that date Antony Watteau
would be painting similar subjects.

This was a very different camp from that of the night
before in the cool and silent pine-woods. It was warm
and even stifling in the valley. The shrill song of frogs,
like the tremolo note of a whistle with a pea in it, rang
up from the riverside before the sun was down. In the
growing dusk, faint rustlings began to run to and fro
among the fallen leaves; from time to time a faint chirping or cheeping noise would fall upon my ear; and from
time to time I thought I could see the movement of something swift and indistinct between the chestnuts. A
profusion of large ants swarmed upon the ground; bats
whisked by, and mosquitoes droned overhead. The long
boughs with their bunches of leaves hung against the sky
like garlands; and those immediately above and around
me had somewhat the air of a trellis which should have
been wrecked and half overthrown in a gale of wind.

Sleep for a long time fled my eyelids; and just as I
was beginning to feel quiet stealing over my limbs, and
settling densely on my mind, a noise at my head startled
me broad awake again, and, I will frankly confess it,
brought my heart into my mouth. It was such a noise
as a person would make scratching loudly with a finger-
nail, it came from under the knapsack which served me
for a pillow, and it was thrice repeated before I had time
to sit up and turn about. Nothing was to be seen, nothing more was to be heard, but a few of these mysterious

rustlings far and near, and the ceaseless accompaniment
of the river and the frogs. I learned next day that the
chestnut gardens are infested by rats; rustling, chirping,
and scraping were probably all due to these; but the
puzzle, for the moment, was insoluble, and I had to compose myself for sleep, as best I could, in wondering un-
certainty about my neighbours.

I was wakened in the grey of the morning (Monday,
30th September) by the sound of footsteps not far off
upon the stones, and opening my eyes, I beheld a peasant
going by among the chestnuts by a foot-path that I had
not hitherto observed. He turned his head neither to the
right nor to the left, and disappeared in a few strides
among the foliage. Here was an escape! But it was
plainly more than time to be moving. The peasantry
were abroad; scarce less terrible to me in my nondescript
position than the soldiers of Captain Poul to an undaunted Camisard. I fed Modestine with what haste I
could; but as I was returning to my sack, I saw a man
and a boy come down the hillside in a direction crossing
mine. They unintelligibly hailed me, and I replied with
inarticulate but cheerful sounds, and hurried forward to
get into my gaiters.

The pair, who seemed to be father and son, came
slowly up to the plateau, and stood close beside me for
some time in silence. The bed was open, and I saw with
regret my revolver lying patiently disclosed on the blue
wool. At last, after they had looked me all over, and
silence had grown laughably embarrassing, the man
demanded in what seemed unfriendly tones:

"You have slept here?"

"Yes," said I. "As you see."

"Why?" he asked.

"My faith," I answered lightly, "I was tired." He next inquired where I was going and what I had had for dinner; and then, without the least transition, "*C'est bien*," he added. "Come along." And he and his son, without another word, turned off to the next chestnut-tree but one, which they set to pruning. The thing had passed off more simply than I hoped. He was a grave, respectable man; and his unfriendly voice did not imply that he thought he was speaking to a criminal, but merely to an inferior.

I was soon on the road, nibbling a cake of chocolate and seriously occupied with a case of conscience. Was I to pay for my night's lodging? I had slept ill, the bed was full of fleas in the shape of ants, there was no water in the room, the very dawn had neglected to call me in the morning. I might have missed a train, had there been any in the neighbourhood to catch. Clearly, I was dissatisfied with my entertainment; and I decided I should not pay unless I met a beggar.

The valley looked even lovelier by morning; and soon the road descended to the level of the river. Here, in a place where many straight and prosperous chestnuts stood together, making an aisle upon a swarded terrace, I made my morning toilette in the water of the Tarn. It was marvellously clear, thrillingly cool; the soap-suds disappeared as if by magic in the swift current, and the white boulders gave one a model for cleanliness. To wash in one of God's rivers in the open air seems to me a sort of cheerful solemnity or semi-pagan act of worship. To dabble among dishes in a bedroom may perhaps make clean the body; but the imagination takes no share in such a cleansing. I went on with a light and peaceful heart, and sang psalms to the spiritual ear as I advanced.

Suddenly up came an old woman, who point-blank demanded alms.

"Good!" thought I; "here comes the waiter with the bill."

And I paid for my night's lodging on the spot. Take it how you please, but this was the first and the last beggar that I met with during all my tour.

A step or two farther I was overtaken by an old man in a brown nightcap, clear-eyed, weather-beaten, with a faint, excited smile. A little girl followed him, driving two sheep and a goat; but she kept in our wake, while the old man walked beside me and talked about the morning and the valley. It was not much past six; and for healthy people who have slept enough, that is an hour of expansion and of open and trustful talk.

"*Connaissez-vous le Seigneur?*" he said at length.

I asked him what Seigneur he meant; but he only repeated the question with more emphasis and a look in his eyes denoting hope and interest.

"Ah!" said I, pointing upwards, "I understand you, now. Yes, I know Him; He is the best of acquaintances."

The old man said he was delighted. "Hold," he added, striking his bosom; "it makes me happy here." There were a few who knew the Lord in these valleys, he went on to tell me; not many, but a few. "Many are called," he quoted, "and few chosen."

"My father," said I, "it is not easy to say who know the Lord; and it is none of our business. Protestants and Catholics, and even those who worship stones, may know Him and be known by Him; for He has made all."

I did not know I was so good a preacher.

The old man assured me he thought as I did, and repeated his expressions of pleasure at meeting me. "We are so few," he said. "They call us Moravians here; but down in the department of Gard, where there are also a good number, they are called Derbists, after an English pastor."

I began to understand that I was figuring, in questionable taste, as a member of some sect to me unknown; but I was more pleased with the pleasure of my companion than embarrassed by my own equivocal position. Indeed I can see no dishonesty in not avowing a difference; and especially in these high matters, where we have all a sufficient assurance that, whoever may be in the wrong, we ourselves are not completely in the right. The truth is much talked about; but this old man in a brown nightcap showed himself so simple, sweet, and friendly that I am not unwilling to profess myself his convert. He was, as a matter of fact, a Plymouth Brother. Of what that involves in the way of doctrine I have no idea nor the time to inform myself; but I know right well that we are all embarked upon a troublesome world, the children of one Father, striving in many essential points to do and to become the same. And although it was somewhat in a mistake that he shook hands with me so often and showed himself so ready to receive my words, that was a mistake of the truth-finding sort. For charity begins blindfold; and only through a series of similar misapprehensions rises at length into a settled principle of love and patience, and a firm belief in all our fellow-men. If I deceived this good old man, in the like manner I would willingly go on to deceive others. And if

ever at length, out of our separate and sad ways, we
should all come together into one common house, I
have a hope, to which I cling dearly, that my mountain
Plymouth Brother will hasten to shake hands with me
again.

Thus, talking like Christian and Faithful by the way,
he and I came down upon a hamlet by the Tarn. It was
but a humble place, called La Vernède, with less than a
dozen houses, and a Protestant chapel on a knoll. Here
he dwelt; and here, at the inn, I ordered my breakfast.
The inn was kept by an agreeable young man, a stone-
breaker on the road, and his sister, a pretty and engaging
girl. The village school-master dropped in to speak with
the stranger. And these were all Protestants — a fact
which pleased me more than I should have expected;
and, what pleased me still more, they seemed all upright
and simple people. The Plymouth Brother hung round
me with a sort of yearning interest, and returned at least
thrice to make sure I was enjoying my meal. His behaviour touched me deeply at the time, and even now
moves me ·in recollection. He feared to intrude, but he
would not willingly forego one moment of my society;
and he seemed never weary of shaking me by the hand.

When all the rest had drifted off to their day's work,
I sat for near half an hour with the young mistress of the
house, who talked pleasantly over her seam of the chestnut harvest, and the beauties of the Tarn, and old family
affections, broken up when young folk go from home, yet
still subsisting. Hers, I am sure, was a sweet nature,
with a country plainness and much delicacy underneath;
and he who takes her to his heart will doubtless be a fortunate young man.

The valley below La Vernède pleased me more and more as I went forward. Now the hills approached from either hand, naked and crumbling, and walled in the river between cliffs; and now the valley widened and became green. The road led me past the old castle of Miral on a steep; past a battlemented monastery, long since broken up and turned into a church and parsonage; and past a cluster of black roofs, the village of Cocurès, sitting among vineyards and meadows and orchards thick with red apples, and where, along the highway, they were knocking down walnuts from the roadside trees, and gathering them in sacks and baskets. The hills, however much the vale might open, were still tall and bare, with cliffy battlements and here and there a pointed summit; and the Tarn still rattled through the stones with a mountain noise. I had been led, by bagmen of a picturesque turn of mind, to expect a horrific country after the heart of Byron; but to my Scotch eyes it seemed smiling and plentiful, as the weather still gave an impression of high summer to my Scotch body; although the chestnuts were already picked out by the autumn, and the poplars, that here began to mingle with them, had turned into pale gold against the approach of winter.

There was something in this landscape, smiling although wild, that explained to me the spirit of the Southern Covenanters. Those who took to the hills for conscience' sake in Scotland had all gloomy and bedevilled thoughts; for once that they received God's comfort they would be twice engaged with Satan; but the Camisards had only bright and supporting visions. They dealt much more in blood, both given and taken; yet I find no obsession of the Evil One in their records. With a light conscience, they pursued their life in these rough times and circumstances. The soul of Séguier, let us not forget, was like a garden. They knew they were on God's side, with a knowledge that has no parallel among the Scots; for the Scots, although they might be certain of the cause, could never rest confident of the person.

"We flew," says one old Camisard, "when we heard the sound of psalm-singing, we flew as if with wings. We felt within us an animating ardour, a transporting desire. The feeling cannot be expressed in words. It is a thing that must have been experienced to be understood. However weary we might be, we thought no more of our weariness and grew light, so soon as the psalms fell upon our ears."

The valley of the Tarn and the people whom I met at La Vernède not only explain to me this passage, but the twenty years of suffering which those, who were so stiff and so bloody when once they betook themselves to war endured with the meekness of children and the constancy of saints and peasants.

Florac

ON a branch of the Tarn stands Florac, the seat of a
subprefecture, with an old castle, an alley of planes,
many quaint street-corners, and a live fountain welling
from the hill. It is notable, besides, for handsome
women, and as one of the two capitals, Alais being the
other, of the country of the Camisards.

The landlord of the inn took me, after I had eaten, to
an adjoining *café*, where I, or rather my journey, became
the topic of the afternoon. Every one had some suggestion for my guidance; and the subprefectorial map was
fetched from the subprefecture itself, and much thumbed
among coffee-cups and glasses of liqueur. Most of these
kind advisers were Protestant, though I observed that
Protestant and Catholic intermingled in a very easy
manner; and it surprised me to see what a lively memory
still subsisted of the religious war. Among the hills of the
south-west, by Mauchline, Cumnock, or Carsphairn, in
isolated farms or in the manse, serious Presbyterian
people still recall the days of the great persecution, and
the graves of local martyrs are still piously regarded.
But in towns and among the so-called better classes, I
fear that these old doings have become an idle tale. If
you met a mixed company in the King's Arms at Wig-
town, it is not likely that the talk would run on Covenanters. Nay, at Muirkirk of Glenluce, I found the beadle's
wife had not so much as heard of Prophet Peden. But

these Cévenols were proud of their ancestors in quite another sense; the war was their chosen topic; its exploits were their own patent of nobility; and where a man or a race has had but one adventure, and that heroic, we must expect and pardon some prolixity of reference. They told me the country was still full of legends hitherto uncollected; I heard from them about Cavalier's descendants — not direct descendants, be it understood, but only cousins or nephews — who were still prosperous people in the scene of the boy-general's exploits; and one farmer had seen the bones of old combatants dug up into the air of an afternoon in the nineteenth century, in a field where the ancestors had fought, and the great-grandchildren were peaceably ditching.

Later in the day one of the Protestant pastors was so good as to visit me: a young man, intelligent and polite, with whom I passed an hour or two in talk. Florac, he told me, is part Protestant, part Catholic; and the difference in religion is usually doubled by the difference in politics. You may judge of my surprise, coming as I did from such a babbling purgatorial Poland of a place as Monastier, when I learned that the population lived together on very quiet terms; and there was even an exchange of hospitalities between households thus doubly separated. Black Camisard and White Camisard, militia-man and Miquelet and dragoon, Protestant prophet and Catholic cadet of the White Cross, they had all been sabring and shooting, burning, pillaging, and murdering, their hearts hot with indignant passion; and here, after a hundred and seventy years, Protestant is still Protestant, Catholic still Catholic, in mutual toleration and mild amity of life. But the race of man, like that indomitable

nature whence it sprang, has medicating virtues of its
own; the years and seasons bring various harvests; the
sun returns after the rain; and mankind outlives secular
animosities, as a single man awakens from the passions of
a day. We judge our ancestors from a more divine position; and the dust being a little laid with several centuries, we can see both sides adorned with human virtues
and fighting with a show of right.

THE MARKET PLACE AT LE PUY

I have never thought it easy to be just, and find it
daily even harder than I thought. I own I met these
Protestants with delight and a sense of coming home. I
was accustomed to speak their language, in another and
deeper sense of the word than that which distinguishes
between French and English; for the true babel is a
divergence upon morals. And hence I could hold more
free communication with the Protestants, and judge
them more justly, than the Catholics. Father Apollinaris

may pair off with my mountain Plymouth Brother as two guileless and devout old men; yet I ask myself if I had as ready a feeling for the virtues of the Trappist; or had I been a Catholic, if I should have felt so warmly to the dissenter of La Vernède.   With the first I was on terms of mere forbearance; but with the other, although only on a misunderstanding and by keeping on selected points, it was still possible to hold converse and exchange some honest thoughts.   In this world of imperfection we gladly welcome even partial intimacies.   If we find but one to whom we can speak out of our heart freely, with whom we can walk in love and simplicity without dissimulation, we have no ground of quarrel with the world or God.

In the Valley of the Mimente

On Tuesday, 1st October, we left Florac late in the afternoon, a tired donkey and tired donkey-driver. A little way up the Tarnon, a covered bridge of wood introduced us into the valley of the Mimente. Steep rocky red mountains overhung the stream; great oaks and chestnuts grew upon the slopes or in stony terraces; here and there was a red field of millet or a few apple-trees studded with red apples; and the road passed hard by two black hamlets, one with an old castle atop to please the heart of the tourist.

It was difficult here again to find a spot fit for my encampment. Even under the oaks and chestnuts the ground had not only a very rapid slope, but was heaped with loose stones; and where there was no timber the hills descended to the stream in a red precipice tufted with heather. The sun had left the highest peak in front of me, and the valley was full of the lowing sound of herdsmen's horns as they recalled the flocks into the stable, when I spied a bight of meadow some way below the roadway in an angle of the river. Thither I descended, and, tying Modestine provisionally to a tree, proceeded to investigate the neighbourhood. A grey pearly evening shadow filled the glen; objects at a little distance grew indistinct and melted bafflingly into each other; and the darkness was rising steadily like an exhalation. I approached a great oak which grew in the meadow, hard

by the river's brink; when to my disgust the voices of
children fell upon my ear, and I beheld a house round
the angle on the other bank. I had half a mind to pack
and be gone again, but the growing darkness moved me
to remain. I had only to make no noise until the night
was fairly come, and trust to the dawn to call me early
in the morning. But it was hard to be annoyed by
neighbours in such a great hotel.

A hollow underneath the oak was my bed. Before I
had fed Modestine and arranged my sack, three stars
were already brightly shining, and the others were beginning dimly to appear. I slipped down to the river,
which looked very black among its rocks, to fill my can;
and dined with a good appetite in the dark, for I scrupled
to light a lantern while so near a house. The moon,
which I had seen, a pallid crescent, all afternoon, faintly
illuminated the summit of the hills, but not a ray fell into
the bottom of the glen where I was lying. The oak rose
before me like a pillar of darkness; and overhead the
heartsome stars were set in the face of the night. No
one knows the stars who has not slept, as the French
happily put it, *à la belle étoile*. He may know all their
names and distances and magnitudes, and yet be ignorant
of what alone concerns mankind, their serene and gladsome influence on the mind. The greater part of poetry
is about the stars; and very justly, for they are themselves the most classical of poets. These same far-away
worlds, sprinkled like tapers or shaken together like a
diamond dust upon the sky, had looked not otherwise to
Roland or Cavalier, when, in the words of the latter, they
had "no other tent but the sky, and no other bed than
my mother earth."

All night a strong wind blew up the valley, and the acorns fell pattering over me from the oak. Yet, on this first night of October, the air was as mild as May, and I slept with the fur thrown back.

I was much disturbed by the barking of a dog, an animal that I fear more than any wolf. A dog is vastly braver, and is besides supported by the sense of duty. If you kill a wolf, you meet with encouragement and praise; but if you kill a dog, the sacred rights of property and the domestic affections come clamouring round you for redress. At the end of a fagging day, the sharp, cruel note of a dog's bark is in itself a keen annoyance; and to a tramp like myself, he represents the sedentary and respectable world in its most hostile form. There is something of the clergyman or the lawyer about this engaging animal; and if he were not amenable to stones, the boldest man would shrink from travelling afoot. I respect dogs much in the domestic circle; but on the highway or sleeping afield, I both detest and fear them.

I was wakened next morning (Wednesday, October 2d) by the same dog — for I knew his bark — making a charge down the bank, and then, seeing me sit up, retreating again with great alacrity. The stars were not yet quite extinguished. The heaven was of that enchanting mild grey-blue of the early morn. A still clear light began to fall, and the trees on the hillside were outlined sharply against the sky. The wind had veered more to the north, and no longer reached me in the glen; but as I was going on with my preparations, it drove a white cloud very swiftly over the hill-top; and looking up, I was surprised to see the cloud dyed with gold. In these high regions of the air, the sun was already shining as at noon. If only the clouds travelled high enough, we should see the same thing all night long. For it is always daylight in the fields of space.

As I began to go up the valley, a draught of wind came down it out of the seat of the sunrise, although the clouds continued to run overhead in an almost contrary direction. A few steps farther, and I saw a whole hillside gilded with the sun; and still a little beyond, between two peaks, a centre of dazzling brilliancy appeared floating in the sky, and I was once more face to face with the big bonfire that occupies the kernel of our system.

I met but one human being that forenoon, a dark military-looking wayfarer, who carried a game-bag on a baldric; but he made a remark that seems worthy of record. For when I asked him if he were Protestant or Catholic ——

"O," said he, "I make no shame of my religion. I am a Catholic."

He made no shame of it! The phrase is a piece of natural statistics; for it is the language of one in a minority. I thought with a smile of Bavile and his dragoons, and how you may ride rough-shod over a religion for a century, and leave it only the more lively for the friction. Ireland is still Catholic; the Cévennes still Protestant. It is not a basketful of law-papers, nor the hoofs and pistol-butts of a regiment of horse, that can change one tittle of a ploughman's thoughts. Outdoor rustic people have not many ideas, but such as they have are hardy plants and thrive flourishingly in persecution. One who has grown a long while in the sweat of laborious noons, and under the stars at night, a frequenter of hills and forests, an old honest countryman, has, in the end, a sense of communion with the powers of the universe, and amicable relations towards his God. Like my mountain Plymouth Brother, he knows the Lord. His religion does not repose upon a choice of logic; it is the poetry of the man's experience, the philosophy of the history of his life. God, like a great power, like a great shining sun, has appeared to this simple fellow in the course of years, and become the ground and essence of his least reflections; and you may change creeds and dogmas by authority, or proclaim a new religion with the sound of trumpets, if you will; but here is a man who has his own thoughts, and will stubbornly adhere to them in good and evil. He is a Catholic, a Protestant, or a Plymouth Brother, in the same indefeasible sense that a man is not a woman, or a woman not a man. For he could not vary from his faith, unless he could eradicate all memory of the past, and, in a strict and not a conventional meaning, change his mind.

The Heart of the Country

I was now drawing near to Cassagnas, a cluster of black roofs upon the hillside, in this wild valley, among chestnut gardens, and looked upon in the clear air by many rocky peaks. The road along the Mimente is yet new, nor have the mountaineers recovered their surprise when the first cart arrived at Cassagnas. But although it lay thus apart from the current of men's business, this hamlet had already made a figure in the history of France. Hard by, in caverns of the mountain, was one of the five arsenals of the Camisards; where they laid up clothes and corn and arms against necessity, forged bayonets and sabres, and made themselves gunpowder with willow charcoal and saltpetre boiled in kettles. To the same caves, amid this multifarious industry, the sick and wounded were brought up to heal; and there they were visited by the two surgeons, Chabrier and Tavan, and secretly nursed by women of the neighbourhood.

Of the five legions into which the Camisards were divided, it was the oldest and the most obscure that had its magazines by Cassagnas. This was the band of Spirit Séguier; men who had joined their voices with his in the 68th Psalm as they marched down by night on the archpriest of the Cévennes. Séguier, promoted to heaven, was succeeded by Salomon Couderc, whom Cavalier treats in his memoirs as chaplain-general to the whole army of the Camisards. He was a prophet; a great

reader of the heart, who admitted people to the sacrament
or refused them by "intentively viewing every man"
between the eyes; and had the most of the Scriptures
off by rote. And this was surely happy; since in a surprise in August, 1703, he lost his mule, his portfolios, and
his Bible. It is only strange that they were not surprised more often and more effectually; for this legion
of Cassagnas was truly patriarchal in its theory of war,
and camped without sentries, leaving that duty to the
angels of the God for whom they fought. This is a token,
not only of their faith, but of the trackless country where
they harboured. M. de Caladon, taking a stroll one fine
day, walked without warning into their midst, as he
might have walked into "a flock of sheep in a plain," and
found some asleep and some awake and psalm-singing.
A traitor had need of no recommendation to insinuate
himself among their ranks, beyond "his faculty of singing psalms"; and even the prophet Salomon "took him
into a particular friendship." Thus, among their intricate hills, the rustic troop subsisted; and history can
attribute few exploits to them but sacraments and ecstasies.

People of this tough and simple stock will not, as I
have just been saying, prove variable in religion; nor
will they get nearer to apostasy than a mere external con-
formity like that of Naaman in the house of Rimmon.
When Louis XVI., in the words of the edict, "convinced
by the uselessness of a century of persecutions, and rather
from necessity than sympathy," granted at last a royal
grace of toleration, Cassagnas was still Protestant; and
to a man, it is so to this day. There is, indeed, one family
that is not Protestant, but neither is it Catholic. It is
that of a Catholic *curé* in revolt, who has taken to his

bosom a schoolmistress. And his conduct, it's worth noting, is disapproved by the Protestant villagers.

"It is a bad idea for a man," said one, "to go back from his engagements."

The villagers whom I saw seemed intelligent after a countrified fashion, and were all plain and dignified in manner. As a Protestant myself, I was well looked upon, and my acquaintance with history gained me farther respect. For we had something not unlike a religious controversy at table, a gendarme and a merchant with whom I dined being both strangers to the place and Catholics. The young men of the house stood round and supported me; and the whole discussion was tolerantly conducted, and surprised a man brought up among the infinitesimal and contentious differences of Scotland. The merchant, indeed, grew a little warm, and was far less pleased than some others with my historical acquirements. But the gendarme was mighty easy over it all.

"It's a bad idea for a man to change," said he; and the remark was generally applauded.

That was not the opinion of the priest and soldier at our Lady of the Snows. But this is a different race; and perhaps the same great-heartedness that upheld them to resist, now enables them to differ in a kind spirit. For courage respects courage; but where a faith has been trodden out, we may look for a mean and narrow population. The true work of Bruce and Wallace was the union of the nations; not that they should stand apart awhile longer, skirmishing upon their borders; but that, when the time came, they might unite with self-respect. The merchant was much interested in my journey, and thought it dangerous to sleep afield.

"There are the wolves," said he; "and then it is known you are an Englishman. The English have always long purses, and it might very well enter into some one's head to deal you an ill blow some night."

I told him I was not much afraid of such accidents; and at any rate judged it unwise to dwell upon alarms or consider small perils in the arrangement of life. Life itself, I submitted, was a far too risky business as a whole to make each additional particular of danger worth regard. "Something," said I, "might burst in your inside any day of the week, and there would be an end of you, if you were locked into your room with three turns of the key."

"*Cependant*," said he, "*coucher dehors!*"

"God," said I, "is everywhere."

"*Cependant, coucher dehors!*" he repeated, and his voice was eloquent of terror.

He was the only person, in all my voyage, who saw anything hardy in so simple a proceeding; although many considered it superfluous. Only one, on the other hand, professed much delight in the idea; and that was my Plymouth Brother, who cried out, when I told him I sometimes preferred sleeping under the stars to a close and noisy alehouse, "Now I see that you know the Lord!"

The merchant asked me for one of my cards as I was leaving, for he said I should be something to talk of in the future, and desired me to make a note of his request and reason; a desire with which I have thus complied.

A little after two I struck across the Mimente, and took a rugged path southward up a hillside covered with loose stones and tufts of heather. At the top, as is the

habit of the country, the path disappeared; and I left
my she-ass munching heather, and went forward alone
to seek a road.

I was now on the separation of two vast watersheds;
behind me all the streams were bound for the Garonne
and the Western Ocean; before me was the basin of the
Rhone. Hence, as from the Lozère, you can see in clear
weather the shining of the Gulf of Lyons; and perhaps
from here the soldiers of Salomon may have watched for
the topsails of Sir Cloudesley Shovel, and the long-
promised aid from England. You may take this ridge
as lying in the heart of the country of the Camisards;
four of the five legions camped all round it and almost
within view — Salomon and Joani to the north, Castanet
and Roland to the south; and when Julein had finished
his famous work, the devastation of the High Cévennes,
which lasted all through October and November, 1703,
and during which four hundred and sixty villages and
hamlets were, with fire and pickaxe, utterly subverted, a
man standing on this eminence would have looked forth
upon a silent, smokeless, and dispeopled land. Time and
man's activity have now repaired these ruins; Cassagnas
is once more roofed and sending up domestic smoke;
and in the chestnut gardens, in low and leafy corners,
many a prosperous farmer returns, when the day's work
is done, to his children and bright hearth. And still it
was perhaps the wildest view of all my journey. Peak
upon peak, chain upon chain of hills ran surging southward, channelled and sculptured by the winter streams,
feathered from head to foot with chestnuts, and here and
there breaking out into a coronal of cliffs. The sun,
which was still far from setting, sent a drift of misty gold

across the hill-tops, but the valleys were already plunged in a profound and quiet shadow.

A very old shepherd, hobbling on a pair of sticks, and wearing a black cap of liberty, as if in honour of his nearness to the grave, directed me to the road for St. Germain de Calberte. There was something solemn in the isolation of this infirm and ancient creature. Where he dwelt, how he got upon this high ridge, or how he proposed to get down again, were more than I could fancy. Not far off upon my right was the famous Plan de Font Morte, where Poul with his Armenian sabre slashed down the Camisards of Séguier. This, methought, might be some Rip van Winkle of the war, who had lost his comrades, fleeing before Poul, and wandered ever since upon the mountains. It might be news to him that Cavalier had surrendered, or Roland had fallen fighting with his back against an olive. And while I was thus working on my fancy, I heard him hailing in broken tones, and saw him waving me to come back with one of his two sticks. I had already got some way past him; but, leaving Modestine once more, retraced my steps.

Alas, it was a very commonplace affair. The old gentleman had forgot to ask the pedlar what he sold, and wished to remedy this neglect.

I told him sternly, "Nothing."

"Nothing?" cried he.

I repeated "Nothing," and made off.

It's odd to think of, but perhaps I thus became as inexplicable to the old man as he had been to me.

The road lay under chestnuts, and though I saw a hamlet or two below me in the vale, and many lone houses of the chestnut farmers, it was a very solitary

march all afternoon; and the evening began early underneath the trees. But I heard the voice of a woman singing some sad, old, endless ballad not far off. It seemed to
be about love and a *bel amoureux*, her handsome sweet-
heart; and I wished I could have taken up the strain and
answered her, as I went on upon my invisible woodland
way, weaving, like Pippa in the poem, my own thoughts
with hers. What could I have told her? Little enough;
and yet all the heart requires. How the world gives and
takes away, and brings sweethearts near, only to separate
them again into distant and strange lands; but to love
is the great amulet which makes the world a garden;
and "hope, which comes to all," outwears the accidents
of life, and reaches with tremulous hand beyond the
grave and death. Easy to say: yea, but also, by God's
mercy, both easy and grateful to believe!

We struck at last into a wide white highroad, carpeted
with noiseless dust. The night had come; the moon had
been shining for a long while upon the opposite mountain; when on turning a corner my donkey and I issued
ourselves into her light. I had emptied out my brandy
at Florac, for I could bear the stuff no longer, and re-
placed it with some generous and scented Volnay; and
now I drank to the moon's sacred majesty upon the road.
It was but a couple of mouthfuls; yet I became thenceforth unconscious of my limbs, and my blood flowed with
luxury. Even Modestine was inspired by this purified
nocturnal sunshine, and bestirred her little hoofs as to a
livelier measure. The road wound and descended swiftly
among masses of chestnuts. Hot dust rose from our feet
and flowed away. Our two shadows — mine deformed
with the knapsack, hers comically bestridden by the pack

— now lay before us clearly outlined on the road, and now, as we turned a corner, went off into the ghostly distance, and sailed along the mountainlike clouds. From time to time a warm wind rustled down the valley, and set all the chestnuts dangling their bunches of foliage and fruit; the ear was filled with whispering music, and the shadows danced in tune. And next moment the breeze had gone by, and in all the valley nothing moved except our travelling feet. On the opposite slope, the monstrous ribs and gullies of the mountain were faintly designed in the moonshine; and high overhead, in some lone house, there burned one lighted window, one square spark of red in the huge field of sad nocturnal colouring.

At a certain point, as I went downward, turning many acute angles, the moon disappeared behind the hill; and I pursued my way in great darkness, until another turning shot me without preparation into St. Germain de Calberte. The place was asleep and silent, and buried in opaque night. Only from a single open door, some lamplight escaped upon the road to show me I was come among men's habitations. The two last gossips of the evening, still talking by a garden wall, directed me to the inn. The landlady was getting her chicks to bed; the fire was already out, and had, not without grumbling, to be rekindled; half an hour later, and I must have gone supperless to roost.

The Last Day

When I awoke (Thursday, 3d October), and, hearing a great flourishing of cocks and chuckling of contented hens, betook me to the window of the clean and comfortable room where I had slept the night, I looked forth on a sunshiny morning in a deep vale of chestnut gardens. It was still early, and the cock-crows, and the slanting lights, and the long shadows encouraged me to be out and look round me.

St. Germain de Calberte is a great parish nine leagues round about. At the period of the wars, and immediately before the devastation, it was inhabited by two hundred and seventy-five families, of which only nine were Catholic, and it took the *curé* seventeen September days to go from house to house on horseback for a census. But the place itself, although capital of a canton, is scarce larger than a hamlet. It lies terraced across a steep slope in the midst of mighty chestnuts. The Protestant chapel stands below upon a shoulder; in the midst of the town is the quaint old Catholic church.

It was here that poor Du Chayla, the Christian martyr, kept his library and held a court of missionaries; here he had built his tomb, thinking to lie among a grateful population whom he had redeemed from error; and hither on the morrow of his death they brought the body, pierced with two-and-fifty wounds, to be interred. Clad in his priestly robes, he was laid out in state in the church.

The *curé*, taking his text from Second Samuel, twentieth chapter and twelfth verse, "And Amasa wallowed in his blood in the highway," preached a rousing sermon, and exhorted his brethren to die each at his post, like their unhappy and illustrious superior. In the midst of this eloquence there came a breeze that Spirit Séguier was near at hand; and behold! all the assembly took to their horses' heels, some east, some west, and the *curé* himself as far as Alais.

Strange was the position of this little Catholic metropolis, a thimbleful of Rome, in such a wild and contrary neighbourhood. On the one hand, the legion of Salomon overlooked it from Cassagnas; on the other, it was cut off from assistance by the legion of Roland at Mialet. The *curé*, Louvrelenil, although he took a panic at the archpriest's funeral, and so hurriedly decamped to Alais, stood well by his isolated pulpit, and thence uttered fulminations against the crimes of the Protestants. Salomon besieged the village for an hour and a half, but was beat back. The militiamen, on guard before the *curé's* door, could be heard, in the black hours, singing Protestant psalms and holding friendly talk with the insurgents. And in the morning, although not a shot had been fired, there would not be a round of powder in their flasks. Where was it gone? All handed over to the Camisards for a consideration. Untrusty guardians for an isolated priest!

That these continual stirs were once busy in St. Germain de Calberte, the imagination with difficulty receives; all is now so quiet, the pulse of human life now beats so low and still in this hamlet of the mountains. Boys followed me a great way off, like a timid sort of lion-hunters; and people turned round to have a second look, or came out of their houses, as I went by. My passage was the first event, you would have fancied, since the Camisards. There was nothing rude or forward in this observation; it was but a pleased and wondering scrutiny, like that of oxen or the human infant; yet it wearied my spirits, and soon drove me from the street.

I took refuge on the terraces, which are here greenly carpeted with sward, and tried to imitate with a pencil the inimitable attitudes of the chestnuts as they bear up their canopy of leaves. Ever and again a little wind went by, and the nuts dropped all around me, with a light and dull sound, upon the sward. The noise was as of a thin fall of great hailstones; but there went with it a cheerful human sentiment of an approaching harvest and farmers rejoicing in their gains. Looking up, I could see the brown nut peering through the husk, which was already gaping; and between the stems the eye embraced an amphitheatre of hill, sunlit and green with leaves.

I have not often enjoyed a place more deeply. I moved in an atmosphere of pleasure, and felt light and quiet and content. But perhaps it was not the place alone that so disposed my spirit. Perhaps some one was thinking of me in another country; or perhaps some thought of my own had come and gone unnoticed, and yet done me good. For some thoughts, which sure would be the most beautiful, vanish before we can rightly scan their features; as though a god, travelling by our green highways, should but ope the door, give one smiling look into the house, and go again for ever. Was it Apollo, or Mercury, or Love with folded wings? Who shall say?

But we go the lighter about our business, and feel peace and pleasure in our hearts.

I dined with a pair of Catholics. They agreed in the condemnation of a young man, a Catholic, who had married a Protestant girl and gone over to the religion of his wife. A Protestant born they could understand and respect; indeed, they seemed to be of the mind of an old Catholic woman, who told me that same day there was no difference between the two sects, save that "wrong was more wrong for the Catholic," who had more light and guidance; but this of a man's desertion filled them with contempt.

"It is a bad idea for a man to change," said one.

It may have been accidental, but you see how this phrase pursued me; and for myself, I believe it is the current philosophy in these parts. I have some difficulty in imagining a better. It's not only a great flight of confidence for a man to change his creed and go out of his family for heaven's sake; but the odds are — nay and the hope is — that, with all this great transition in the eyes of man, he has not changed himself a hair's-breadth to the eyes of God. Honour to those who do so, for the wrench is sore. But it argues something narrow, whether of strength or weakness, whether of the prophet or the fool, in those who can take a sufficient interest in such infinitesimal and human operations, or who can quit a friendship for a doubtful process of the mind. And I think I should not leave my old creed for another, changing only words for other words; but by some brave reading, embrace it in spirit and truth, and find wrong as wrong for me as for the best of other communions.

The phylloxera was in the neighbourhood; and instead of wine we drank at dinner a more economical juice of the grape — la Parisienne, they call it. It is made by putting the fruit whole into a cask with water; one by one the berries ferment and burst; what is drunk during the day is supplied at night in water; so, with ever another pitcher from the well, and ever another grape exploding and giving out its strength, one cask of Parisienne may last a family till spring. It is, as the reader will anticipate, a feeble beverage, but very pleasant to the taste.

What with dinner and coffee, it was long past three before I left St. Germain de Calberte. I went down beside the Gardon of Mialet, a great glaring watercourse devoid of water, and through St. Etienne de Vallée Française, or Val Francesque, as they used to call it; and towards evening began to ascend the hill of St. Pierre. It was a long and steep ascent. Behind me an empty carriage returning to St. Jean du Gard kept hard upon my tracks, and near the summit overtook me. The driver, like the rest of the world, was sure I was a pedlar; but, unlike others, he was sure of what I had to sell. He had noticed the blue wool which hung out of my pack at either end; and from this he had decided, beyond my power to alter his decision, that I dealt in blue-wool collars, such as decorate the neck of the French draught-horse.

I had hurried to the topmost powers of Modestine, for I dearly desired to see the view upon the other side before the day had faded. But it was night when I reached the summit; the moon was riding high and clear; and only a few grey streaks of twilight lingered in the west. A

yawning valley, gulfed in blackness, lay like a hole in
created Nature at my feet; but the outline of the hills
was sharp against the sky. There was Mount Aigoal,
the stronghold of Castanet. And Castanet, not only as
an active undertaking leader, deserves some mention
among Camisards; for there is a spray of rose among his
laurel; and he showed how, even in a public tragedy,
love will have its way. In the high tide of war he married,
in his mountain citadel, a young and pretty lass called
Mariette. There were great rejoicings; and the bridegroom released five-and-twenty prisoners in honour of the
glad event. Seven months afterwards Mariette, the
Princess of the Cévennes, as they called her in derision,
fell into the hands of the authorities, where it was like
to have gone hard with her. But Castanet was a man of
execution, and loved his wife. He fell on Valleraugue,
and got a lady there for a hostage; and for the first and
last time in that war there was an exchange of prisoners.
Their daughter, pledge of some starry night upon Mount
Aigoal, has left descendants to this day.

Modestine and I — it was our last meal together —
had a snack upon the top of St. Pierre, I on a heap of
stones, she standing by me in the moonlight and deco-
rously eating bread out of my hand. The poor brute
would eat more heartily in this manner; for she had a
sort of affection for me, which I was soon to betray.

It was a long descent upon St. Jean du Gard, and we
met no one but a carter, visible afar off by the glint of
the moon on his extinguished lantern.

Before ten o'clock we had got in and were at supper;
fifteen miles and a stiff hill in little beyond six hours!

Farewell, Modestine

On examination, on the morning of October 4th, Modestine was pronounced unfit for travel. She would need at least two days' repose according to the ostler; but I was now eager to reach Alais for my letters; and, being in a civilised country of stage-coaches, I determined to sell my lady-friend and be off by the diligence that afternoon. Our yesterday's march, with the testimony of the driver who had pursued us up the long hill of St. Pierre, spread a favourable notion of my donkey's capabilities. Intending purchasers were aware of an unrivalled opportunity. Before ten I had an offer of twenty-five francs; and before noon, after a desperate engagement, I sold her, saddle and all, for five-and-thirty. The pecuniary gain is not obvious, but I had bought freedom into the bargain.

St. Jean du Gard is a large place and largely Protestant. The maire, a Protestant, asked me to help him in a small matter which is itself characteristic of the country. The young women of the Cévennes profit by the common religion and the difference of the language to go largely as governesses into England; and here was one, a native of Mialet, struggling with English circulars from two different agencies in London. I gave what help I could; and volunteered some advice, which struck me as being excellent.

One thing more I note. The phylloxera has ravaged the vineyards in this neighbourhood; and in the early

morning, under some chestnuts by the river, I found a
party of men working with a cider-press. I could not
at first make out what they were after, and asked one
fellow to explain.

"Making cider," he said. *"Oui, c'est comme ça.
Comme dans le nord!"*

There was a ring of sarcasm in his voice; the country
was going to the devil.

It was not until I was fairly seated by the driver, and
rattling through a rocky valley with dwarf olives, that
I became aware of my bereavement. I had lost Modestine. Up to that moment I had thought I hated her;
but now she was gone,

> "And, O,
> The difference to me!"

For twelve days we had been fast companions; we
had travelled upwards of a hundred and twenty miles,
crossed several respectable ridges, and jogged along with
our six legs by many a rocky and many a boggy by-road.
After the first day, although sometimes I was hurt and
distant in manner, I still kept my patience; and as for
her, poor soul! she had come to regard me as a god.
She loved to eat out of my hand. She was patient, elegant in form, the colour of an ideal mouse, and inimitably
small. Her faults were those of her race and sex; her
virtues were her own. Farewell, and if for ever ——

Father Adam wept when he sold her to me; after I
had sold her in my turn, I was tempted to follow his
example; and being alone with a stage-driver and four
or five agreeable young men, I did not hesitate to yield
to my emotion.

NOTES

PAGE **iv**. **Sidney Colvin**: An English essayist and critic. He was one of Stevenson's intimate friends, and his literary editor. **John Bunyan**: the author of *Pilgrim's Progress*, a book which Stevenson knew intimately. See Stevenson's essay, *Books which have influenced me*.

PAGE **v**. **Antigone**: a tragedy by Sophocles, a Greek dramatist of the fourth century B.C. **Job**: See *Job*, xxxix, 5.

PAGE **1**. **Velay**: an ancient territory in southwestern France. **Le Monastier**: for a fuller description of this highland village, see Stevenson's *A Mountain Town in France*, an essay which was originally intended as the opening chapter of *Travels with a Donkey*. **Le Puy**: the ancient capital of Velay; one of the most picturesque towns in Europe. **Legitimists**: supporters of the elder Bourbon line of Louis XIV to the throne of France. **Orleanists**: supporters of the junior line of the younger brother of Louis XIV, the Duke of Orleans. **Imperialists**: supporters of the son of Louis Napoleon. **Republicans**: opposed to monarchy and empire; supporters of the republic established after the Franco-Prussian War. **Cévennes**: a mountain chain in southern France.

PAGE **4**. **Modestine**: the name playfully suggests the modesty and the small size of the beast.

PAGE **5**. **revolver**: "It was of an antiquated pattern, uncertain in its mechanism, and more likely to be a menace than a protection to its owner." — Mrs. Stevenson. **spencer**: a knitted coat or jacket similar to a buttoned sweater. **Beaujolais**: a local wine named from the district which produced it.

PAGE **6**. **vaticinations**: "prophecies," "predictions." **Christian**: the hero of *Pilgrim's Progress*.

PAGE **7**. **as an ox goeth to the slaughter**: cf. *Proverbs*, vii, 22.

PAGE **9**. **Alais**: a town on the left bank of the Gardon. "**Et vous marchez comme ça!**": "And you walk like that!"

PAGE 10.   My deus ex machina: literally, " A god [let down] from a machine." Descriptive of an ancient stage device employed for solving abruptly a dramatic difficulty in Greek tragedy. Here the peasant has helped Stevenson in time of need.   Sabbath: the Scotch Presbyterians held to a strict observance of Sunday.   ascetic feast: a felicitous allusion to cold Sunday dinner.

PAGE 11.   Homer's Cyclops: man-monsters who dwelt in caves on the crests of hills. See *Odyssey*, Book IX.   like a sucking-dove: cf. to Bottom in Shakespeare's *Midsummer Night's Dream*, I, ii, 84.

PAGE 12.   instantly: " constantly," " every instant."   hypothec: originally, the lien that the Scotch landlord took on the crop and chattels of his tenant; later, colloquially used for " the whole lot."

PAGE 13.   acolytes: those belonging to the four minor orders of the clergy; aspirants for the priesthood.

PAGE 16.   Mount Mézenc, St. Julien: peaks in the mountains of Vivarais.

PAGE 18.   in a suite: " connected."   grouting: " rooting with the snout."

PAGE 19.   amateur: " lover."

PAGE 20.   dur comme un âne: " tough as a donkey."   St. Etienne: a large manufacturing town in the department of Loire.

PAGE 23.   common wolf: in 1765, this wolf suddenly appeared in Lozere; it was killed in 1787.   Alexander Pope: one of the leading English poets of the eighteenth century; he was very small of stature. The exact quotation has not been located.   little corporal: Napoleon.   M. Elie Berthet: a French novelist (1815–1891); the reference here is to his novel *Bête du Gévaudan* (Beast of Gévaudan).

PAGE 24.   caryatides: columns of sculptured female figures supporting the cornices of Greek buildings.   " D'où'st que vous venez ? "   " Where did you come from ? "

PAGE 28.   Herbert Spencer: a celebrated English philosopher (1820–1903); founder of the system of thought known as the synthetic philosophy.

PAGE 31.   " a little farther lend thy guiding hand ": the exact line of Milton's *Samson Agonistes* is " A little onward lend thy guiding hand." " **C'est que, voyez-vous, il fait noir** " : " It is, you see, dark." " **mais — c'est — de la peine** " : " but — that is — some trouble," or " it would cause me trouble." " **Ce n'est pas ça** " : " It is not that."

PAGE **32.** " **C'est vrai, ça,**" . . . " **oui, c'est vrai. Et d'où venez-vous ?** " " That is true," . . . " yes, that is true. And where do you come from ? " **farceuse** : " a roguish jester."

PAGE **33.** **Filia barbara pater barbarior** : " a barbarous daughter, a more barbarous father."

PAGE **34.** **bambino** : the image of the child Jesus, as seen in many Catholic churches.

PAGE **36.** **Pastors of the Desert** : *Histoire des Pasteurs du Desert.* The history of the Protestant insurrection in France between 1765 and 1789. **Ulysses** : after his return home from the Trojan war, he was still restless for adventure. See Dante's *Inferno*, Canto XXVI, and Tennyson's *Ulysses*.

PAGE **39.** **Lady of all Graces** : " the Virgin Mary." **What went ye out for to see ?** Cf. *Matthew*, ii, 7. **Balquidder, Dunrossness** : remote Protestant parishes in West Perthshire, Scotland, and in the Shetland Islands.

PAGE **41.** **Æsop** : the traditional author of the most famous collection of Greek fables. Stevenson, however, had in mind La Fontaine's *Le Meunier, son Fils et l'Ane* (*The Miller, his Son, and the Donkey*). See La Fontaine's *Fables*, Book iii, No. 1.

PAGE **42.** **quintals** : one quintal is equal to about 220 pounds.

PAGE **45.** **Matthew Arnold** : Matthew Arnold (1822–1888), English poet and critic. The quotation is from *Stanzas from the Grande Chartreuse*, a description of a Carthusian monastery, situated high in the Alps.

PAGE **47.** **Our Lady of the Snows** : a monastery, named from its location in the snow-covered mountains. See also Stevenson's poem, *Our Lady of the Snows*.

PAGE **48.** **Languedocian** : from Languedoc, formerly an independent kingdom, now southern France, the home of the most famous poets of Mediæval France. **Wordsworth** : William Wordsworth (1770–1850). The quotation which follows is from the sonnet beginning, " Proud were ye mountains when in time of old." **Trappist** : an especially austere order ; one of the branches of the Cistercian monastery of La Trappe in Normandy, France.   **sheets of characters**: the reference is to the pictures Stevenson, as a boy, used to represent characters in his toy theatre. See his essay, *A Penny Plain and Two-pence Colored*, in *Memories and Portraits*.

PAGE **49**.   **Marco Sadeler**: a Dutch engraver of the early seventeenth century, the son of Giles Sadeler, the celebrated engraver.

PAGE **50**.   **Dr. Pusey**: Edward Bouverie Pusey (1800–1882), a leader in the Oxford Movement, which sought to counteract the growing liberalism by emphasizing creeds and rites.

PAGE **51**.   **the Father Hospitaller**: one whose office it was to receive and entertain guests.

PAGE **54**.   **MM. les retraitants**: those who retire from active life to the monastery for meditation and prayer, but who do not take the vows.   **the late Pope**: Pope Pius IX (d. 1878).   **Imitation**: *The Imitation of Christ*, attributed to Thomas à Kempis, a German mystic of the fifteenth century.   **Life of Elizabeth Seton**: Mrs. Elizabeth Ann Bayley Seton (1774–1821), founder of the order of Sisters of Charity (1809), and first Mother Superior.   **Cotton Mather**: a famous Puritan divine (1663–1728). Most often remembered for his persecution of witches and for his *Magnalia*, an ecclesiastical history of New England.   **everlasting psalm**: see *Revelation*, v, 13.   " **Le temps libre est employé à l'examen de conscience, à la confession, à faire de bonnes résolutions** ": " The free time (leisure) is employed in the examination of the conscience, in confession, and in making good resolutions."

PAGE **56**.   **breviaries**: service books for public and private devotion, for use in the Roman Catholic church.   **Waverley novels**: novels of Sir Walter Scott (1771–1832).   **Basil**: St. Basil (329–379), a father of the Greek church.   **Hilarion**: St. Hilarion (300(?)–371), a hermit who introduced monasticism into Palestine.   **Raphael**: St. Raphael (1614–1693), a Benedictine monk and historian of Portugal.   **Pacifique**: St. Pacifique (1575–1653), a French monk and missionary.   **Veuillot**: Louis Veuillot (1813–1883), a French writer of polemical works, who emphasized the extreme doctrines of the Church of Rome.   **Chateaubriand**: François René Auguste, Vicomte de Chateaubriand (1768–1848), a French statesman and romancer.   **Molière**: the stage-name of Jean Baptiste Poquelin (1622–1673), the leading French dramatist.

Notes

PAGE **58**. **lay phalansteries**: as used here, the communities of artists at Fontainebleau. **Cistercian rule**: referring especially to the laws of silence and to the exclusion of women among the Cistercian monks.

PAGE **60**. **compline**: the last service of the day. **Salve Regina**: "Hail Queen," a hymn to the Virgin Mary, sung after the compline.

PAGE **61**.
> " **Que t'as de belles filles,**
>   **Giroflé!**
>   **Girofla!**
>   **Que t'as de belles filles,**
>   **L'Amour les comptera!** "

> " How many beautiful daughters you have,
>   Giroflé, Girofla,
>   How many beautiful daughters you have,
>   Love will count them."

PAGE **63**. **kilted**: " tucked-up."

PAGE **64**. **Gambetta's**: Leon Gambetta (1838–1882), a prominent French statesman after the Franco-Prussian War. " **Comment, monsieur?** " " How, sir? " " **Et vous prétendez mourir dans cette espèce de croyance?** " " And you mean to die in that kind of faith? "

PAGE **65**. **my father's face**: see Balfour's *Life of Stevenson*, Vol. I, p. 95. **Gætulian lion**: the translation of the expression *Gaetulus leo*, which occurs in Horace's *Odes*, I, xxiii, 10.

PAGE **66**. " **C'est mon conseil comme ancien militaire,**" observed the Commandant; " **et celui de monsieur comme prêtre** ": " This is my advice as an old soldier," observed the Commandant; " and this gentleman's as a priest." " **Oui,**" added the curé, **sententiously nodding**; " **comme ancien militaire — et comme prêtre** ": " Yes," added the parish priest, sententiously nodding; " as an old soldier and as a priest." **grig**: " grasshopper " or " cricket."

PAGE **67**. " **a faddling hedonist** ": a trifler who seeks pleasure as the chief end in life.

PAGE **68**. " **La parole est à vous** ": " The word is yours "; that is, " it is for you to give your opinion."

PAGE **69**. **Old Play**: the quotation is from Stevenson's own poems. In thus attributing it to an old play, he is following a custom of Sir Walter Scott.

PAGE **71.** **inconsiderable burn**: "small stream."   "**Hé, bourgeois; il est cinq heures!** " "Hey, sir; it is five o'clock."

PAGE **72.** **bourrée**: "a country dance."

PAGE **73.** **feyness**: from the old English *fey ;* "doomed."

PAGE **75.** "**In a more sacred or sequestered bower — nor nymph nor faunus haunted** ": a paraphrase of the description of Eve's bower; see Milton's *Paradise Lost*, Book IV, ll. 705–708.

PAGE **76.** **arcana**: "mysteries."   **Montaigne**: Michel Eyquem de Montaigne (1533–1592). The celebrated French essayist. The quotation which follows is from his essay on *Experience*.   **Bastille**: the Bastile was the state prison of France; it was destroyed during the French Revolution.

PAGE **80.** **caravanserai**: "an inn."

PAGE **83.** **W. P. Bannatyne**: an assumed name for Stevenson himself.

PAGE **86.** "**like stout Cortez when, with eagle eyes, he stared on the Pacific** ": the quotation is from Keats's sonnet, *On First Looking into Chapman's Homer*.   **Pic de Finiels**: a mountain peak.   **Montpellier and Cette**: the seaport of Montpellier.

PAGE **87.** **Grand Monarch**: Louis XIV (1638–1715), king of France.   **Camisards**: the French Protestants of the Cevennes, who raised an insurrection against the persecutions which followed the revocation of the Edict of Nantes in 1685.   "**the discourse of every coffee-house** ": coffee-houses were places of entertainment in London during the seventeenth and eighteenth centuries, where people gathered not only to eat but also for the purpose of political and literary conversation. See Macaulay's *History of England*, Vol. I, Chap. iii, and the *Spectator*, No. I, 49, 403, 568.   **Roland**: Roland Laporte (1675(?)–1705). The leader of the Camisards. **Castanet**: André Castanet (1674–1705). A captain of the Camisards under Roland.

PAGE **92.** **squired**: "attended as a squire."   **patet dea**: "appears like a goddess."

PAGE **93.** **Archbishop Sharpe**: James Sharpe (1613–1679), Archbishop of St. Andrews, Scotland; murdered by the Scotch Covenanters when he attempted to force episcopacy upon them.   **Mar-**

shal Villars: Claude Louis Hector, Duke of Villars (1653–1732), Marshal of France; he suppressed the insurrection of the Camisards.

PAGE **94. Lamoignon de Bavile:** a distinguished lawyer and Governor of Languedoc (1648–1724). He persecuted the Camisards with great cruelty. **François de Langlade du Chayla:** Abbé de Chayla (1650 (?)–1702), Archpriest of the Cevennes; he also cruelly persecuted the Camisards. **pariah:** " a menial servant," " a person of no social standing."

PAGE **95. Scavenger's Daughter:** a mediæval instrument of torture; by means of it the victim was slowly squeezed to death. **Baal:** see *1 Kings*, xviii.

PAGE **97. Captain Poul:** he commanded a large force of horse and foot soldiers in Germany and Hungary, and in the Alps. **"Because the Spirit of the Lord is with me":** see *Luke*, iv, 18.

PAGE **98. Killiecrankie:** a pass in Perthshire, Scotland, where, in 1689, Claverhouse fell.

PAGE **101. Antony Watteau:** a French genre painter (1684–1721), who was especially noted for his representation of shepherd life, rustic festivals, etc.

PAGE **103.** " **C'est bien** ": " That's good."

PAGE **104.** " **Connaissez-vous le Seigneur?** " " Do you know the Lord? " **"Many are called,"** . . . " **and few chosen** ": see *Matthew*, xx, 16, and xxii, 14.

PAGE **105. Moravians:** a religious sect which traces its origin to John Huss; it began in Bohemia and Moravia, and later scattered to Great Britain, Germany, and the United States. **Derbists:** The founder was John Nelson Darby (1800–1882), a clergyman of the Church of England; the sect aimed at one universal Christian brotherhood. **Plymouth Brother:** also called Derbist.

PAGE **106. Christian and Faithful:** see Bunyan's *Pilgrim's Progress*, Part I, Chap. xi.

PAGE **107. horrific:** a country whose wildness causes the feeling of horror. **Byron:** George Gordon, Lord Byron (1788–1824). For his love of wild scenery see his description of the Alps in *Childe Harold*, Book III.

PAGE **109. subprefecture:** the subdivision of a department in France. **Mauchline, Cumnock, Carsphairn:** these three towns are situated in southeastern Scotland, and are associated with the

struggles and persecutions of the Covenanters. **Prophet Peden:**
Alexander Peden (1626(?)–1686), the leading preacher of the Scotch
Covenanters; he suffered many persecutions.

PAGE **110. Black Camisard, White Camisard:** bandits distinguished by the color of their uniforms. **White Cross:** so called
on account of the white cross sewed on the hat.

PAGE **112. dissenter:** one who refuses to conform to the Established Church.

PAGE **114. à la belle étoile:** "in the open air."

PAGE **119. house of Rimmon:** see 2 *Kings*, v, 18. **Louis XVI:**
king of France from 1774 to 1792.

PAGE **120. Bruce:** Robert Bruce (1274–1329). The hero of
Bannockburn, and king of Scotland. **Wallace:** Sir William Wallace
(1274(?)–1305), a Scottish hero. See Burns's poem, *Scots wha ha'e
wi' Wallace bled*.

PAGE **121.** "**Cependant, coucher dehors!**" "But to sleep out-
of-doors."

PAGE **122. Sir Cloudesley Shovel:** a British admiral (1650–
1707), who, at the time referred to, was commander of a fleet in the
Mediterranean.

PAGE **123. Rip van Winkle:** see Irving's *Sketch Book*.

PAGE **124. Pippa:** *Pippa Passes*, a dramatic poem by Robert
Browning. **Volnay:** red Burgundy wine, produced in the district
of Volnay.

PAGE **128. Apollo:** the Olympian god, representing light and life-
giving power. **Mercury:** the messenger of the gods, representing
darkness. **Love:** Cupid.

PAGE **130. phylloxera:** an insect which destroys grapevines.

PAGE **133.** "Oui,. c'est comme ça. Comme dans le nord!"
"Yes, it is like that. Just as in the North."

"And, O,
The difference to me!"

Quoted from Wordsworth's poem, *She Dwelt among Untrodden Ways*.

34589